In Praise of Supervision Matters

" . . . Rita Sever captures the essentials and artistry of working with the hearts and minds of those we manage."
—Renato P. Almanzor, PhD, Senior Director of
Programs, LeaderSpring

"A gem of a resource . . . full of support, advice, tools, and tips for those who supervise others."
—Kathryn Gaines, Ph.D., President, Leading Pace, LLC

"With her years of hands-on experience and wisdom, Rita Sever has captured the heart of supervision . . . *Supervision Matters* deserves to be on every leader's book shelf!"
—Diane Foster, MA, Career Development and Master Certified
Coach, Author, *The Skill Kit for Leaders*

"*Supervision Matters* is practical, useful, and packs a quiet punch that, cumulatively, can lead to lasting transformational effects."
—sujin lee, Project Director, CompassPoint Nonprofit Services

Supervision Matters

Supervision
Matters

---

100 BITE-SIZED IDEAS TO
TRANSFORM YOU AND YOUR TEAM

RITA SEVER

SHE WRITES PRESS

Published 2016
Printed in the United States of America
Print ISBN: 978-1-63152-145-4
E-ISBN: 978-1-63152-146-1
Library of Congress Control Number: 2016937340

For information, address:
She Writes Press
1563 Solano Ave #546
Berkeley, CA 94707

Cover design © Rebecca Lown
Interior design © Tabitha Lahr

She Writes Press is a division of SparkPoint Studio, LLC.

Most of this work has been previously published in the "Matters of Supervision" newsletters published by Rita Sever over the last ten years.

To Mark,

who has always heard my voice
even when it was just a whisper

CONTENTS

Chapter 6: How You Communicate Expectations ... 133

Chapter 7: How You Give (and Get) Feedback ... 155

Chapter 8: How You Act When Things Aren't Working ... 183

Chapter 12: How You Are Part of the Organization

Afterword

Appendix

INTRODUCTION:

Supervision Matters

In 1989, I worked in an AIDS service organization in Northern California. I was the sixth employee to work there. One day the executive director came in and announced to the entire staff that we'd just received a large grant. "We're going to double our staff in a month," she said. "I need someone to take care of these personnel files. Who wants to do it?" I raised my hand. That was the unanticipated start of my career in human resources.

As I learned how to do HR, I learned a lot about how people work. I learned what makes some people give their all and what makes others take shortcuts. I learned how to help people get along with each other and get their work done. By the time I left that organization nine years later, we had fifty employees. Along the way, I learned the rules and procedures of HR, but even more I learned how to work with people and how to build a culture together.

The next organization I worked at had 230 employees. This organization was across town and a world away in terms of the staff. It was another nonprofit but functioned more like a business. At the AIDS organization, people worked there because of their commitment to the mission. At CAP Sonoma, some people were there for the mission (to provide services to low-income people), but for many it was just a job. This made my job very different. I learned a whole lot more about HR and about people. When I started my own business many years later, I decided to focus on the most important component of day-to-day work for the staff: supervision.

While working at CAP, I earned my MA in organizational psychology. I would attend classes after working all day and go back to work the next day to observe the dynamics I studied and apply what I learned. Although I was exhausted from the long days, I was fascinated by the way organizations can either work well or not. What I learned reinforced my commitment to help people be better supervisors.

Supervision is a part of management, but it is not the same thing. Merriam-Webster defines management as "the act or skill of controlling and making decisions about a business, department, sports team, etc." Management therefore includes working with projects, budgets, other departments, and products. Supervision is the management of people. Similarly, leadership is a part of supervision, but it is not the same thing. A supervisor is expected to lead his or her staff, but leadership can arise anywhere within an organization. A solitary staff member can be a leader at times and a designated leader may or may not supervise people. (They also may or may not be an actual leader, but that's another story!)

Studies show that supervision matters. To most people, their supervisor *is* the organization. If their supervisor is thoughtless and demanding, then that's how they see the organization. If their supervisor is supportive and fair, then so is the organization.

I saw the impact of individual supervision play out time after time while I was an HR director. The quality of supervision impacted productivity, quality of work, team interaction, conflict, and the culture of departments.

During exit interviews, when I would ask people, "Why are you leaving?" the answer usually led back to their individual supervisor. Even if employees did not directly say, "I'm leaving because of my supervisor," it often came down to that if I asked a few follow-up questions about why they started looking for another job.

The supervisor sets the tone for each department. The supervisor gathers the troops to get the work done. The supervisor connects the work to the mission (or doesn't) and sets the standards for work in each department. The supervisor harasses employees or doesn't. The supervisor recognizes liability or creates it. The supervisor makes day-to-day organizational life go round.

And the sad truth in many organizations is that there is often very little training for supervisors. The assumption is that supervision will take care of itself. If someone is good at their job, they are promoted and then they are often told as an afterthought, "Oh by the way, part of your job now is to supervise your former coworkers."

Even on the rare occasions when supervisors are trained, that training is often on generic techniques focused on productivity, and the supervisor still doesn't know how to handle the interpersonal dynamics that make or break relationships with their employees.

This book was written for supervisors. The role of supervision is hugely underappreciated in most organizations. Every step a supervisor takes to implement an idea from this book will help them be more successful as a supervisor, which in turn will help their employees be successful and ultimately those actions will help the organization. It's a win-win-win!

This book does not lay out a roadmap for how to be a supervisor. It instead focuses on helping you think about your role, your approach, and your interactions with your staff. You can read one section a week or one section a day, or read whole chapters at a time. You can read the book from front to back, or jump in at any point that interests you. I do recommend that you pause along the way and take time to honestly reflect on your own supervisory style and how these ideas apply to your unique situation.

Any way you choose to enter this book will serve you and help you better understand how to approach this critical work of being a supervisor. It will help you ask some important questions about your organization, your team, and yourself. Whether you work in a small organization or a large one, whether you are a new supervisor or a seasoned supervisor, this book is designed to be your partner in the important work you do.

The reason I raised my hand when our executive director held out those files almost thirty years ago and asked someone to take them was that I cared about the people part of my organization. I knew that those files represented people who mattered. And I wanted to make work life easier and better. I still do.

Your work as a supervisor directly impacts the success of your team and the lives of your team members. Your work as a supervisor also has the potential to transform—or to negatively influence—your organization. Have fun and be thoughtful as you read this book; you just might learn how to transform your work, your team, and yourself.

A Note About Coaching Corners

To help you think about how these ideas apply to you, I offer a few questions following each section. Take a little time to reflect on these questions, especially when a particular chapter intrigues you. It's also a good idea to take a little more time considering a topic if you have a strong resistance to what I write. One approach that works is to set a timer for five or ten minutes and then to write nonstop in response to the question(s). Just see what comes up for you.

A Note About Details in the Book

This is not a book that I wrote to report on specific events from my career. Most of the particular names used in this book are pseudonyms and some of the situations are composites of actual experiences. They all tell the truth about a facet of supervision.

I also want to acknowledge that I often make general statements within a particular section to make a point relative to that section, but of course there are exceptions to these broad suggestions. For example in Chapter 3 in the section entitled "Don't Just Do Something, Stand There" I am obviously not recommending that supervisors always stand there!

One More Important Note

I am not an attorney and therefore nothing in this book should be construed as legal advice.

CHAPTER 1:

How You Relate to People

IT'S ABOUT YOU

I don't always give money to people who are asking for money on the street, but when I do, I remind myself that the act is more about me than about them. I figured this out a few years ago and it's helped me immensely. Before that, I would wage a little argument in my head: "They'll just use it to buy alcohol," or, "This guy is probably a scammer." One day I realized, so what? My giving away my money was not about what the other person did with the money. If I choose to give someone a dollar, then it's not my dollar anymore and they can do what they want with it. The question for me was, "Am I the kind of person who gives money to homeless people?" Sometimes I am and sometimes I'm not. But the lesson I realized was that it is much more about me than about them.

This holds true in supervision too. What kind of supervisor are you? What kind of supervisor do you want to be? Are you controlling or are you collaborative? Are you focused on a coaching approach or a monitoring approach? Do you engage in two-way conversations or deliver one-way lectures? Are you focused on results or methods? The answers to these questions will help you determine how you want to act in any given moment.

I was recently coaching someone—let's call her Joyce—who wanted to be a supportive supervisor but kept talking down to her staff. We were talking about the difference between being authoritative and being respectful and clear. The difference between these two ways of being shows up in tone and language. I asked Joyce to consider the difference between these two statements: "Stop your gossiping and get back to work," versus "It is important that the work take precedence over social visits at work. I need you to cut down on your personal visits with your coworkers. How can you do that?"

Joyce listened to my examples, then immediately replied, "It won't make a difference what I say to them or how I say it." She was so focused on the actions of her staff that she overlooked her own actions.

In helping Joyce to understand that we needed to focus on her actions, I reminded her that, even as a supervisor, you can't control what other people do. This is a bottom-line truth of life, and it's an important truth to remember in the workplace too. The only person you **can** control is you. You can influence other people's actions but you cannot make anyone change. What can **you** do differently? What changes in your tone or approach might work to influence the employee to change? It's true that what you do might not make a difference, but you won't know until you try it. And if you're going to try something, you need to try it clearly and carefully by focusing on your own actions.

Granted, the authoritative approach may get immediate short-term results, but at what cost? Chances are that when you're out of the office the employees will revert to bad habits **and** that they will leave their jobs when presented with the opportunity. They also might develop resentment that will affect their work in other ways.

None of this is to suggest that your staff can do whatever they want with no consequences. If you try something and it doesn't work, then you need to figure out another strategy, whether that strategy is to try another approach or to move on to a discipline process. The point is that you can only directly control what you do and hope to affect what your employees do through your actions.

Actively changing what you say and do can indeed make a difference. You can choose to be collaborative. You can choose to listen. You can be respectful **and** clear and direct. You can support your staff to make choices about their actions.

So the question remains, what kind of supervisor do you choose to be and how does that transform your actions? It's about you.

Coaching Corner

- Take two minutes to write out an answer to the question in this section: What kind of supervisor are you? Then take one minute to reflect on how that image of yourself matches up with your daily actions.
- Are there particular times when you seem to act in a way that doesn't reflect who you want to be as a supervisor? What are the circumstances? Are there particular actions, or people, that trigger a different response from you?
- Do you tend to worry about how others will respond to your words and actions? How might it be different if you focused on making sure you are saying and doing what you need to say and do instead of spending your time in hypothetical "what if"-land?

IT'S ABOUT THEM TOO

I was minding my own business sipping a cup of tea at a local Starbucks when a man and a woman sat down near me and started talking. I couldn't help but overhear their conversation, and it soon became clear that this was their first meeting. They had apparently met online. During the half hour that I remained sitting there before I left to attend to the rest of my day, I heard more of their conversation than I wanted to. And what did I hear of their conversation? I heard the man talking. And talking and talking. Establishing his pedigree and expertise. Clearly trying to impress. I couldn't help but think: "Shut up. Ask her a question! Let her have a chance to talk!"

This happens far too often in supervision as well as on first dates. The supervisor is so intent on showing her staff that she is an expert that she doesn't stop talking. The conversation is one-sided and becomes a lecture. That doesn't work well when you're trying to communicate information and it works even less well when you are also trying to build relationships.

We all have an instinctive need to be seen. We want to be recognized, known, and valued for who we are and what we bring to the world. This need does not stop at work. When staff members feel unseen, they disengage a little bit—or a lot. And you, as a supervisor, are the person most responsible for seeing them.

This seeing is not about making them feel good, although it might do that. It feels good to be seen for who you are. This kind of seeing is about knowing who people are in terms of their work. It means seeing the strengths and weaknesses they bring to the job at hand. The relationship building that needs to happen as a part of supervision is based on the basic principle that people are different from each other and we all want to be seen and respected. It is about basic respect. When you can respect who people are, and understand how to help them succeed, you will be a more successful supervisor and the organization will be more successful. It is that simple—and that complex.

One of the foundations of being a good supervisor is cultivating strong, healthy, and appropriate relationships with the people you supervise. This does not mean being friends with people. Being friends can get in the way of good supervision. "Healthy" means respecting the boundaries of the relationship. You're not trying to know everything about your staff. You're not trying to heal their childhood wounds. You are trying to help them do their job well.

Relationships, whether personal or professional, grow through time and conversation. That's how we get to know people, by talking to them and spending time with them. We like to think work is different and we can just throw directions at someone and everything will be fine. And it might be, for a while. But if you want your team to be successful, you have to actually know who the team members are and how they work—individually and together. And that means you have to set aside time to connect with them, individually and together. It doesn't have to be a lot of time, but it does need to be consistent time.

Your relationships with your staff are built, or eroded, every time you talk. When you stop to say hello, when you scream at them that they did something wrong, when you explain a new work assignment, or when you ask how their injured dog is doing. It all matters.

Your time and your conversations with your staff are the foundation of a strong relationship with the people you supervise. These relationships continue to evolve based on the way you give assignments, how you give feedback, how you collaborate with your team, and how you display your power and authority. You make the relationship stronger when you keep your appointments with your staff. When you are trustworthy you let people know that you respect them and the work. All of these actions show how you see people, or how you don't.

In the overheard date at the coffee shop, the man was definitely being seen and heard. The woman, not so much. I have no idea if this initial date progressed to a second date, but unless the guy changed his approach, I doubt it. People need to be seen—on dates and at work.

Coaching Corner

- Think of your relationship with someone close to you. How did you build the relationship? Did you ever stay up all night talking? Did you do things together? Did you talk it through when you had misunderstandings? Think about the parallels of these kinds of interactions in supervision. You're not going to stay up all night talking, but you can commit to regular meetings so you know you have time to talk.
- When have you felt unseen or unheard? What did it feel like? What did you do about it?
- What comes up for you if you think of getting to know your staff? Perhaps you already know them well? When I suggest you can support people by paying attention to who they are, does that make sense to you or do you have an argument? Perhaps you have been advised to not get too close to your staff. Make a list of your concerns and then reread this chapter to see if your concerns are answered.

MY WAY OR THE HIGHWAY

I coached a supervisor, Diane, who practiced many good supervision habits. However, when she had me interview her staff, I found out that she drove them nuts! The reason? She insisted that each and every member of her team accomplish their tasks the way she would accomplish them.

Robert was a strong assistant to her but he was not overly organized. Although he responded to every request from Diane in a timely manner and had never misplaced a file, Diane continually rated him poorly on "organizing skills" and reminded him at least monthly that he needed to clean his desk.

Another one of her staff members, Katri, worked with clients and had never had a complaint about her work. Diane berated her for being too chatty and for letting her client documentation pile up throughout the day. If Diane was in Katri's job she knew she would be friendly but not chatty, and with the time she saved she would complete the paperwork after each client and file it away immediately. Katri preferred to chat with each person and keep a pile of paperwork to be completed in her desk. At the end of the day, she filed all the paperwork.

Diane's third employee David was another matter. He handled the financial records for the organization. He was an exempt employee, and he insisted that it worked better for him to come into work after hours to do his work. Diane was frustrated when she needed reports or data and David was not there to give them to her. They communicated through e-mail and David would get her the information she needed in the evenings when he came into work. She didn't doubt that he was working, but she was constantly begging him to shift his work hours to match the rest of the team.

Diane was a well-intentioned supervisor but she needed to let go of her "my way or the highway" attitude. There are times when it is essential to change the manner in which staff members are doing their jobs. For example, Diane was well within her rights to insist that David work during regular business hours. His absence affected her ability to do her work, and impacted other members of the team also. I worked with Diane to tell David that his work was part of the team process and that he needed to participate accordingly. While he was exempt, that did not mean he got to set his own hours. Diane reviewed the meaning of being an exempt employee with David and then told him that the basic hours of this job were eight to five. If those hours had not worked for David, Diane could have considered whether some compromise hours would work or if she did in fact need to find someone who could work the regular schedule. Fortunately, David adjusted his schedule and his team involvement improved.

For the other staff members, however, Diane was confusing

the way **she** would handle a situation with the requirements of the job. The basic question for Diane and other supervisors is "How does this impact the employee's ability to do his or her work?" If the answer is that it doesn't, then the concern may just be a matter of style differences. If the work is adequately completed but the way someone does it annoys you, then you might need to look inward for the solution to the problem. Can you articulate how a person's style is impacting the work in a negative manner? If not, consider letting it go and focusing instead on the results.

Instead of a "my way or the highway" attitude, develop an approach of "my way or your way—as long as the requirements of the job get done."

Coaching Corner

- Are there any members of your team who have a different style than you? How do you usually respond to that difference?
- Reflect on what meaning you give to the fact that someone does something in a completely different way than you do. Do you think they are wrong? Or that they might be criticizing your style? What do you tell yourself about the difference?
- Is there any staff member who you struggle with about how they do something? If so, use the basic question of "How does this impact the employee's ability to do his or her work?" to ensure that the change is required by the work and not your own personal style.
- Imagine how you would frame a conversation with Robert, Katri, or David to either change a work practice or apologize for your hypervigilance and tell them you're willing to try it their way as long as they get the needed results.

INTENTIONAL CONVERSATIONS

> *Accidental:* unintentional, unintended,
> inadvertent, chance, unplanned.
> **Example:**
> Buying a tire because you had a blowout and now
> need a replacement immediately.
>
> *Intentional:* deliberate, on purpose, planned,
> intended, premeditated.
> **Example:**
> Carefully monitoring your tire treads so you are
> prepared when it's time to buy a new one.

To be an effective supervisor you must thoughtfully build relationships that help you help your staff be successful. To do that you must know what makes each one of them tick in relation to their job. This requires intentional conversations.

An intentional conversation is a two-way conversation designed to help both you and your employee understand each other better, relative to the work. For instance, part of your job as a supervisor is to motivate your staff. So you might ask the question that's on your mind: "What motivates you?" They will often ask for more money because that seems like the most likely way to motivate someone. But if you word the question differently, you might get more helpful answers and the question won't seem as artificial.

"So, Joanne, I'm going to try something new to help us both do our work the best we can. I'm going to start each of our one-on-one meetings with a question that we'll both take a turn answering. We'll just take two minutes each. I promise the questions won't be intrusive and will always be about work. So let's give it a try. Tell me which parts of your job you enjoy most."

The following week you might ask, "What is one thing you would change about your job if you could?"

You can learn a lot in two minutes. (See more ideas for intentional questions at the end of this section.) This type of exchange does several things. You're building your relationship by listening and talking as partners. And you're learning how the person you supervise works. It is very important that this be a safe exchange. Focus on simply listening and understanding both sides of the conversation. This is not the time to judge their answers or correct their feelings. If you listen thoughtfully, you will learn a lot. These conversations will not be useful if you shut down their honest answers by your reaction. If you need to clarify objective information, do it at another time.

You might learn concrete information that you can directly apply to their jobs. You might learn they love to do a task that someone else on your team hates to do; that's an easy fix that will leave both people feeling heard and valued. Or you might realize that this particular employee loves a challenge. Good to know. Keep that in mind. In these conversations you might together learn something about your preferences as a supervisor that will help both of you. (Like the fact that you hate to organize the department potlucks and your staff member would enjoy it.)

Even if what you hear doesn't immediately help you help them do their job better, pay attention. Listen. Take it in. It might prove valuable later. At the very least, the act of really listening makes a difference.

It works. Take time to ask intentional questions and, most importantly, listen to their answers. And let them listen to yours. You may find that these few moments of intentional conversations can add up to big changes.

Coaching Corner

- Often supervisors consider that their input to their staff is a one-way flow of information. The practice described in this section focuses on the two-way communication required in a supervisory relationship. How do you feel about answering questions about your work style or priorities? If revealing this kind of information to your staff makes you nervous, think about what that means. Does it imply a lack of trust or a fear of giving away power? Simply consider what it means to you as a supervisor.

- Make a plan to try a two-way, two-minute per person, intentional exchange within the next week with the people you supervise. Time the two minutes for each person and then note what you heard and what you learned. Was it worth it?

- If you heard that someone "loved a challenge," how could you use that information to be a better supervisor to him or her?

Sample Questions for Intentional Conversations

MOTIVATION

- What makes you want to come to work?
- Tell me about a time you were really excited about a project you were working on.
- What parts of your job do you like the best?
- If you could change one thing about your job, what would it be?
- If you could design your perfect job, what would you do?
- When do you feel most engaged with your work?
- What is one skill you wish you could use more at work?
- What do you wish you had more time to do during work?
- What inspires you?

WORK STYLES

- How did you come to work here?
- What kinds of tasks do you find most engaging?
- What do you enjoy least about your job?
- When do you generally prefer to work on your own and when do you prefer to work as part of a team?
- Are there parts of your work that you'd like to approach in a different manner?
- What time of day do you do your best work?

continued ⇨

COMMUNICATION

- How do you like to communicate with someone
    - For routine matters?
    - For updates?
    - For problem-solving?
    - For feedback?
- When do you feel comfortable disagreeing with someone?
- What drives you crazy in terms of communication?
- How do you generally respond to deadlines?
- When have you found feedback helpful and when has it been delivered in a way that made it hard for you to hear?

LEARNING

- In general, how do you learn best?
- Tell me about a time when you learned something.
- What did you notice about your learning process the last time you tried something new? Or do you notice anything in telling about it now?
- What would make it safe to make a mistake while you were learning?
- What might get in the way of your learning?

RECOGNITION

- Tell me about a time you felt really appreciated.
- How can I best let you know that your work is valued?
- If there was a parade in your honor, what might it be about?
- What kind of recognition would make you want to "write home" about it?

RELATIONSHIPS IN MINUTES

It takes time and conversation to build a relationship. But how much time does it take? Years? Days? Hours? How about a few minutes? There are so many variables, of course, but over time, even small encounters can lead to connections and relationships.

When the Golden Gate Bridge became the first major bridge in the country to fully convert to electronic toll taking, twenty-eight full-time toll workers lost their jobs. What amazed me in the stories that surrounded this event were the countless stories of relationships formed with these people. Relationships had formed in the ten seconds it took to drive through the tollbooth! Over weeks, months, and years, relationships were formed. People were bringing flowers and crying over the loss of those ten-second exchanges.

One poignant story emerged of a child who waved to the toll woman every day of his life. When it was time for him to give up his pacifier, he decided to give it to the toll woman to keep for him! When this woman lost her job because of the elimination of her position, the boy was twelve years old and he held up a sign to the window that said: "We will miss you" as he and his family rolled through her tollbooth for the last time.

Relationships are built on people seeing each other. Seeing who each other is and what each other does. Although these toll workers did not know much of anything about the drivers, or vice versa, they saw each other every day. This seeing was more than the physical sight; it was about recognizing each other as unique individuals and making a human connection in those seconds. Over time that seeing led to a connection that was trusted and valued on both sides.

See the people you work with and let them really see you. Have conversations, large and small, that help you know each other. Don't pry into their personal lives to try to force connection, but simply listen, be open, and notice who they are and how they work. Notice what matters to them. How many of your employees have pets? Do you know the last movie they saw? Again, it's not about using conversations or questions to grill someone; it's about paying attention. Build on what you know. Talk about your best work together. Ask them what they hope to learn on the job. Ask if they have ideas on how to do their work better. Make sure the conversations are two-way conversations. And if there are any employees that you haven't talked to in a while, maybe because they do good work, go out of your way to see them and talk to them.

Relationships can be established second by second, over time. It can make all the difference in the world and build a bridge to long-term connections.

Coaching Corner

- What is one relationship that you can improve by focusing on quick intentional conversations? Make a plan to practice that focused conversation for a period of time—say over three weeks—and see what happens.
- Are there people in your life that you have a casual but meaningful relationship with, like the toll workers? Take a second the next time you see them to acknowledge that fact. It can be a simple appreciation like, "Thanks

for being so friendly," or a statement of what the relationship is, like, "It's great to see you every day."

- Are there any people you interact with on a daily basis where you are consistently not present? Do you ignore cashiers when they make change or look at your phone instead of saying hello? Try noticing and seeing them for a change and see how it feels.

THE IMPORTANCE OF SEEING

Part One

When I go to Starbucks I always get the same drink: a strong chai tea. One day, when I ordered my regular drink, the cashier charged me twenty cents extra for my two extra pumps of chai. I politely told her, "No, that doesn't cost extra. I never have to pay more for it."

She just looked at me. She didn't say anything. She didn't nod; she didn't smile; she just looked at me, waiting for me to pay. Even if she didn't want to deduct the extra charge, she could have said something simple like, "I'll check that out," or, "That's how I was trained." But she didn't say anything! She acted like she didn't hear me. This made me feel like she didn't **see** me. As if I weren't even there.

I felt myself get so angry. Really angry. Out of proportion angry. It wasn't the twenty cents; it was how she made me feel invisible. I paid for my drink and left and I carried the anger with me into my day. I drove away feeling furious. After a block, I talked myself down and let it go.

This incident was a visceral reminder of how important it is to be seen and heard.

Part Two

Studies have shown that 80 percent of complaints can be resolved by simply hearing the complainants' concerns. Not even necessarily doing anything, just listening and hearing. When they are heard, people feel seen.

This explains the importance of good customer service but it applies to all of us in every part of our lives, as complainers and as those who receive complaints.

Part Three

In supervision, the supervisor **will** be seen and heard. By virtue of their positional power and the communications flow in organizations, a supervisor will get their message across. Hopefully, as a supervisor, you are attentive to your message and convey your expectations, information, and feedback in a thoughtful and coherent manner.

In many organizations, however, the employees being supervised feel unheard and unseen. Communication flows down but never up. Directives are delivered on the fly as the supervisor passes someone's desk. In too many situations, the employee only hears from their supervisor when there is a problem. All of these common practices leave employees feeling invisible.

Scheduling regular individual meetings with your staff is necessary to counteract the prevailing invisibility. When you meet with your staff on a regular basis you can establish a clear practice of listening and learning about the people you supervise. Put specific effort into having two-way conversations. It is also important to have clearly defined and structured team meetings in which you facilitate communication between all team members.

Some people are more visible by virtue of their extroversion or confidence. Other people are more quiet and reserved. That does not mean that the quiet ones don't need to be seen and heard. Nor does it mean that they don't have good ideas to contribute. It is your job to invite, encourage, and expect people's participation—in individual and group meetings.

Seeing the people you supervise will help you build relationships with them, will help them see and respect you in turn, and will ultimately create a stronger team and more effective and productive work. You'll see!

Coaching Corner

- Have you ever had an experience like the one I describe in Part One? Did you realize that you felt unheard and unseen? Remember what that was like and stretch your empathy muscles by imagining how it might feel for your employees to feel that at work.
- What do you know about the strengths and challenges of the individuals you supervise? Do you take those into consideration when you delegate work?
- Have you established regularly scheduled one-on-one meetings with the people you supervise? If not, when can you start?
- Do your team meetings have a clearly agreed upon purpose and process? Does everyone know what those are? If not, how can you build an interactive process to identify a way that sees every team member?

ASSUME THE BEST

Capers are tiny round pickled spice pods used in Mediterranean cooking. Their flavor is potent and permeates whatever dish they are added to. I don't like capers. I ordered fish at a restaurant recently and the description didn't mention the capers in the tomato sauce. It's not something you can pick out, either, so the meal was not very enjoyable to me.

A short time after this meal I was working with a group that was experiencing difficulties. I realized as I met with each person in the group that their problem was caper-like. They had one bad habit that had permeated the group: the practice of assuming bad intentions. In and of itself, the habit appeared to be fairly minor and innocuous, but like capers, the impact of adding it to this group was intense. When I interviewed these team members, staff actively distrusted each other. They said things like, "I don't know if she's telling me the truth." And "If I'm lucky, I'll get the data from her by the deadline." Every staff member spoke of their work in individual terms: I/me/mine. A healthy team uses words like we/us/our. But there was no space for the flavor of collective work, or the "we," to develop with that distrust of each other's intentions infusing their expectations.

This habit of assuming bad intentions can develop in a group when there is distance, disconnection, or lack of communication. The distance may be physical or emotional. Departments that work together all the time can still be distant if they don't actively work on building common ground and human connections. People who don't know each other well enough can easily become "other." It becomes a matter of me versus them, my work is more important than theirs. Once that happens, it is easy to slip into the habit of assuming bad intentions.

Here's what happened: Gretchen, the administrative assistant, made a mistake on someone's monthly report. Although she corrected it right away, Sally (whose report was wrong) told her coworkers to make sure they studied their reports because Gretchen didn't know what she was doing. If any one of Sally's coworkers knew and trusted Gretchen, they would have walked over to her and found out what happened. "Hey Gretchen, I need to talk to you. I heard there was a problem with Sally's report. Do I need to be worried about my report?" Gretchen would have answered honestly and said, "No. Somebody spilled a soda on her input sheet and I misread a number that got smudged. I am very careful with the monthly reports; I know people depend on them." The team would have realized that it was an innocent mistake and moved on in their work.

What happened with this team, however, was that no one knew Gretchen personally. She was new and hadn't yet connected with her coworkers. So no one talked to Gretchen, in general or when it came to this mistake. No one checked it out. They didn't even consider that option because they saw Gretchen as "other." Their focus remained on their own work. It felt to them like Gretchen didn't care about their work. Maybe she even did it on purpose. And then they ran with that assumption. That one mistake built into questions and assumptions about administration. The administrative team became defensive and started pointing out mistakes that the service team was making, trying to "share the blame" but in reality creating more of a culture of distrust. Before long people within the same organization were acting like enemies based on numerous assumptions and interpretations that may or may not have had any root in reality. When situations like this begin, they can even permeate the whole organization so that everyone is seen as "other" and bad intentions are assumed at every turn. That makes workplace cooperation, communication, and productivity much more difficult and seriously hinders the mission.

This negative spiral is avoidable. And as a supervisor you have a big role to play in this whether you are directly involved or observe such interactions percolating between staff. Hopefully you prevent many situations like this from beginning in the first place by fostering healthy workplace relationships, trust, and communications. But even when there is distance or disconnection, you have a choice about your response to mistakes or conflicts. First of all, you can acknowledge the distance or disconnect and see if you can find a way to get together and connect. In the meantime, you can stop yourself from assuming bad intention. Listen to this hypothetical internal monologue in response to the Gretchen incident: "Wow. My monthly report is really important and it feels like Gretchen doesn't care about that. In fact, she doesn't care about any of us. I'll show her . . . wait—wait—wait a minute. What am I assuming? Maybe Gretchen didn't do this on purpose. Maybe she doesn't even know there was a mistake on my report. Maybe Gretchen cares about us and tries to do a good job. I need to talk to Gretchen."

The assumption of good intention is the part that takes this internal commentary in a whole new direction. If I assume that Gretchen is working as hard as I am, then I will proceed very differently. If I assume that Gretchen means well, then I will stop myself from making assumptions about what she did. If I assume bad intention, then I won't bother to give Gretchen the benefit of the doubt. As a supervisor, you can examine your own assumptions about others, but you also can help members of your team question the assumptions they're making about coworkers in order to promote problem-solving and communication.

Of course there are times when there **is** bad intention. Occasionally people **are** out to make trouble, and when you truly have reason to distrust someone, you must address that. These cases are not routine, however, and letting your staff act with distrust and lack of communication would be like throwing capers in every dish you make—it just doesn't work!

Coaching Corner

- What is your usual response when someone makes trouble in your life? Do you automatically assume bad intention behind the action?
- Do you routinely "check out" your assumptions? If not, what stops you?
- Is there anyone whom you have assumed to have bad intentions? Do you need to formulate a plan to meet with this person or group to start over, or at least to examine that assumption?
- Does your team know that each person on the team has the good of the organization in mind? If you answer yes, how do you know that? Is that an assumption in itself?

RITA'S RULES OF ENGAGEMENT

As a supervisor there will be times when you need to engage with someone who has a different opinion, approach, or need concerning the outcomes of a project or action. This might involve a conversation with your supervisor, a peer, a staff member, a union, a vendor, or a customer/client. No matter what you are negotiating, it is imperative that you pay attention to how this interaction is impacting the relationship, especially if the relationship is going to continue.

When I was working to build and maintain relationships across the union negotiating table, I developed four basic practices that reminded me how I wanted to do negotiations. Even more important, these practices reminded me of who I wanted to be during negotiations. I encourage you to use these if you like them, or develop your own rules of engagement.

✓ Be My Best Self

The primary practice while dealing with other people is to remember that I can control and change only my own behavior. In all transactions I need to listen for the voice that calls me to be my own best self and not give into any temptation to be small or untrustworthy. While it is important to agree on rules of conduct and methods for discussion as we negotiate, we cannot direct the actual actions of anyone but ourselves.

✓ Hear and See Each Individual

I need to recognize the other person as an individual, not just an opponent or a position. I can take time to engage in conversation, mentioning what I did over the weekend and inquiring about theirs. In order to see and hear each other, we need to know each other. We don't have to be friends but it never hurts to know what kind of movies someone enjoys. Bring curiosity to the table to learn who people are and what matters to them.

✓ Play Nice with Other People

When engaged in any conflict, it is easy to designate sides: our side and their side, us and them, good and bad. This sets up an adversarial relationship from which it is difficult to then build common language, interests, and solutions. Early in my marriage my husband and I learned how powerful it was, in the midst of an argument, if one of us would get up and cross the room to stand beside the other. This became a direct physical metaphor: we're on the same side. In almost every relationship there is some bottom line that we are both working toward. Reframing the issue in terms of the common side can be a compelling first step that sets the tone for the remaining conversation. Once we remember that we're working as partners to solve a common problem, it is more possible to listen well and be present.

✓ Share My Candy

The final practice that I use to build relationships is one that is as old as civilization itself—the act of breaking bread together. When people share a meal, or a snack, it can be an opening to our shared humanity. People can often talk easier over a cup of coffee. It will not create instant solutions, but it can build the relationship.

Coaching Corner

- What does it mean to you to be your best self? How do you know if you are working and living in line with the values that matter most to you?
- Have you ever gotten pulled into an adversarial relationship that didn't solve the problem at hand? What can you do to remind yourself that you're "on the same side," or at least share a common interest in a solution?
- Do you believe that relationships can make a difference in conflict? What do you do to intentionally build relationships?

INVITING STAFF TO PUSH BACK

"Costco called to tell me my contacts are in," I mentioned casually during lunch with my son and his family. My delightful three-year old grandson who has been to Costco countless times looked at me with confusion in his face and asked, "Where is Costco's mouth?"

This was a funny reminder of how easily we can slip into jargon and turns of phrase that we assume everyone understands. Most of the time we are probably right in our assumption that people are on the same page as us, but sometimes we're not. New people or people who come from different cultures than our own (including different work cultures) may be left confused and embarrassed that they don't understand what you're talking about. It's important to take the extra time and consideration to ensure that everyone is on the same page and understands the same thing.

If you, as the supervisor, do not occasionally (and respectfully) pause to check for understanding, you will not know that there wasn't understanding until it is too late. Remember that it is hard to be the one to stop the conversation and ask, "What are you talking about?" Or "What does PCN stand for?" Or "How exactly do you handle that procedure here?"

Given the inherent power differential in the supervisory relationship, most of the time employees are going to assume that they *should* understand what you're telling them and that if they don't, they're supposed to figure it out on their own. It would be quicker and easier if they could just ask you, but most people don't think this way. Even if you've thrown out the offer, "Ask me any question at any time," most employees don't feel comfortable asking questions unless you repeat the offer over and over again, and wait for a response. Or if you set up those one-on-one conversations that give them an opportunity to come to you with their issues, questions, and concerns.

Practice catching yourself using idioms, initials, or shorthand, and pause. It isn't enough to simply ask, "Do you know what PCN stands for?" because that can seem like a test. A test that they should know what it stands for. Better to pause and explain, "PCN is the acronym for Personnel Change Notice. We use that all the time." Only if an employee says something like, "Yeah, I know," can you safely assume that they know it. If they say, "Okay," or "Oh yeah, right," those are signs that they didn't know and you just saved them some confusion.

In addition to this practice of catching and explaining yourself, it's good to build the overarching practice of encouraging your staff to "push back." You want your staff to know that not only is it okay to push back, but that you expect it. By "push back" I mean that they ask questions—about acronyms, procedures, strategy, mistakes, confusions, practices—about everything that impacts their job. And that they proactively tell you things. Allow them to offer their opinions: to tell you when they think something isn't going to work; that they don't see how they can fit another project on their plate; when they have lost sight of their priorities; when they are feeling bored and underutilized. These are all things that are good for you to know.

You will not know these things if you don't actively encourage pushback and make it safe for them to do so. Let them know that you expect them to have questions. Tell them to stop you if a question is getting in the way of them understanding you. You can tell them, "Ask me anything anytime" but don't stop there. Follow up with consistent check-ins and clarifications. "Do you have any questions?" "Let's make sure we're on the same page. What are your plans for this week?" "Are there any phrases or jargon you've heard that you don't understand?" "What do we need to consider as we move forward with this project?" "What do you think about this plan?" By actively and consistently asking these kinds of questions, you make your offer real and not just a theoretical idea.

It's imperative that you practice the next step in this interaction with your employees with absolute attention: Listen. Listen intently. Listen actively. Listen even if they initially have nothing to say. Do not just pause and go on. Stop. Wait for them to respond.

Wait through occasionally uncomfortable silences. Wait. Listen. Even if they end up saying, "No, I don't have any questions." In that silence, in that waiting, you've let them know that this is real. You want to hear what they have to say. You **really** do. There is room for pushback.

The next step is also important. Respond respectfully to whatever they say. Even if they say something that astounds you, like, "What's a Personnel Change Notice?" when they are holding one in their hands and you've reviewed the form every day for a week. We all have our moments. Let them have theirs and don't berate them or shame them. If you ask for their opinion about something, listen and treat them respectfully, even if you don't like the idea.

It doesn't mean you have to do anything about their opinion, but if you asked for it, hear it. You can simply respond neutrally, "Thanks for telling me what you think." This will make it safe for them to ask what they need to ask and to tell you what they need to tell you. It will also give you a good idea of what they are thinking about. You need to know these things. But if you respond with any kind of judgment, "No, that's never going to work." Or, "We've tried that a million times," or even with no comment but let out a big sigh, they will hear that you don't really want to hear their ideas. They will stop offering them, even if you ask for them. It doesn't mean you can't tell them what you think if they ask. "That's an interesting idea but I don't think it will work. Let me tell you why."

Catch your jargon. Invite pushback. In doing so, you'll invite a strong partnership that can help you both be successful. And no one will be left silently wondering, "Where is Costco's mouth?"

Coaching Corner

- Monitor your jargon count for a day and see how often you use phrases or idioms that outsiders might not understand.
- Do you welcome "pushback" from your staff? If so, how

have you let them know it? If not, how will you let them
know that you're open to it?

- How comfortable are you with listening? Especially
  through moments of silence? If you are not comfortable
  with this, how could you practice it in small increments
  so you can build your tolerance level?
- How have you actively made your work environment
  safe for employees to ask questions or make
  comments? How have you passively or inadvertently
  made it unsafe?

CHAPTER 2:

How You Talk

GOOD MORNING

I once received a thank-you note from someone that read in part, "Thank you for your warm 'Good Mornings.'" This was not a person I supervised. This was not a person I even saw every day, but when I did see him I said "Good morning. How are you today?" Or, "How was your weekend?" And I waited to hear his answer.

Apparently this meant something to him. In my work, I've heard people say, "I can be standing right in front of my boss and say 'hi' and he doesn't even reply. I don't even bother anymore." I can't count how many times people have told me, "She doesn't even say good morning to me. It's like she doesn't even see me." In those moments, when these employees felt unseen because of the lack of a basic friendly greeting, they became a bit disengaged from their work. As discussed in the previous chapter, seeing the people you supervise is a crucial component of the job. You must see them as people—not just as clerks, or caseworkers, or programmers. People are not their jobs. They have lives and feelings and events going on.

I can hear you saying, "Well of course they do. I know that!" But do you act like you know it? Do you know that, really? What does Brayden love to do on the weekend? What's important to him? What is he most worried about these days? Knowing the people you supervise as people, not just as workers, is one of the first steps in building an effective framework of supervision.

This is not to say that you should be nosy or pushy or intrusive. It is up to each person to open up and to share any facts of his or her personal lives. Or to choose not to share. But if you don't ever ask a general question, then they won't feel that you even recognize that they are individuals. Open-ended questions open the door for a person to step through: "How was your weekend?" "Did you do anything fun last night?" "How's Fido doing?" (If you know they have a Fido pet in their lives.) They may choose to give you a one-word answer, especially if this is a change from your usual interaction with them. And that's a clear sign to stop. But just asking will let people know that you see them and recognize that they have lives.

When this door to conversation opens, it is also important that you respond authentically—that you let the people you supervise see you as a real person also. Slowly, this recognition and door opening can build into a relationship. These don't have to be long heart-to-heart conversations. They can be brief exchanges that build on each other. Maybe you hear that someone has gone to the movies four out of five times when you've asked what they did over the weekend. Then you can start asking, "Did you see that new action movie that just came out?" Or give them a gift certificate to the local movie theater as a special thank-you for a job well done. They will know that you are paying attention and that you are seeing them.

The second half of the equation is even more essential. If you take time to ask a question, you **must** stand there and wait for an answer. Otherwise, it is worse than not asking at all. If you don't have time to listen to an answer, then don't ask. Asking as you pass in the hall, without slowing down, marks you as someone going through the motions who clearly does **not** care. Sometimes you really don't have time, so don't ask.

But you can always say, "Good Morning!"

Coaching Corner

- How do you feel when people pass you in the halls at work without saying hello? Do you care? If you do, notice what that feels like. If you don't care, simply consider that it does matter to some people.
- Think about what you are comfortable sharing about your personal life with your staff and where your line of privacy lies.
- What can you do this month to ensure that each person you supervise feels seen by you?

PRAISE AND THANK-YOUS

"I only hear from my boss when something goes wrong," Elsa told me with real sadness. She loved her job but she was tired of "getting in trouble." She told me she was starting to look for another job. She thought that if her work didn't matter, then she might as well try to get a job that paid better. I knew that her boss did in fact appreciate her work; he had told **me** how great she was many times, but unfortunately he rarely told her.

Avoid being the kind of boss who interacts with your staff only when there are problems or mistakes. Be proactive about noticing, appreciating, and praising when things are going well. It may feel awkward at first if you are not used to it, but try to give compliments and praise for a job well done, and become familiar with it.

In one study done at Wichita State University, 58 percent of employees said they never received positive feedback from their managers. Never! The same study showed that a personal thanks from a manager was one of the most motivating things for employees. Personal recognition and appreciation can create a world of difference.

It's a sad fact of modern life that we all have way too much to do. When you are feeling overwhelmed it's easy to focus on the next item on your list and to take the things that are working for granted. So you might need to add this task of acknowledging people for their good work to your to-do list to remind yourself to do it. However, it must be sincere. If you just walk out of your office at 4:15 every day and say, "Good job everyone!" that will not work. You need to find real things to appreciate. Your praise needs to be specific and timely. General appreciation for a job well done is appropriate, but it will mean more if it is done in conjunction with specific recognition. When you receive a report, thank the person who sent it to you. When you hear from a client how helpful someone was, share the news and add your appreciation for the excellent representation of the organization. When a major project is well done, praise the people who made it happen.

Here are a few ideas to help you get started:

- ✓ Write the names of each person you supervise on your weekly or monthly calendar. Put a check next to their name every time you find a sincere way to appreciate them.
- ✓ Set aside a specific time every week, like Friday morning, to write a note to a staff member or

coworker, thanking them for something they did that week that impacted your job.

✓ On special holidays or events, like the company's anniversary celebration, send a note to their home telling your staff how much they contribute to the organization.

✓ Make a note of birthdays and anniversaries and give your staff members balloons or a few hours off.

✓ Send an e-mail or voice mail after hours or over the weekend just to say thanks. Imagine how good it would feel if you received something like that on a Monday morning!

✓ Throw a dart at a calendar to determine an unexpected date to take your staff out to lunch. Be sure to let them know that the lunch is in recognition for the work they do all year long. (Make sure you block off extraordinarily busy times so this doesn't become a setup.)

✓ When you say goodnight at the end of a busy day, say, "Thank you for the hard work you did today"—as long as you mean it.

Don't be the kind of boss whom your employees only see when there is trouble. Do something on a regular basis to let people know that you notice their work and their efforts. It's a little thing that can keep employees satisfied with their jobs—and their supervisor.

Coaching Corner

• Think about the last few times you spoke directly to each of your staff members when you weren't giving them directives. How many of those times were critical and how many were appreciative?

- How does it feel for you to say "thank you" and mean it to someone? If it is hard for you, what is that about?
- How do you recognize yourself for work well done?

CURIOSITY: WAKE IT UP TO SLOW DOWN

"That's it, she's late again and hasn't called me. I'm firing her!" Carl was furious. His employee, Mary, had been late repeatedly and he was fed up with it. Now she was late again.

"Okay, you may be right but before you decide what to do, talk to her. Ask her what's going on. Find out why she was late. You need to make sure there wasn't an accident or something else that you find out about **after** you've fired her," I counseled him.

As it turned out, there wasn't a radical reason why she was late. But the fact that he stopped to ask the question opened a new conversation between them. Mary felt respected and acknowledged by the fact that he did not assume what was going on and that he cared enough to ask. She responded with the truth and was able to hear his concerns in a way she hadn't before. It shifted their entire relationship.

It was certainly relevant to the employee that she didn't get fired, but the pertinent lesson I saw in all of this was the understanding on the part of the manager that it was important to slow down to ask questions. It is crucial that as a supervisor you make sure you have all the facts, especially before you take a drastic step like firing someone. So often we look at things only from our perspective and we forget that there even is another perspective. That's a big mistake—in supervision and in life.

Curiosity is a sense that we can outgrow. Children are so curious. Once they learn to talk, the questions pop out of them nonstop. Why is the sky blue? How does the phone work? Why did you tell that lady she looked nice? Why do people die? Why? Why? Why? They wonder and they ask. They don't censor themselves.

As we grow up we learn about life and we don't ask so many questions. At some point, we seem to decide that we know enough and then we might stop asking questions altogether. Even worse, we might stop wondering. We don't even let ourselves hear the questions, never mind asking them out loud.

A traditional view of supervision frames the supervisor as the expert. They are assumed to be the one who knows where the team is going, how they are going to get there, and what the rules are. In this view of the work world, there is no need to get input from the ones being supervised. The supervisor knows all the relevant information. In reality, it works much better when the supervisor acknowledges that they have important information and so do the staff they supervise. Each person has his or her unique view of the project. When important choices need to be made, making sure all the information is on the table ensures that the supervisor is in the best position to decide how to move forward.

Taking time to ask questions not only assures that you will have the information you need to make decisions but also opens the door to have conversations. It can strengthen your relationship with the people you supervise and help to build the team. Be curious. You might wonder what their intention was in their approach to a problem. Are they having any problems with their project? What do they see as their top priorities for the week? How do they think their work impacts their coworkers? What happens for their teammates when they show up late for work? Is there any information they need to move forward on the report that is due next week?

Asking questions and getting relevant information makes you a better supervisor. Check in. Be curious. Ask questions. Slow down and listen to their responses before you decide how to proceed. Make curiosity your friend and it will serve you well.

Coaching Corner

• What stops you from asking questions that pop into your mind? How is that helping you and how is that hurting you?

• Is there a situation where you wondered, "What were they thinking!" How can you phrase that as a question or statement of curiosity so you can really get the information and not just shut down communication? (Perhaps a version of "Tell me what your plan was when you took that step.")

• Is there a decision you're facing in which you haven't considered relevant information from your staff ?

SHOW UP AND TELL THE TRUTH

What do you do when you just don't want to do anything? Is showing up ever enough, in and of itself?

For me, this is not a rhetorical question. There are many times, in my writing and in my consulting, when I feel like I have nothing to say. I know that is not literally true. Sometimes I just feel disconnected.

So I show up and I tell the truth. Sometimes that is all you can do. And sometimes it is the very best you can do. It sounds deceptively simple: show up and tell the truth. And yet, oftentimes, it is more than enough.

Show up and be present. As a supervisor, it is essential that you do this. I have seen many supervisory relationships fall apart simply because the supervisors were not present. Either they literally were not present or they were so engrossed in their own tasks that they forgot that they were supervisors. Being present and available is one of the essential tasks of supervision. You set the direction for the team. If you are not there, then things can get misdirected or take a wrong turn. Your staff needs to be able to count on your help in answering questions and in offering support. Sometimes this support means you need to run interference for them and sometimes it means offering a kind word or a clarifying comment. Often it simply means being there in case you are needed.

Show up at meetings. This means being there physically, but also being there mentally. Be attentive. Once I did a training where a team leader came late, left early, and was holding side conversations while I was presenting. She was very clearly telling her team that this training did not matter. She wasn't engaged, so why should they bother? Part of supervision is building effective actions, and this is an area where modeling behavior is crucial. Show others the type of behavior you expect from them. Be there. Be prepared. Offer ideas. Listen to other ideas. Respond. Interact and participate.

Just as you need to recognize your staff as individuals, not just as workers, you need to be there as an individual also. This doesn't mean bringing all your dirty laundry to work or making your personal life available for inspection, but it does mean being real. Being yourself and responding in real time as you recognize ideas, thoughts, reflections, feelings, and problems.

It also means telling the truth in good times and in bad. Your staff needs to trust that they can count on you to tell the truth, even if the news is not great. This seems counterintuitive but it is true. There is nothing worse than a manager telling someone, "Don't worry, everything is fine," and then announcing five days (or five minutes) later, "Uh-oh! TROUBLE!" People prefer to know about trouble when it happens rather than to have people pretend it is not happening. Plus, if there's trouble—with something at work or with their performance, your employees have a right to know about it.

The power of telling the truth in the moment was exhibited for me after a sexual harassment training I did. A few days after the training, a supervisor I trained heard someone making an inappropriate sexual comment.

If she didn't say anything in that very moment, she would have been condoning the behavior. She had to let the whole team know that the comment was out of line and wouldn't be tolerated. Acting in the moment set the tone for the kind of work environment they were striving for as a team, as well as protecting them in any potential harassment claims.

This kind of thing happens to supervisors often and in many ways it is the hardest part of being a supervisor. We all want to just look the other way sometimes. Not just with inappropriate comments, but with any number of little problems: people coming in late, complaints, missed deadlines, whatever—it feels easier in the moment to let it slide. But that is almost always a mistake. Show up and tell the truth. Address problems as they arise.

Sometimes showing up and telling the truth is not only all you can do—sometimes it is the best you can do.

Coaching Corner

- When are you not showing up? Is there an area of your work or your life when you are either literally not showing up or mentally not present?
- Where in your life is there a truth that needs to be spoken? What is holding you back from telling the truth?
- What obstacle do you need to address to become more skillful at showing up and telling the truth?

DO I HEAR YOU NOW?

Have you ever had the experience of spending a considerable amount of time listening to someone only to hear him or her proclaim, "You never listen to me!" I have been baffled by this experience in my life—both personally and professionally. Sometimes I recognize the frustration behind the sentiment. Perhaps it was a group of disgruntled employees who were lobbying for a change and when they didn't get the change they wanted, they assumed they were not heard. If their bosses had heard them, surely they would have understood their point of view and made a change! Or an employee tells her supervisor that she was late meeting a deadline because of a crisis in her life, and the supervisor does not mention the crisis in her response.

So how can you make sure people feel heard, regardless of what comes next? Active listening is the practice of listening with full attention to focus on understanding what another person is communicating and then reflecting it back to that person. It can help people feel heard no matter the outcome of the conversation. Consider this conversation in which an employee is expressing her frustration and her supervisor is reflecting what is heard so the employee knows she is being heard:

> "You never listen to me! I talk and talk and talk and you just talk over me. It makes me angry."
>
> "I hear that you feel angry because you think I don't listen to you."
>
> "Yes. It's like you think you know what I'm going to say and don't even bother to hear if it is what I'm really saying. Sometimes I wonder why I even bother to talk to you."
>
> "Wow! You feel like I assume what you're going to say and don't listen to what you really do say. You're so frustrated you don't even feel like talking to me sometimes."
>
> "YES!"

Active listening is a powerful tool. Sometimes it feels artificial, but if it is done well, it can make a big difference in communication. The process works in part because of the reflecting back. You are more engaged in what they're actually saying when you force yourself to repeat back what you've heard in your own words.

In my experience, I've learned that making sure that the other person feels heard is as important as active listening, if not more so. You might hear and understand what another person is saying to you, but that may be irrelevant if they do not feel heard. If you understand, but the speaker doesn't think you do, then the conversation cannot move forward. Until the speaker feels heard and understood, you are still at square one.

The best way to know if a person feels heard is to ask him or her. Check it out. After reflecting what you heard, ask: "Did I get it right?" Or, "Did I hear you correctly?" Or, "Did I miss anything?" Then the conversation can move forward. You might have to do this a few times—even going over the same information until you get agreement that you did in fact hear them. Only when the person acknowledges that you have heard and understood them correctly should you move on.

This type of interaction doesn't need to happen in every single conversation you have with people, of course, but it is very helpful for difficult conversations, new assignments to a staff member, complicated instructions, or confusion. If you find yourself frustrated, or sense that the person you're speaking to is frustrated, slow down and practice active listening. Ask, "Did I get it?" This is an investment of time that will pay off in the long run. Or maybe even in the short run. Once a person experiences you as a real listener, then trust starts to build and it won't take so long next time. And they won't spend time telling other people how unheard they feel.

Coaching Corner

- When have you felt really heard? How did this affect the situation you were in?
- Is there a situation where someone repeats himself or herself over and over about the same topic? Is there a

way you can practice active listening with them to help
them feel heard so they can move on?

• What gets in the way of really listening to someone?
Are you rushed? Are you thinking about your response?
Are you thinking about something else you have to do?
Are assumptions getting in the way? What do you need
to do to prepare yourself to be present and attentive
for a conversation?

AVOID THESE COMMUNICATION TRAPS

Crevasses are deep fissures in the snow that mountain climbers
occasionally fall into without warning. The danger of crevasses is
that you can't see them until you fall in. Often they are covered by
snow or thin ice and it is only when a person falls through that the
crevasse reveals itself.

After reading about this particular icy danger, I led a workshop
on Communication Skills and thought about how communication
traps can act like mountain crevasses. People can get themselves
into trouble before they even know it if they aren't careful about
how they communicate. As a supervisor, communication is a major
component of your work. It is up to you to make sure that each person you supervise knows his or her job and how it impacts the work
of the organization. You must explain work projects, assign tasks,
pass on news, give feedback, orient new employees, build the team,
and navigate through myriad organizational and political paths to
keep your entire team on track.

If you fall into a communication trap, it can lead to confusion and functional mistakes that may have severe impact. Here
are some of the traps supervisors fall into when they're presenting
information to their teams, along with thoughts on how to avoid
each trap.

⊠ **The Confusion Trap.** Your team leaves the meeting asking, "What was that about?!"

Avoid this trap by identifying and articulating your bottom line for the conversation before you start. What exactly are you trying to convey? If your team hears nothing else, what do you want them to know? Once you identify that, you can figure out how best to say it so that the bottom line doesn't get lost in the message.

⊠ **The Vagueness Trap.** Your team leaves with more questions than answers.

Avoid this trap by preparing answers to the basic questions of reporters: Who, what, when, where, why, how? Answer these key questions to make sure you are filling in the entire picture and leaving little room for speculation or interpretation. If it's an assignment you are explaining, give the context and the parameters of the assignment. If it is news about the organization, answer as many of these questions as you can and acknowledge the information you don't have. Leave time for the team to ask their own clarifying questions.

⊠ **The Lecture Trap.** Your team's eyes glaze over.

Avoid this trap by being clear and concise. Resist the urge to explain too much. This might sound contradictory to The Vagueness Trap, but it is not. You want to give pertinent information, but you don't want to give irrelevant information or repeat answers over and over. Say it clearly and concisely, ask if there are any questions, and move on.

⊠ **The Leave-Them-Guessing Trap.** Your team leaves thinking they have a choice but they don't.

Avoid this trap by clearly stating what is nego-tiable and what isn't. When you are explaining an assignment, a change in practice, or a decision, be clear before you begin as to whether you are issuing a directive or asking your team for their opinion. Are you asking your employees to consider an option or are you directing them to do something different? Know the answer to this question and deliver the message in a manner that makes it clear. Being direct does not have to come across as bossy or demanding. If objections arise, you can listen and respond, but if you know that the decision has been made, say that: "I hear your concerns and this decision is final." On the other hand, if this is an informational meeting, present it as such, saying something like, "I'm con-sidering a change and I'd like your thoughts before I make my final decision." The important thing is that you know what your objective is.

☒ **The Closed-Door Trap.** Your team has something to say but no chance to say it.

Avoid this trap by participating in two-way con-versations. Keep the door open. Even when a defin-itive decision has been handed down and you need to deliver it directly, you can still listen to reactions, concerns, and feelings generated by the decision. Listen to concerns in an authentic manner, but also draw the line if you need to by saying something like, "If there is more that you want to say, we can meet after the meeting." And then give them an opportu-nity to follow up with you.

Take a few minutes to prepare before you deliver important information. Review these five traps to make sure that you avoid them. Being vague, rambling, or unclear may be easier in the short run, but if it leads to your team wandering dangerously through unknown territory, the comfort and time saved will be lost in a blizzard of confusion.

Coaching Corner

- What trap are you most prone to fall into? How can you develop a detector to remind you to avoid this trap?
- What is the danger for your team if communication falters? On a scale of 1 to 10, how important is communication as a priority for your work? Do you give it the appropriate amount of preparation time relative to its importance?
- When have you experienced any of these traps from a listener's perspective? What did it feel like and how did you respond?

WHAT'S IN YOUR POCKET?

What do you typically keep in your pocket? For most people, it's keys, money, maybe an ID. In other words, the essential items you need to get through your day.

What are the essential items you need to get through messy situations at work? I recommend that supervisors have a few prepared statements ready to use when necessary, to keep in your metaphorical pocket, if you will. We all face situations that take us by surprise. We like to think we would know exactly how to respond to any given situation, but the reality is that too often people aren't prepared and don't know how to respond. There is also a danger that you might just react and say something abruptly, which may or may not be the best response.

Most often the situation goes like this: You see someone do something inappropriate, perhaps even in a group situation. You know you have to say or do something, but your brain freezes up and all you can think is: *I don't know what to say! I've got to say something!! What should I say?!!* Too often you end up walking away without saying anything because you were afraid of saying the wrong thing.

What you need to do is fill up your pocket. You want to have useful phrases ready to go so you don't have to think about how to say something awkward or challenging in the moment. In most cases, using a phrase like this will buy you time. You can use that time to make a plan for following up with the employee in a clear and direct manner soon after the incident when you will have time to address the whole situation.

Here are a few phrases to consider putting in your pocket:

✓ **"Let me think about it and I'll get back to you."**
Keep this phrase handy for when you're asked to make a commitment to something. In your quick scan, what's been said sounds okay, but you realize you might not be thinking of everything you need to consider.

✓ **"Remind me to talk to you about this next time we meet."** Use this one when you see an employee say or do something that was not quite right but doesn't require an immediate intervention. Also handy when a topic comes up at the end of a meeting and you don't have time to address it right away.

✓ **"Tell me more."** This one is for when you hear something that you find hard to believe or you sense there is more to the story.

✓ **"Anything else?"** Use this when you meet with a particular employee and you find yourself feeling like they're trying to tell you something but you don't know what it is.

✓ **"That's not okay."** This is the phrase to use when you need to let an employee, and possibly a group that witnessed an action, know that a line has been crossed. This simple phrase draws the line without shaming or punishing; it simply states a fact.

All of these phrases need to be delivered in a calm neutral tone or they'll lose their effectiveness. Any hint of impatience or judgment from you can make them weapons, not tools.

Remember that all these phrases simply address the immediate situation. You may still need to follow up later, but now you have time to be thoughtful and prepare for a secondary conversation.

Fill up your pocket with a few simple yet powerful phrases and you can be ready to respond to situations that demand attention, even when you don't have time to think it through.

Coaching Corner

- What kind of situations leave you panicked about what to say or do? What phrase could you develop to carry you through the immediate demand?
- Practice saying the phrase so that you can say it calmly and neutrally. You don't want to ruin your phrase by adding an inappropriate tone to your delivery.
- Is there any situation that you've been avoiding because you don't know what to say? Make a plan to address it.

THE WORDS YOU USE

When we were first together, if my husband noticed I was getting upset, he would tell me to relax. It did not take him long to realize that using that particular word in that particular situation had the opposite effect than what he intended. When he told me to relax, I felt furious. He quickly stopped telling me to relax!

The words you use impact how you feel, how you remember, and how you respond to a given situation. A psychologist named Elisabeth Loftus conducted a study in which she showed people a video clip of a minor traffic accident. She then questioned them about what they saw. What she discovered was that how she worded her question directly affected what people remembered about what they saw.

If she asked them, "How fast would you estimate the car was going when it contacted the other vehicle?" people estimated the speed of the car as considerably lower than when she asked, "How fast would you estimate the car was going when it smashed into the other vehicle?" When people heard the word "smashed" they "remembered" that the car was traveling at a faster speed. A week later, Ms. Loftus brought the participants back and asked them, "Did you see broken glass in the video I showed you last week?" More than twice as many people in the "smashed" group reported seeing broken glass than those in the "contact" group. There was no broken glass visible in the video.

This study clearly shows the impact word choice has on memory. Particular words trigger reactions. When a person is told they have a bad attitude, the response is fairly universal: most of us get defensive. Some words invite us to participate and others only pretend to invite participation. ("Does anyone have anything they want to add?" versus "No one disagrees with this, do they?") The way you say things matters!

The words we say out loud affect other people and our own actions. In addition, the words we use internally have as much of an effect on us as what we say out loud.

Consider the difference between these statements:

INITIAL CONCERN	REFRAME
We've got so much to do; we're all totally overwhelmed.	We are a busy group doing a lot of great work.
I have to take care of my kids/parents/pets; someone always wants a piece of me.	I love my kids/parents/pets. It is demanding to take care of them, but I know that my attention is how I show my love.
Just give me a yes or no answer.	Tell me what you're thinking.
I know change is hard for all of us.	Change is unsettling and it is exciting too.
A meeting with each staff member takes up too much time.	The time I invest with my staff is a priority to accomplish our goals.
We don't have any pressing agenda items so we can skip our staff meeting this week.	We have an open agenda this week. What's important for us to discuss?

The actions that you take will be different based on the words you think. Pay attention to how you speak, to yourself and to others. The words you choose matter.

Coaching Corner

- What do you say to yourself when you're feeling stressed or overwhelmed? How does that affect how you feel and how you act?
- Have you ever invited a response in a way that clearly indicated that you didn't want any? If so, what led you to that and how could you have changed the situation?
- Are there any particular words that trigger a response in you? If so, what is your plan to deal with it?
- Is there a way you can actively monitor the words you choose? Perhaps you could pick a day to watch your word choice and reflect at the end of the day on what impact your words had.

Reference: IB Psychology, accessed 1/13/16. http://ibpsychologyast.blogspot.com/2010/10/loftus-and-palmer-study-of-memory-1974.html

---

EITHER/OR TALK RARELY HELPS

Here's a secret of supervision, work, and life: things are rarely mutually exclusive, though people often act as if they are. We act as if there are only two choices and that one choice invalidates the other. We ignore the vast landscape between the extremes. We tend to think in dichotomies and make our way through the world in a constant consideration of either/or thinking:

Right/Wrong
Lie/Truth
Happy/Sad
Success/Failure
Us/Them

Win/Lose
Good/Bad
My way/The Highway
With me/Against me

This way of thinking is more than a matter of semantics. It is a matter of how we formulate the words we use to describe situations, which then frame the conversation and the actions available to us. If I think my only choices are A or B, then by definition I don't consider that A **and** B might be a solution when combined, or that other options might include C, D, E, or F.

The duality of seeing the world as this **or** that impedes us from seeing the vast area in between the two extremes. If we can't see the in-between area, then we can't talk to each other about it or work to build mutually satisfying solutions. In mediation, the most critical step is to get the participants to calm down enough to hear each other. Part of the hearing each other is allowing for more complicated answers. We're used to seeing things in a clear-cut manner, when in truth reality is rarely simple. People are good **and** bad. Staff work hard **and** they make mistakes.

Either/or thinking can show up in supervision in any number of ways:

- ✓ **John** is a manager who has the expectations that there is one answer to a problem in his department. Therefore he does not allow any time to explore options to get to the best solution.

- ✓ **Carrie** has an employee who reported that he saw another employee taking something. When Carrie confronts the alleged thief, she says, "You either stole it or you didn't."

- ✓ **Joan** is another manager who can only see one way of doing things. Her employee, Lisa, does things in a

different way. Because Joan doesn't see Lisa's different way as viable, Lisa will never be successful with
Joan as her manager.

✓ **Gary**'s employee comes to him and lets him know
that there are some problems with the upcoming
deadline. Gary just says, "Are we going to meet the
deadline or not?"

✓ **Chenille** is a manager who is confronted with two
employees telling two versions of an incident. "One
of you must be lying," she exclaims. "And I'm going
to find out who." There is no room to find their common ground or even to discover why they have two
different versions of what happened.

If unfettered, this approach to work can lead to a culture of
blame. In this situation, when there is a mistake the conclusion is
often that someone did something wrong and we are going to find
and punish that one person, instead of figuring out how to move
forward in a productive manner and as a team. It is much more
complicated and much richer to explore the middle ground. Ask
questions. Allow for ambiguity and the possibility that there are
more than two options. Consider the following differences:

EITHER/OR THINKING	MORE OPEN THINKING
You are right or I am right.	We both have part of the story.
You lied or you told the truth.	You told the truth as you knew it at the time.

continued ⇨

EITHER/OR THINKING	MORE OPEN THINKING
You finished the project or you didn't.	You finished a draft of the project and thought you were done, but since then more information has come to ilght, which changes the project.
You are happy or you are sad.	Sometimes you are both happy and sad at the same time.
You succeeded or you failed.	You were successful in meeting your goals and someone else did more than you did.
You are with us or with them.	Perhaps we can all find a way to work together.
An option is good or it's bad.	Usually the best options are combinations of a number of ideas. Prematurely limiting or maligning your options reduces your chances of finding the best solution.
You're either with me or against me.	Consider the possibility that I can be working for the same goals and still challenge your ideas.

The concept of ideas and options being mutually exclusive is a sneaky and insidious worldview that can color any number of workplace scenarios. Watch out for it. When you find it, see if you can find another option to consider.

Coaching Corner

- Is there an area where you have created a dichotomy of right/wrong or us/them? Actively imagine middle ground between these extremes. What could that look like?
- How do you respond, both internally and externally, when you disagree with someone?
- It is not always comfortable standing in the middle areas beyond your own ideas and opinions and knowledge of how things are or should be. What do you need to do to be able to stay in the discomfort without pushing for a resolution before the issue is fully explored?

CHAPTER 3:

How You Act

TRUST IS ESSENTIAL

When I started my last full-time position within an organization, there were two hundred employees. Because I was the Human Resources Director, every employee was important to me and I wanted all of them to feel safe coming to me with any issues they might have. I had to build trust. I had to earn trust. I was so busy, however, that I was inadvertently eroding trust. I would walk from one meeting to another and I'd pass eight people. Six of them would ask me for something. I'd say "okay" and continue on. By the time I got back to my office I was lucky if I remembered half of the things I'd agreed to do. At some point I realized that this lack of follow-through wasn't working to build trust.

People were asking me to do something, I was agreeing, and then I wasn't doing it. I wasn't ignoring their requests on purpose, but that didn't matter. To some of the employees, this casual request and lack of follow-through was their only contact with me. I realized that their experience was that I would agree to do something and then not do it. I had to change my routine. I began to stop when someone asked me for something and write myself a note on the spot. Later, I learned to ask people to e-mail their request to remind me. By making this change, I became more trustworthy. The simple act of doing what I said I would do, whether it was a big item or a minor item, affected trust. It seemed like a simple act but it had a profound effect on whether I was trustworthy or not.

Trust is a firm confidence in the honesty, integrity, and reliability of another person. Trust is a belief that someone's word is good and that they will not lie to you or let you down. Trust is important. If the people you supervise do not trust you, you cannot build an honest relationship with them and you cannot build a true team.

People who don't trust each other can still work together. The work can get done. But when there are stresses or when something goes wrong, trust influences the outcome. If something goes wrong—a report is late, an appointment is missed, or a procedure is skipped, what happens? If there is trust, you assume there's a good reason and you find out what happened. If there is no trust, it is easy to assume the worst and act from that place.

Distrust is contagious in a workplace. When one person or department doesn't trust another one, it starts eroding confidence. I worked with a group that was divided into two camps. It started when one of the leaders took credit for the other's work in a public meeting. Then the other leader actively undermined a project of the first leader by withholding information that she needed to complete the project. Eventually both teams were lined up against each other. This kind of animosity can spread like a virus until an organization is teeming with distrust. Then a whole lot of time is spent second-guessing and covering tracks instead of doing the work, because blame is a quick successor to distrust. It is not a healthy or fun environment. It is not a productive environment. Clients and customers pick up on it quickly and they can start distrusting the organization too.

Everything you do as a supervisor helps to build trust or distrust—your words, your actions, and the manner in which you do and say things. Trust can be lost quickly by a major betrayal and it can be eroded bit by bit over time by seemingly insignificant actions. Here are some supervisory actions that build trust:

- ✓ **Follow through on your talk and promises.** Do what you say you will do and don't do what you say you won't do. This applies to big things and little things. And if you can't keep your word for reasons beyond your control, own up to it and explain it!

- ✓ **Tell the truth.** Good news or bad news, your team needs to trust you to tell the truth. This means you tell it like it is in feedback meetings and evaluations. You let them know what you know about the future of the department or any problems that lie ahead. You don't want them to find out about news that affects them from the grapevine instead of from you.

- ✓ **Listen, ask questions, and understand each person's perspective.** Even if it looks like they did something incredibly crazy, stop and ask them what happened. Hear their side of the story and understand their perspective. It may not change the outcome but it will build trust.

- ✓ **Don't talk behind anyone's back.** If your team hears you talking about anyone behind their backs, whether that someone is part of the team or even unknown to them, they will assume that you talk about them behind their backs. They will not trust you.

✓ **Admit and apologize when you make a mistake.**
Apologizing does not make you weak; it makes you
human. It makes you trustworthy to be able to admit
that you made a mistake and you will do what you
can to fix it.

Trust and communication are the foundation upon which relationships are built. Relationships are the foundation upon which
supervision is built.

When I started handling spur-of-the-moment requests in
a more trustworthy manner, I became a better manager, a better
supervisor, and a better person.

Coaching Corner

- Our values inform our actions. Is trust a real value for
  you? How do you honor this value? Are there actions
  you can take to become more trustworthy at work?
- What situations, environments, or stresses lead you to
  take actions that could be inadvertently eroding trust?
  How could you counteract these situations so you
  could build your trustworthiness?
- Who have you trusted in your work life? Who have
  you distrusted? What impact did trust have on these
  relationships?

BE(A)WARE OF YOUR POWER

Power has not traditionally been well used in work situations.
Abuses of power have historically led to mistreatment of people, the
employment of children, terrible instances of harassment, and even
murderously unsafe work environments. This kind of public history

and perception of what "bosses" are capable of can lead people to instinctively distrust those with power.

Many supervisors do not feel personally powerful. And yet a supervisor has power. Even the most kindhearted, compassionate, soft-spoken supervisor has power by virtue of their position as a supervisor. The nature of a supervisory relationship implies a differential of power. It is imperative that every supervisor be aware of this. Unacknowledged power is often the most dangerous kind of power.

We can all acknowledge that the hierarchical, authoritative "boss" has power. We have an image in our mind of the dictatorial boss who hires and fires on a whim, assigns good or bad tasks to people he or she likes or dislikes, and makes arbitrary decisions. Most of us, however, are not like that. We consider ourselves to be fair and consistent and careful. We intend to be the kind of boss who considers the input of others before we make a decision and maybe we even aim for consensus in our decision-making. We want to be the kind of supervisor who cares about the people we supervise. We would never just issue an order across the room or yell at someone in front of others. Even if this "nicer" perception of ourselves is all true, the power differential still exists and we must be aware of it.

As a supervisor, you have the power to affect the work and lives of the people you supervise. You have the power to hire and fire, to assign tasks, and to micromanage or delegate tasks and responsibilities. You have the power to respond to an infraction or you can choose to look the other way. Even if you do not actually have much power in your organization, the people you supervise perceive that you do. And perception matters. If someone feels you have power over them, they will act accordingly, whether you think it is appropriate or not.

Employees often hold supervisors as "other" unless or until they prove themselves to be trustworthy. Part of being trustworthy is acknowledging the power of your position. You can't pretend it doesn't exist. A supervisor who does not acknowledge this power is less trustworthy than one who does. How can you trust someone who doesn't even know they hold the key to your security? How can you trust a person who's casual about your livelihood?

Many supervisors want to downplay their power. They just want to be one of the guys or gals. "Let's just all do our jobs and then we don't have to worry about who the boss is," they might say. This can work in some situations for a period of time. But eventually, you, as the supervisor, must step up and take responsibility and control; make the decisions and set the tone for the work group. You must be the leader. Becoming the leader does not mean that you must become more "bossy," but you must become more conscious about the lines of authority and responsibility. You must be aware of the power you hold, and perhaps even more importantly, you must be aware of the **perception** of the power you hold.

Acknowledging your power does not mean that you act as a dictator or become authoritarian. The awareness of your power may or may not show up in any overt actions on your part, but the shift in your understanding can lead to actions that are cleaner and clearer to those you supervise. It means that you know where the buck stops. You hold the responsibility for the department and the work. You know that your team is counting on you to lead and you take that responsibility consciously and seriously. You own the responsibility of your position as a supervisor.

There are differentials in our society that make the power issue even greater; these reflect historical and continuing struggles. Consider, for example: a man supervising a woman; a white person supervising a person of color; a straight person supervising a gay person; or an able-bodied person supervising a person with disabilities. In these situations, the relationship you have with the person you supervise can be viewed as a microcosm of society's issues. The differential and history of power are assumed to be in place in this relationship as they are in the greater society unless and until you prove otherwise.

Part of proving this is acknowledging and taking responsibility for the different types of power you have. It also means internally being aware that this historic or identity power is a factor in your relationship. For example when a man asks a woman he supervises out for a drink to discuss a work project, he must understand that this invitation is different than when a peer suggests the same thing. As a man and as a supervisor, there are power dynamics that make the invitation suspect. Is he implying she better go out with him because he's her boss? Is he initiating a sexual encounter as a male? Is there an implied threat to her job in the invitation?

With awareness of this power dynamic, he can take responsibility for clear verbal and nonverbal communication to support his employees' dignity and safety. Recognizing and taking responsibility for the various power dynamics operating in that situation means bearing in mind that those dynamics can affect both the way his words might be interpreted and also the way they might be delivered. It means he would (and in general that supervisors should) consciously choose to think about what/how/when he is communicating, and to whom. This helps to avoid misunderstanding, discomfort that might affect the work, or potential harassment claims. Instead of saying, "Hey Linda, why don't we grab a drink together tonight to discuss the project," he could suggest (also with awareness of his tone and body language), "I'd like to find a time to discuss the project with you when there's not so much going on in the background. Any ideas of how we could manage that?"

Another example is from my own experience of coming to understand that my position as a director in an organization had its own power implications. I couldn't just be "Rita." I carried the power of my position with me in any situation at work, even when I was at lunch or sitting at my desk doing paperwork. I also had to recognize that as a white woman, I could not understand the experience of being a person of color in the world or in our work environment. Having lived in my skin my whole life, I carried the privilege and blind spots of my identity into my work. So it was critical to listen attentively and to work collaboratively to make the workplace safe for every employee and to invite every voice to contribute to problem-solving for the organization.

The following quote from Paulo Freire is an important reminder in supervisory relationships as it is in societal issues: "Washing one's hands of the conflict between the powerful and the powerless means to side with the powerful, not to be neutral."

Coaching Corner

- What comes up for you when you think of yourself as a powerful person?
- Are there ways in which you want to distance yourself from power in order to be more comfortable?
- Who is a positive role model for you of a powerful person? What do they do that shows you they hold their power as a responsibility and not as a hammer?

DON'T JUST DO SOMETHING, STAND THERE

Sometimes the hardest thing to do is to do nothing. And yet there are times when you simply have to wait. One of the traits of a good leader is the ability to wade through periods of ambiguity without rushing to "fix" things. There are times when the most appropriate thing is to let the process unfold. Here are a few examples of good times to metaphorically just stand there.

✓ **Wait for an answer.** As a supervisor, you ask many questions. You ask questions to find out what happened, to encourage problem-solving, to coach an employee to be reflective on their own actions. If the employee does not have a quick answer it can be easy to start guessing. "Maybe you didn't understand my instructions, or maybe you were trying to help, maybe you should try this . . ." You want to help the employee, so you start offering multiple-choice answers to the question you just asked. Resist that temptation. Sit attentively in silence and let the employee come up with an answer. **Make** the employee come up with an answer. He or she will say something eventually. If nothing else, after five minutes they will say, "I don't know." Then you can suggest possible answers at that point or you can continue to probe, "What if you did know? What would you say?" (That question almost always gets an interesting and true answer.) Resist jumping in before he/she answers.

✓ **Investigation.** When an allegation is made or misbehavior is suspected, you must conduct an investigation to gather as much information about the event as possible. It is easy to assume that the first thing you heard is correct (or incorrect depending on what you assume you know about the participants). Don't assume. Whether you do the investigation yourself, your HR department does it, or you hire an external person to investigate, your job is to wait. Wait until all pertinent information has been gathered. Do not act as if you know what happened. You could be guilty of retaliation if you act as if you know the results of the investigation before you do. This is hard. It is hard not to act in the face of bad behavior (or the suspicion of such) but you must wait.

✓ **Improvement and development.** After much informal coaching and clear feedback, you give an employee you supervise a written warning on something that is not working. You tell him or her how to improve the performance. A week later, the problem is still not fixed. There may be some small improvement but it is not enough. You are eager to move this person out and move on. That may or may not be the eventual outcome of this intervention but you must wait yet again. A week is not enough time to improve a performance issue unless it is something very clear like, "Never being late to work again." Even in that case you might have to give the employee time to adjust life circumstances like childcare, depending on the circumstances and history of the issue. In most cases, you must offer support for the change and give a reasonable amount of time for the employee to demonstrate success before you move to the next step.

✓ **Processing change.** When you implement any kind of organizational change, either for your work team or organization-wide, you must be patient with the change process. Change is hard for people, even when it is logical or good change. Rushing through it or not explaining the reasons for the change will ensure that people resist the change. Generally people respond better when you give notice of the change, explain the reasons for the change, invite responses to the change, and give plenty of lead time to make the change. Be patient with people during the change process. Don't rush it.

As a leader, it is often your job to be decisive and to make things happen. Sometimes, however, your best action is to wait. To be patient and give time for the process to complete itself. Sometimes it is helpful to simply ask yourself, "Will this action actually help move anything or am I just impatient to act?" There are times when just standing there, no matter how hard it may be, is valuable.

Coaching Corner

- Is there a situation where you usually feel impatient? How does your impatience show up in your actions?
- When have you felt resistance to change? Remembering the experience of having change thrust upon you can help you build empathy for those you are working with. What helped you move forward through the change?
- If you are someone who just **has** to talk when there is a moment of silence, what is that about? Sit with this question and let the answer rise up within you. Then ask it again and wait for another answer to rise up. And another. Do this several times until new information emerges. This process will give you important information to help you deal with your impatience.

SLOW DOWN TO GET THERE FASTER

In the best of times, we get into the flow of our work: we're productive and happy, and time flies. Other times we plod along and get things accomplished but we know we're not focused or optimally productive. Then there are times when it seems like we are chasing our tails! We pick up a project and find we don't have what we need to complete it; we go to delegate a task and no one is available; we get prepared for a meeting and then the topic is usurped by an urgent need. Sometimes I find myself picking up one piece of paper after another and feel like I'm moving in circles. I am literally not getting anything done.

As a supervisor, I sometimes felt like I was running across the hall every two minutes, either to ask a question, to deliver a task, or simply to tell my staff something.

Between my three-page to-do list, my piles of paperwork, and my cluttered mind, I started feeling crazy. I recognize this cycle now and call this my pinball syndrome. I am like a ball set loose in a pinball—I bounce from one thing to another and don't stay anywhere long enough to get any points (or to be effective). This usually happens when I am most busy; there seems to be an inverse proportion to how busy I am and how effective I am.

Here's the secret I discovered: **Slow down!** It is a counterintuitive solution, but it works. It even works with driving: When I drive in bumper-to-bumper traffic, I have learned that driving in the slow lane gets me there at least as fast as driving in the "fast" lane. I have identified cars that speed by me and then I am right next to them twenty miles later. Often I get where I'm going faster if I slow down. Perhaps it's my calm acceptance of the situation that adds to my contentment with my travel time but it has been an interesting shift in my driving and my life.

Part of what happens when we get overwhelmed is that we lose focus and we start hyperventilating—both literally and figuratively. Slowing down returns you to your body, and we are all more effective when we use our bodies in conjunction with our minds! Sometimes it is helpful to simply shift gears and break the cycle; stop playing pinball. Then after this mental reset, when you return to the task at hand, you can focus on one item at a time and move forward. Shifting gears creates space in your brain and lets your focus catch up with your energy.

Here are some ways that I have effectively implemented this slowing-down magic:

✓ **Moving and dancing.** One evening I was working late to get the group insurance bills paid. I could not get the Kaiser bill to balance; I had added and counted and looked at it every which way at least four times and it kept coming out wrong. Finally, I stopped. I pulled out my iPhone and turned on some loud music. I danced in the night by myself in my office. After one song, I put it away and went back to the bill. When I added it up, it balanced.

✓ **Clean my desk.** The most effective cure I have found to the pinball syndrome is to stop and clean my desk. It makes no logical sense! I am outrageously busy and I stop and take everything off my desk and go through every pile as I rearrange my focus. By the time I am done, I can find the paperwork I need and my mind is ready to proceed calmly and competently. It is really a process of cleaning my mind.

✓ **Take a break.** If I feel the overwhelm coming on, I can curb it by proactively taking a five-minute walk or going out for a cup of tea, either alone or with a colleague. It has the same effect of getting my mind out of the one-track panic of "I can't do it all, I can't do it all." I come back refreshed and ready to tackle my projects.

✓ **Consolidate.** This is the step I know I need to take when I am running to my staff every two minutes. Sometimes I have to ask them to do this also, when they are running to me every two minutes. This step involves making a list of topics, ideas, updates, etc., and then saving the list for a prearranged meeting once a day. Of course, there will be a few things that are time-sensitive and can't wait but at least 90 percent of the disruptions can wait until the assigned meeting time.

✓ **Breathe.** Studies have shown that three deep breaths can reduce stress. Pausing to breathe is not simply a California-New-Age gimmick—it really works. It gets oxygen moving through your body so you are calmer and can think more clearly. At one point I brought a timer to work and set it for an hour. Every hour I would stop, shut my eyes, and concentrate on breathing for one minute. It was a really productive period for me. Over time, I let that practice slip away but I have recently reinstated it. It is even easier now with appropriate apps.

✓ **Vacation.** The ultimate shifting of gears is the act of taking a vacation—for a day or a few weeks. Leave behind your laptop and answer only urgent voice mails. One of the wonderful aspects of vacation is that you don't ever have to rush anywhere. You just do what's next. You can be in the moment and remember who you are. And then when you come back to work, you can hopefully remember that you enjoy the work you do and feel focused and energized for your next project.

Consider the magic of slowing down to get there faster. It will help you with your work, your supervision, and your life if you recognize when it is time for you to slow down and shift gears.

Coaching Corner

- What is your usual response to feeling overwhelmed? How effective is your response?
- Do you resist the idea that a counterintuitive solution could be effective? What if it were? What if slowing down really did get you somewhere faster? How could that affect your daily actions?
- Do you secretly believe that if you are not overwhelmed then you are not important? Do you wear your overwhelm

like a badge of honor? What part of your self-identity
would you lose if you slowed down?

WHAT ARE YOU PRACTICING?

I make my living helping people be more effective supervisors. The
truth is that when I was a supervisor, I did many of the best practices I talk about but I did not do them all. Sometimes I imagine
my former employees thinking, "She never did that with me!" I'm
confessing to not always walking the talk to highlight the concept
that we are all a work in progress. All the time. We are all practicing
one thing or another all the time. But the question here is this: Are
you practicing what you want to be practicing?

I recently heard about a study that said it takes about forty direct,
intentional conversations with employees before supervisors feel completely comfortable with a new style of supervision. For most supervisors, this means that when you decide to try something new, it will
take almost a year before that new approach is fully part of who you
are as a supervisor. In one way, this might feel daunting. But in another
way, it can be liberating. It means you can give yourself permission
to practice and reflect, to practice and correct, and to practice some
more—and don't forget to praise yourself when you get it right—all
while getting the work done and moving forward. You don't have to
learn something and immediately be perfect at it. What a relief!

Other studies say it takes four months to implement a new
habit. The time factor varies, but studies generally agree that it takes
time. And practice. The thing to remember is that time does not
stop while you're practicing. The work goes on. You set up regular
meetings with the people you supervise or you don't. You choose
how to use that time. Are you going to consciously try to improve
your approach, or are you going to just keep doing the same thing—
whether it works or not?

I read once that a pilot flies from one location to another by making constant corrections on the course. If the pilot does not make small corrections along the way, even though the pilot set out on the right course, the plane will not end up where the pilot wants it to go. It is the corrections that keep the plane on track. Isn't that what we all do every day, if we're paying attention? Practice, correct; practice, correct; practice, improve . . . Hopefully over time what we are practicing becomes part of us and we recognize improvement, but we never stop and say, "Okay, I'm good. I never have to do anything different—I've got it now." There is always something new to learn and practice.

Here are some actions you could start practicing to become a better supervisor:

- ✓ Appreciate what's working.
- ✓ Take time to meet with your employees.
- ✓ Be clear about your expectations.
- ✓ Slow down to get all the information you need.
- ✓ Give timely and specific feedback.
- ✓ Build a practice for self-reflection.

Whatever it is, pick a task, an approach, or a new habit and start consciously practicing it. Practice is what makes the difference. Consider this amazing quote:

> *Top performers dislike practicing just as much as others do.*
> *But more than others, they have the will to keep at it anyway.*
> —From *Complications* by Atul Gawande

We can add supervision to that list of top performers. Good supervisors take time to actively supervise and they constantly practice improving how they do supervision. You're practicing something all the time. Why not practice being effective?

Coaching Corner

- What are you practicing? Is it something you want to get better at, or are you just doing what you've always done?
- Do you give your employees time and space to practice? Or do you expect them to do their work perfectly every time as soon as they learn it?
- Do you have a practice to reflect on what is working and what isn't working? If not, what can you commit to doing to start such a practice?

THINGS I KNOW AND FORGET

It's not easy being a supervisor, manager, parent, friend, or even a conscious adult in a complicated world! Recently I was reminded of an important lesson that I know well, but in the heat of the moment, when I needed it most, I somehow forgot what I knew. I was in the midst of an argument with my husband when I heard myself interrupting him and thinking I knew what he was going to say before he said it. It wasn't until he said clearly and succinctly, "You're not listening to me!" that I remembered that I knew how to listen, and that it wasn't by interrupting and assuming. After my sheepish apology, and some attentive listening on my part, we quickly concluded our discussion.

That evening I took time to write in my journal. Off the top of my head I identified ten such important lessons that I consistently forget and must relearn. They all have implications for the work of being a supervisor.

✓ Hearing someone is not enough; they must **feel** heard.
✓ My understanding of a comment, action, or event is not **the** Truth. At best, it is my interpretation.
✓ My words and actions can have unintended consequences.

✓ Just because I know what I mean does not mean everyone else does.

✓ Power dynamics don't go away, even if two or more people tacitly agree to set them aside temporarily.

✓ Starting a sentence with "You" when giving feedback often leads to a defensive response.

✓ Healthy conflict is not an oxymoron. Conflict does not automatically equal fighting, which does not automatically equal danger. Conflict can actually be safe and productive when done well.

✓ Having a clearly stated and agreed upon goal or outcome is essential in making sure we're aiming in the same direction.

✓ Taking care of myself is not a luxury; it is essential.

✓ To do anything well I need time to prepare (both myself and the content).

Coaching Corner

- What do **you** know and forget?
- How do you respond when you act in a manner that you later realize was counterproductive? Are you comfortable apologizing? What does making a mistake mean to you?
- Is there something you want to actively remember during the next week or month? What can you do to remind yourself?

GOLDILOCKS AND THE THREE SUPERVISORS

Goldilocks wandered through the employment forest. She found a cheery organization and decided to work there.

Goldilocks tried on her first supervisor. This supervisor was very attentive and told Goldilocks exactly how to perform her job, when things were due, and how to maneuver through the organization. At first Goldilocks thought this supervisor would be a great fit for her because she didn't have to worry about making any mistakes. The supervisor was right there to correct her when anything wasn't perfect. As time went on, the supervisor continued to watch every move that Goldilocks made: Was her time sheet turned in? Did she remember to complete her report? Did she make that call that they talked about? The supervisor stopped by her desk every day to see what she was working on, rearranging her tasks if she disagreed with the plan. Goldilocks did not have any room to act on her own or to be creative. She longed for an opportunity to do something on her own, even if it got her in trouble. She needed some room and some trust from her supervisor. Finally, Goldilocks decided to move on. "Too tight!" said Goldilocks.

Her next supervisor was a relief to Goldilocks. He gave her lots of room and trusted her to make her own decisions. In fact, after the first week, in which he took her out to lunch and told her the political lay of the land, he told Goldilocks, "I trust my people. If you need help, let me know. Otherwise, I'll leave you alone." *What a relief,* thought Goldilocks. She loved making her own decisions and trying things out. Some of her ideas worked and some didn't. In either case, she just kept working. She didn't hear from her supervisor when things didn't work out. And she didn't hear from him when they did. Sometimes she wasn't even sure if she knew which projects worked and which ones didn't. Goldilocks began to wonder if her supervisor even remembered her name. She remembered that he had said, "If you need help, let me know," so the next time she faced a tricky decision she decided to run it by him before she acted. He didn't return her call for over a week. When she ran into him in the hall and asked for his help, he said, "Just decide what to do. That's what I pay you for." Goldilocks eventually decided to look for another supervisor. "Too loose!" said Goldilocks.

Her third supervisor worked closely with Goldilocks to help her learn the terrain of the new job. Then she set up a regular weekly meeting time with Goldilocks. When they met, the supervisor gave her updates and asked her how her projects were going. She listened to Goldilocks when she had ideas or suggestions. If Goldilocks asked for help with a decision, the supervisor would often ask, "What do you think?" and then would sometimes say, "That sounds good." But sometimes she would say, "Have you considered the impact that action would have on your coworkers?" or something else that Goldilocks found helpful. Goldilocks left meetings feeling more focused on her work. Once Goldilocks found herself stuck in a towering stack of priorities. She called her supervisor frantically. "Help!" she cried. Her supervisor called her back the same day. "Okay, let's review what you're working on," she stated calmly. "What is the overall purpose of your job?" When Goldilocks repeated the key focus area the supervisor had shown her during orientation, the supervisor praised her and said, "Okay, that's your guiding light in prioritizing these tasks." Then she helped her review the tasks and approved the newly updated task list. Her supervisor often told Goldilocks what a good job she was doing and how happy she was to have her on the team. Goldilocks thrived. She took on more and more responsibility. More importantly, she looked forward to going to work every day, knowing that she was making a difference and being successful. "Just right!" said Goldilocks.

Coaching Corner

- Which supervisor does your style most closely match? Would the people you supervise see it the same? Is that style working for the people you supervise?
- Rank the top ten tasks of your job. Does supervision show up on the list? If not, should it? If so, how does the time you spend doing supervision reflect that priority?

- How do you honestly respond when the people you supervise ask for help or a moment of your time? Does your internal frenzy spill out in a way that lets them know you don't have time for them? Is that the message you want to give them? If it is, is there another approach you can take to the conversation?

THE DANGEROUS DOZEN AND THE DILIGENT DOZEN

When I work with supervisors, I am often surprised by the particulars of a situation but I am rarely surprised by the underlying problems or practices. Here is a quick summary of bad practices that supervisors practice on a regular basis.

1. Being confused about their relationship with their employees. One minute they're their best friends and the next they come down hard and heavy on their work. Keep 'em guessing!

2. Being equally confusing about what they expect from each employee. They give them vague assignments and fuzzy due dates, then hold them accountable for clear results.

3. Not bothering to give any feedback. These supervisors tell their staff members, "If you don't hear from me, you're doing fine." And then they wait until they're ready to fire them to let them know there are problems.

4. Letting things go. If someone asks them for some guidance, they lead him or her on. They say they'll get to it, but they really feel too busy to actually follow up on any of their promises.

5. Ignoring the law and the organization's policies. They think the policies are made just to keep HR busy; the rules don't have anything to do with how the real world works.

6. Meeting with their employees one-on-one only when they give them their annual evaluations. They think this will make it seem really special.

7. Showing the staff who their favorite employees are by letting them get away with things. In fact, they let most people get away with things. The staff are all doing their best after all.

8. Making sure that no one ever forgets who is the boss. They remind their employees of this every day by looking down at them, giving orders, never using please or thank you, and expecting them to say "How high?" when they're told to jump.

9. Not giving their employees a forum to discuss ideas or talk directly with them. These supervisors believe that "If you give them an inch, they'll take a mile. And it all starts when you listen to them—even for a minute."

10. Never letting the staff see them laugh, play any silly icebreakers, or participate in gift giving or office events. Any of that kind of frivolity would make them seem soft.

11. Working every employee as hard as possible. Anyone might quit tomorrow and you need to get as much out of them as you can.

12. Not caring about the specifics of the work their organization does. To these supervisors, work is work; it doesn't matter if their employees make widgets or do childcare. If someone mentions the organization's mission or values, they tune out and hum "Row, row your boat" to distract themselves.

On the other side of the coin, there are good practices that supervisors work at diligently to invest in their employees and the success of the organization.

1. Building healthy, appropriate relationships with the people they supervise. They know who each person is and how to help him or her do his or her best work.
2. Establishing clear expectations so each person knows what their job is, how it supports the mission, and how to do the job.
3. Giving prompt and specific feedback.
4. Following up; they do what they say they're going to do.
5. Following the law and the policies of the organization.
6. Establishing and maintaining regular and frequent one-on-one meetings with those they supervise (at least monthly).
7. Holding people accountable for their work and their agreements.
8. Working in partnership with their coworkers, including the people they supervise.
9. Listening at least as much as they talk.
10. Being kind and playing often.
11. Paying attention to sustainability: of themselves, their team, and their organization.
12. Keeping the mission in mind at all times.

Most supervisors in reality do some things from both lists, at least some of the time. You may not win a "Best Supervisor of the Year" award right away, but you can begin to intentionally determine how you fulfill the role. It's not an accident whether you are a good or a bad supervisor. What kind of supervisor do you want to be?

Coaching Corner

- Have you been on the receiving end of any of the Dangerous Dozen? If so, consider how those actions impacted your work.
- Is there one point of the Diligent Dozen that you notice as something you could improve? If so, design a plan to take one small step toward it and practice it intentionally for a month. At the end of the month, see how it affected your work and your employees' work.
- Set up a one-on-one meeting with each employee you supervise. Ask them if there is anything specific you can do to help them be more successful in their work. Listen carefully to how they respond. Listen for the actual answer and notice how comfortable they are in this situation. This will show you how accustomed they are to a two-way exchange with you.

STOP BEING SO NICE

When I was an HR director, I once met with a manager, Darla, about one of her employees, Carlos, who was in serious danger of losing his job. Darla talked through the situation with me and we agreed that Carlos needed to know that this was a serious situation. I knew the conversation would be hard for Darla because she was, above all else, a nice person and her identity as a nice person was important to her. She didn't want to hurt Carlos's feelings. However, by the time she left my office, she was clear about how she was going to approach the conversation with Carlos.

Later that afternoon, I happened to cross paths with Carlos and stopped to say hello. When I asked him how it had been going, he told me it was going great! "I just had a meeting with my supervisor and she's really happy with my work. I only have one thing I need to work on, but it's no big deal. As Darla said, everyone has something to work on." He went on his way whistling.

The message we had identified had clearly not been delivered! Or rather, it had been delivered in such a vague and sugarcoated manner that Carlos had not heard it. Darla had been too nice!

This situation is too common. And if Darla were to proceed down this road for a few months, Carlos might "suddenly" be terminated and would feel it was unfair and that he had no idea he was in such trouble! By being so afraid to hurt his feelings, Darla could also be preventing Carlos from correcting his behavior and saving his job.

This scenario gets even more complicated and problematic when a supervisor such as Darla is not an isolated individual in an organization but rather is emblematic of a "culture of nice" throughout an organization. Things get so mired down in niceness that nothing is ever addressed directly. Discipline issues are tolerated way beyond the point of acceptable, conflict is pushed underground, and trust is nowhere to be found. YIKES! Through all of this "niceness" the organization and the mission flounder and slip into mediocrity. Not so nice after all!

I understand the desire to be nice. Too often people think that the only alternative to being nice is being mean! There is a whole lot of territory between these two extremes. Let me assure you that there is a way to be clear that is not mean.

First, let's look at a few definitions. Nice is defined by Merriam-Webster as giving pleasure or joy; good and enjoyable. Notice that this definition focuses on the feelings of the recipient of the nice action. We experience niceness as pleasing, agreeable, and pleasant. Interestingly, an obsolete definition of "nice" is wanton. "Wanton" means not limited or controlled. This obsolete definition hints at some of the problems of niceness. Niceness can be perceived as a veneer that is unfettered and irrelevant.

Consider another word: kind. The definition of kind is: having or showing a gentle nature and a desire to help others, affectionate, loving. Notice the difference here: nice is defined by how it is received; kind is defined by how it is delivered.

Now when I engage someone in a difficult conversation, I consider three key factors:

1. Why am I having this conversation?
2. What is the bottom line?
3. How can I say what I want to say in a way that is clear and kind?

Let's break each of these down a little further:

1. **Why am I having this conversation?** Is my intention to support the work of the organization? Am I trying to help this employee understand something that is getting in the way of his or her success on the job? Am I trying to help the employee be more effective in her work? Does she need to know that her actions could lead to discipline or even termination? I've found that as long as my answer to the "why" question is job-related and connects to the mission of the organization and the purpose of the employee's job, then the conversation needs to happen.

2. **What is the bottom line?** What does the employee need to hear? If he hears nothing else, what do I want him to understand when he leaves our conversation? Some examples: "Your job is in jeopardy." "You could be more successful if you stop doing X." "You will never get promoted if you don't improve this skill." Answering the bottom-line question will help you be better prepared for your conversation.

3. **How can I say what I want to say in a way that is
   clear and kind?** Find a way to say what you want to
   say that is both clear and kind; one without the other
   is not acceptable. Your message needs to be clear
   enough that the employee understands the bottom
   line and it needs to be kind. This means removing any
   judgmental or shaming words or tone, and speaking
   to the reason for having the conversation in the first
   place (see number one above). You are not addressing
   the employee's behavior to be mean; you are addressing it for the good of the organization and, hopefully,
   it will also be helpful for the employee.

Notice that there is no step that asks, Is this easy for me to say?
Nor is there a step that asks, Will they still like me after this?

Being nice can be a fatal flaw for a supervisor, and an organizational culture. It can lead to the avoidance of important conversations. Being clear and kind, however, can go a long way toward
building a respectful organization that delivers on its mission. So
stop being so nice and focus instead on being clear and kind.

Coaching Corner

- When has being nice gotten in the way of your being
  clear? Consider a situation you have experienced or
  witnessed and how it could have been handled better.
- How does it change an action when the focus is on the
  intention of the actor rather than the response of the
  recipient? Which one can you really control?
- Is there a conversation that you need to have? Prepare
  for it using the three-step process outlined above.

BEWARE OF SHORTCUTS

When my daughter was eleven, she went to a summer camp. On the last day of the camp, her group had planned to take a three-mile hike in a nearby forest. So up a hill they went, had a picnic near a lake, and then began to hike back down. Halfway down the hill, someone remembered a shortcut to the parking lot. Happy to get back sooner, the group turned off onto the smaller path. It took a while to realize it definitely wasn't a shortcut. Rather than taking the time to track back to the known route, they decided to turn again onto yet another trail that seemed like it too would save time. Soon enough, the group was thoroughly lost in the woods. Eventually they made it back, late that evening. The three-mile walk in the woods had turned into an exhausting, potentially dangerous, seventeen-mile hike. Some shortcut!

Shortcuts are often illusions. They look like they're going to save time and money, but often they don't. The magician doesn't really saw a woman in half and shortcuts don't really save you time.

Here are a few shortcuts that I've seen supervisors take that offer that same illusion of saving time. Beware!

☒ **Skipping your regularly scheduled one-on-one meeting with the people you supervise.** This seems like it's not a big deal, right? "Everything is fine. Nothing is going to get off track if I skip one meeting. I've just got so many more important things to take care of!" It's true that one meeting probably won't derail the relationship, but the problem is that one missed meeting leads to two and then three and it becomes an easy habit. Pretty soon you're not catching problems you should know about. And you're not aware of successes that need to be acknowledged. You're not guiding and supporting. Your people are feeling abandoned and before you know it you've eroded trust in this important relationship. It happens gradually, but over time you have eroded your relationship and possibly have some misunderstanding or messes to clean up. Those regular meetings matter. They're too important to take a shortcut around them.

☒ **Not bothering to start meetings with a connection activity.** Whether it's a check-in question, an icebreaker, or a quick game, spending two to three minutes at the start of your team meetings on something lighthearted is worth its weight in gold. This short time does several things quickly: it helps people connect to each other in a human way that is about more than job titles or positions; it relaxes everyone and opens them up to be creative and attentive; and it gets people in the room. Studies have shown that until a person speaks in a group setting, their attention is often elsewhere. By inviting every participant to speak during a start-up activity, they are primed to be involved in the meeting. Every time I was pressed for time and skipped this step, I regretted it. It would take half the meeting to get everyone focused and on target with our meeting topic. Take the time. It will make the meeting and the team work better.

☒ **Overlooking details on compliance issues.** "Well, I know this is not really an exempt position but it will be so much easier if we classify it that way." "No one will know if we don't count that half hour this person worked after closing." "We'll just include your final check in the next payroll run." "It's too much trouble to hire them as an employee; let's just make them an independent contractor." Compliance matters, and specific laws wouldn't have been written if it were okay to gloss over them. Don't take these potentially costly shortcuts.

☒ **Not dealing with problem employees.** "I just don't have the time or energy to deal with Archie. I know I told him last time was his last chance, but I can't fire him now. Let's just give him a little more time. He'll either figure it out or leave." That may be true but it may take a long time. And in the meantime, all your performing employees are going to get frustrated and either leave or cut back their efforts because why should they work so hard when obviously it doesn't matter how good or bad you are at your job—everyone is treated just the same.

It may be tempting to find a quicker way to go, and sometimes these actions may save you a few minutes now but could cost you big time in the long run. Don't fall for these shortcuts.

Coaching Corner

- Have you fallen for any of these shortcuts? If so, make a plan now for how you will change or amend your actions.
- Are there other shortcuts that have tripped you up? What did you expect and what did you get? What did you learn from those mistakes?
- What can you do or say when you are tempted by a shortcut? Perhaps it's asking yourself, "Is this really worth it?" or "What have I already decided to do about this?"

TINY STEPS CAN CHANGE OUR BRAINS

I've always thought it would be fun to participate in a book club. But whenever I've tried to join one, I rebel. As soon as I have a book I **must** read, I won't do it! I'll read other books but not that one. There is some part of me that reacts to the assignment as if I were an eight-year-old saying, "You can't make me!" And that's right, I can't make me.

That's why I am so intrigued by a little book I recently read called *One Small Step Can Change Your Life—The Kaizen Way*, by Robert Maurer, PhD. It describes the importance of tricking our brains. The book describes research that shows how our brains become primitive and fearful in the face of big changes. So they resist the change. It's like when someone tells you not to think about elephants and suddenly that's all you can think about. When we're consciously trying to make a big change, all our brains can think about is how they don't want to change.

The Kaizen Way suggests making small changes so that we don't scare our brains. Instead of committing to thirty minutes of exercise a day and then resisting it to the point of doing nothing, this book says try one minute of exercise a day. Then if/when you want to do more, add another minute. But only if you want to. Just by doing one minute a day, you'll start changing your brain. Exercise won't seem like such a big deal.

The idea here is to think about the change you want to make and then to design a small step toward that change. Make the step so tiny that you know you can do it. Then you can guarantee success, and the success itself becomes an important component in changing the brain.

In the spirit of kaizen (a Japanese word that means improvement), here are some tiny steps you can take to be a better supervisor. Pick one of these and commit to it. Or choose your own tiny step toward becoming an even better supervisor than you currently are.

✓ **If you've been struggling to set up regular meetings with your employees, start small.** Ten minutes per week (even five, two, or one if that's all you know you can realistically do right now). Schedule it with the employee so you both can count on it and keep it. As important as keeping the meeting is making it two-way. This is not a ten-minute lecture. Listen at least as much as you talk.

✓ **Set aside time once a month to review your expectations.** Whatever amount of time you commit to this purpose, spend half the time on your own, clarifying what you need and want from this person, project, or job. Then meet with the employee to review your expectations. A helpful phrase to use is, "I want to make sure we're on the same page." Again, make sure you listen.

✓ **Find and use one icebreaker at your staff meeting.** Just try it. Within twenty-four hours of that meeting, jot down impressions of how it went, what difference it made to the meeting, and if/when you'd like to try it again.

✓ **Take each of your direct reports out to lunch or coffee.** Within twenty-four hours of the lunch, jot down a few reactions to how it went.

✓ **Ask your employees how your style of supervision works for them.** Tell them you really want to get feedback. Ask them on a regular basis until they actually tell you what they think. Don't accept, "Oh, you know, it's fine." And when they do tell you something, no matter what it is, or if it pushes your buttons, simply say, "Thank you for letting me know." Do not defend. Do not argue. Just listen.

✓ **When you are frustrated with an employee or a coworker, stop and ask yourself, "What is my contribution to this situation?"** Allow enough silence for an answer to emerge and listen to it.

✓ **Say good morning to everyone you supervise once a day or once a week.**

✓ **Say thank you to everyone you supervise once a week or once a month.** Check it off in your datebook when you've done it for the week.

✓ **Write a note of appreciation to each person you supervise.** Once this year.

✓ **Take time, after you've done any of these tiny steps, to reflect on how it went and what the impact was.**

Tiny steps can change our brains and our lives. One of my projects was to write two words a day in my journal. Two words. I set that tiny goal when I realized I hadn't written in my journal for weeks. I wanted to jump-start my writing practice. I noticed that at two weeks, I had been 100 percent successful. Many days I simply wrote two words but sometimes I realized I wanted to write more and that felt good too. My brain remembered that it liked to write on a daily basis. And it felt good to be successful. Try it. You'll like it and you'll be an even better supervisor.

Coaching Corner

- Watch yourself try on this idea of tiny steps. Do you feel hopeful or skeptical?
- What if supervision were the most important part of your job? Try on that idea and then take one minute to think of a foolproof tiny step you can take to make a change to improve your supervision.
- If you decide to do one of the suggested steps, make it definitive. When will you do it? How will you remember? What exactly will you do and when will you do it?
- If you find yourself not believing that tiny steps can make a difference, ask yourself "what if it could?" If one minute a day of exercise could make you healthier, wouldn't it be worth a try?

CHAPTER 4:

How You Think About Others

WHAT'S YOUR VIEW OF THE WORLD?

My mother died when I was eight years old. Her death has colored every interaction in my life. Sometimes the effect is obvious and conscious, but even when it is the furthest thing from my mind, it's still there. The memory of it is in my bones, the knowledge of it is in my approach to life, and my way of being is formed from it.

We are all formed by the circumstances and relationships of our lives. When we are growing up, we learn how to make meaning, how to interpret events, and how to protect ourselves. We learn our language, our culture, the purpose of work, how to handle conflict, what words to use, how to read people, the meaning of power and authority, and countless other things. We take this all in and we develop a lens through which we see the world. Our lens is individual but we share traits with others who grew up in similar circumstances to us: race, class, school systems, age, gender, geography, pop culture, etc.

Then we enter the workforce and act as if we all see and experience the same thing. It's crazy to think this would be the case, but we have all silently agreed to pretend that we see through the same lens—at least at work. With this pretending, it's miraculous that we get anything done.

We make the best of this most of the time and we usually see enough of the same things that we can get work accomplished. But this lens issue is there and causes problems. People interpret offense where none was intended, they misunderstand the meaning and importance of words, they feel left out, they create opposite priorities, they unintentionally harass others, and they don't see how others are impacted by their words or tones. The list goes on and on. Usually we ride through these instances where we miss each other's meaning, but over time relationships can deteriorate because of our different understanding of events. And sometimes these misunderstandings blow up.

This can happen most dramatically when someone does something that makes absolutely no sense to you. They overreact, yell, walk away when you're talking to them, and then before you know it, you are yelling at them or following them out into the hall. Your lens has just run headlong into their lens and you are in a battle that you can never win. It's as if you're yelling at each other, "The world is yellow." "No, it's blue." No one will win that argument because, of course, you're both right. Your perspective is what you experience.

This is not to say that anyone can do anything they want just because it makes sense according to his or her lens. There are actions that are permitted in the workplace and there are actions that are not. And as a supervisor, you are often the arbiter of what's okay and what isn't.

Here's a critical practice: Pause. Take a step back and remind yourself, "They are seeing this differently than I am." In that five-second pause, you can decide how to proceed. But the pause and the decision about how to proceed make all the difference in the world. This practice keeps you from overreacting in defense of your lens. During the pause, you might frame your immediate response. Some possible options include:

> "Hey, we need to finish talking about this."
> "Okay, let's take a break and talk about this tomorrow."
> "You can walk out for a quick break but come back in three minutes so we can finish this."
> "It is not okay to yell at me, or anyone else, in the workplace."

Recognizing that we see the world differently changes things. A good supervisor will always keep his or her own perspective in mind such as in the following thoughts:

- ✔ "My view is not the only view."
- ✔ "Let me understand how this other person is seeing and interpreting this."
- ✔ "Mmm, I don't think we mean the same thing even though we're saying the same words."
- ✔ "Wow! This person really got upset when I said that. I don't understand why but this must be important to them."
- ✔ "I thought I was clear about what I wanted here, but for some reason it didn't land the way I thought it would."
- ✔ "I know what I mean by initiative, but I don't know what it means to this employee."
- ✔ "We clearly have different ideas of teamwork around this table. Let me be clear about what I expect from this team."

When you recognize that different lenses are at play, you can work through the differences, but until you recognize it, you are bound to be talking past people.

Because I lost my mother when I was young, I am always ready for people to abandon me. I don't have to tell people that. I don't need to make this a part of my interactions with people. But I do need to recognize this in myself before I can respond objectively to what's in front of me.

Pause, remember you are both wearing lenses, and then decide how to respond.

Coaching Corner

- What plays into your personal lens? How does that show up in your work?
- Have you ever had an interaction where the other person's actions made no sense to you? How did you respond? How did that response impact the interaction and/or the relationship?
- When I tell you to pause, do you feel impatient? Count to five. Are you willing to invest that much time in being a better supervisor?

FACT OR INTERPRETATION?

On a flight a few years ago, we hit some rough air. There were a few episodes of turbulence in which the plane dropped several feet. After one particularly surprising drop there was a collective gasp from the passengers; we could feel the tension rising. Suddenly, through the attentive silence a little girl called out, "Whee!" Everyone laughed and the tension seemed almost to burst. This little girl did not know that turbulence might be scary. To her, the bumps were fun.

This is a delightful example of reframing. I think of that little girl whenever I hit turbulence now—on a plane or in life! It might be scary, or it might be something else. It might even be fun if I let go of my preconceived ideas. My thoughts do not change the dynamics of being on a plane through turbulence, but they can drastically change my response to it.

The distinction between fact and interpretation is vitally important. The fact is that planes hit unstable air. My interpretation in this situation is the meaning I give to the fact, which might be that my plane is going to crash. My interpretation then influences my response to the original fact. If I think turbulence means that we're going down, I am terrified. If I think the plane is a fun ride, then I can relax and even enjoy the surprises. When I can remind myself of the basic fact, "The plane is going through unstable air," then I can choose how to respond to that information.

Most of the time, we go immediately from fact to interpretation without even realizing it. The plane bumps and I interpret danger. I become very afraid in response to this interpretation of danger. Because of these thoughts, I may continue to be afraid or become terrified, perhaps even after the fact of the turbulence has ended.

This instantaneous jump from fact to interpretation can get us into trouble. Sometimes it is harmless: I see someone yawn in a meeting and I assume they are bored. No big deal. It doesn't really matter to me why they yawned and it doesn't impact my actions. We don't have to stop and analyze every fact and consciously decide our next step. The important thing is to realize it is happening and to be able to slow down to check our interpretation when appropriate.

Here are a few examples of how this might show up at work:

FACT	INTERPRETATION
A coworker doesn't say hello.	She thinks she's better than me; she can't even be bothered to acknowledge me.
A person you supervise repeatedly misses deadlines.	He doesn't respect me or the organization or he would honor his commitments.
A person you supervise comes late to meetings and she doesn't participate when she does come.	She's got a bad attitude. She's not a team player.
You hear through the grapevine that someone repeated information that you told him privately.	He betrayed me. He is not trustworthy.

If you race from fact to interpretation, your response will be dramatically different than if you're able to separate the fact from the interpretation before deciding what to do next. In each of these examples, you don't know enough to reach the conclusion listed above.

Maybe the coworker that didn't greet you was late for a presentation and so caught up in what she was going to say that she didn't even see you. Maybe the person you supervise needs help with time management skills or doesn't understand their assignments or deadlines. Maybe the person who comes late to meetings has a legitimate time conflict. Or maybe it's hard for her to jump into rambunctious meetings and she needs an invitation to share her ideas in the meeting. As for what you may have heard through the grapevine, how trustworthy are your sources? Did the person you shared with know that the information was being shared in confidence? Did you explicitly state that?

See how it works? You just don't know. Your interpretation may be spot on, or it may not be, and if you take action on your interpretation, you might make the situation worse. Especially when it comes to supervision. When employees see their supervisor react to situations without getting all the facts, trust is broken.

Slowing down can help you separate fact from interpretation. You might need more information to determine if your interpretation is correct. Or you might just need to stay with the facts and set your interpretation aside. In each of the scenarios listed above, one alternative would have been to simply respond to the basic facts. To talk to the people about what happened, get their side of the story, and let them know what's needed. Holding our interpretations aside lets us address the actions more cleanly and clearly.

Recognizing that you are adding an interpretation onto the basic facts can free you to reframe your interpretation and then to choose your response. That reframing can make all the difference. It can make the ride much more fun. Whee!

Coaching Corner

- Are you responding to anyone in a negative manner because of an interpretation you made about his or her actions or intentions? If you separate your interpretation from the basic facts, how might that shift your response?
- When do you tend to jump to interpretation? What else might be going on besides what you initially assumed? How can you practice slowing down to separate fact from interpretation?
- Look at a difficult situation from different perspectives

to practice reframing: How might the employee see the situation? How might your customers/clients see the situation? How might a jury see the situation? Do any of those different perspectives shift your response to the situation?

WISHFUL THINKING

It happened in a split second. I was fine and then suddenly I fell and broke my wrist. I had to have surgery and now I have a titanium plate and a dozen screws in my wrist. There were many components to this unexpected "adventure," but the one that surprised me the most was how unconscious, wishful thinking about my recovery kept showing up.

The first time I noticed my wishful thinking was when I went to my post-surgery appointment and the doctor undressed my bandages. I heard my brain say "Oh—blood!" as he took them off. Now, obviously I knew I'd had surgery and I knew that surgery involved cutting and blood, but because I had not consciously thought about it, there was a primitive part of my brain that was surprised to see bloodstains. It was as if some part of me wanted the quick fix and hoped that, after the surgery, everything would be fine. I was unconsciously thinking that I could go back in time, or that what had happened wouldn't make any difference in my life. And the sight of blood made me quickly face the falseness of my wishful thinking.

The second time I noticed my wishful thinking was two weeks later when the doctor removed my bright green cast. Somehow, the focus of my energy and concern had shifted from my broken wrist to my cast. It was heavy, cumbersome, and itchy. When they took it off I found myself surprised again. "Oh, my wrist is still a mess," I thought. Taking off the cast did not make the wrist all better. Now again, this was obvious to my logical mind. But my wishful mind had focused on the cast and decided that if I could just get rid of that—all would be well.

Where supervision is concerned, there are many ways we can engage in wishful thinking, but the most common is similar to my broken-wrist thinking: if we just look at the immediate surface issue and take a small step (or no step) everything will be just fine. We can see a problem and still let wishful thinking convince us that if we ignore it, it will go away. We can wonder how our staff is doing but trust in our wishful thinking that's telling us people would speak up if they needed anything and therefore we don't have to ask. We can ignore signs pointing to the contrary and listen only to the wishful thinking that says of course people know how their job supports the mission and values of your organization. All of these examples of wishful thinking keep us focused on the surface and hoping that things will magically fix themselves. When we do that, we do not see or attend to what is actually happening. Wishful thinking depends on us not recognizing our own assumptions and therefore we act from what we think is true but may or may not be true.

Let's look at the following examples of supervisors catching their own wishful thinking and then shifting focus to move forward.

✓ In the finance department, Ofelia notices that unpaid bills always get held up on the account clerk's desk. Ofelia assumes that if someone else had that position, the bills would be paid more quickly. So Ofelia focuses on that particular person as the problem. The wishful thinking is that this is a personnel problem and not a systems problem. Before she actually terminates the account clerk, though, she talks to her and realizes that she has twelve steps to do before she can write the checks. When Ofelia looks at the process as a whole, she sees that many more people have a hand in this process. She realizes she has to change the whole bill-paying system before she can fairly judge whether the account clerk is a problem or not.

✓ Jeannette is a new leader who has been hired to take the team in a new direction. Within a month, Jeannette hears from HR that people are unhappy. She hears a lot of her staff grumbling and a few people quit. Jeannette assumes this has nothing to do with her. When HR helps her step back and look at what's going on, Jeannette sees how her wishful thinking had led her to believe that the transition would be easy, and that everyone would be ready to follow her. With this recognition, she was able to slow down and bring people with her. She needed to do more explaining about why the change was important and listen to the concerns of her staff.

When my cast came off, I was reminded that my wrist had indeed been broken (shattered was the official diagnosis) and I was able to see that I had significant work to do to rehabilitate it. I had to acknowledge my wishful thinking and look beyond the focus of that magic to address the real issue. Take time to catch your own wishful thinking so that you can look beyond the initial presentation of a problem. Once you uncover your wishful thinking, your logical mind can step in and ask the intriguing questions that can lead to real solutions.

Coaching Corner

· When do you encounter wishful thinking in your own life? What are you avoiding by ignoring what's going on or by focusing only on the surface? (Don't edit your response—just listen with curiosity.)

- What is one problem that is consuming your attention? Ask yourself what's underneath that problem to see if there is an underlying concern that is not being addressed. Ask the question three times in a row and see what answers come up.
- Are you assuming that you know the cause of any conflict or disruption in your team? Are there other team members who need to be asked for their perspective?

DUALISM GETS IN THE WAY

Dualism is defined by Merriam-Webster as the quality or state of having two different or opposite parts or elements. Dualism is an either/or, us-versus-them perspective. Dualism happens, for instance, when protests about the shooting of unarmed black men are met by the immediate defense of the police on a universal level. The ones defending the police often present themselves in a dualistic paradigm: "You either support the police or you support the protesters." In this paradigm, there is no room for understanding, dialogue, or learning.

Dualism draws a line. The mutually exclusive mind-set denies the possibility that both sides can have a piece of the truth. You can support the work and valor of police in a general way while still holding them accountable and calling for a thoughtful study of the training methods and actions of the police. You can look at the statistics and recognize that there is clearly something going on that needs attention. When the opportunity for dialogue is reduced to, "You're either with us or against us," the opportunity is lost.

Dualistic behaviors play out far too often in the work world, as well as in the world at large. I met with a work group recently where the staff had some concerns that their supervisor was treating people harshly. Instead of listening and considering their concerns, the supervisor moved into a dualistic stance. "You either support the staff or you support me." Drawing that line in the sand entrenches both sides and makes it hard to move forward. The challenge for me in facilitating work from there was to help them all get back on the same side of supporting the mission so they could hear each other and move forward together.

Too often lines are drawn before people even hear each other. The line-drawing often stems from defensiveness. Sometimes the defensiveness is in response to how topics are presented; if a presentation of concerns feels like a threat or an attack, we're more likely to respond as if we're in physical danger. This can lead directly to an ultimatum.

Sometimes defensiveness is just something we bring with us from our personal life: our learned, typical reaction to feedback or perceived threat. Either way, we have to learn to recognize and reframe the situation before we create a dualistic trap for ourselves and our organization. Ideally the initiator of the conversation would reframe the dualistic thoughts before they speak, by acknowledging that they are speaking from their own experience and want to hear about the other's experience.

Here are a few examples of what a reframing might look like:

DUALISM	REFRAME
You're either with me or against me.	I hear you have a strong reaction to what I said and I'd like to talk about this.
One of you is lying.	I hear you both have a different perspective on this. Let me hear from both of you and then we'll see from there.

continued ⇨

DUALISM	REFRAME
You either support the organization or you can leave.	I hear you have some concerns about how we do things here. Can you tell me how your concerns relate to our mission so I can listen better?
We either change or we die.	There is a strong indication that we need to change. Let me lay out my thinking and then hear your concerns.
Either he leaves or I leave.	I find it hard to imagine how I can keep working here. Tell me how you think we can resolve our differences so we can both get our needs met.

Notice that the reframe is almost always in the form of an "I-statement," which underlines that this is **my** opinion. It is not the-one-and-only truth. It is **my** truth. That helps people hear your perspective much more clearly than the dualistic either/or statement.

Watch for dualism in the workplace, in the world, and in your thinking. If you see it, try to reframe it to name one perspective in a way that does not discount the possibility that the other perspective may have some truth to tell also.

Catching and reframing dualistic thoughts helped me countless times during meetings, mediations, and conflict resolution. In my worldview, it's an invaluable practice. But remember, you don't have to be with me or against me.

Coaching Corner

- Can you think of a time when you have been presented with a dualistic scenario? How did you react? What did it feel like? If you can't think of one, imagine someone telling you, "It's him or me." How would you react?
- Listen for examples of dualism at work or in the world. Notice how you react. Do you feel drawn to take a side? Practice trying on both sides to simply open up the dialogue, at least for yourself. Notice if that changes your initial feeling at all.
- If you find yourself reacting to something defensively, and therefore moving to mutually exclusive thinking, what can you say to yourself to open up your reaction?

COMPARED TO PERFECT

Once you had the perfect employee. Or maybe you've never actually had a perfect employee, but you know what he or she would be like. They would:

- be punctual
- be attentive
- be competent
- follow through on every assignment
- be pleasant
- bring ideas to the table
- tell you about problems early enough so that you could solve them
- look up to you but not treat you as an alien
- share your work ethic
- have a work style that was similar to your own
- laugh a lot, but not too much . . .
- Etc. . . . etc. . . . etc. . . .

Your list may be similar or different than mine, but most of us have a list in our mind, even if we've never thought about it. We know what perfect would be. And we don't have it!

So we keep noticing how our actual employees don't measure up. If you've had that elusive perfect employee, you may compare your current employee to him or her. "Elaine would have let me know that the project was stalled the minute it happened!" "Fred would never have handled a complaint like that!"

If you have never worked with the perfect employee, your imagination knows that she is out there. You might find yourself wondering what kind of an ad would manifest this perfect person. You may compare your current staff to this imaginary employee. "If only my staff would follow through!" "My life would be better if I had a staff who knew how to work together!" "What would it be like to work with staff who brought ideas, not just problems to the table?"

While it is important to know what you want, it is just as important to recognize what you have. Look at what and who is right in front of you. Focus on being the perfect (or at least good) supervisor and working with the employees you have. Help them be successful and it will help you and your organization be successful.

- ✔ What are his strengths?
- ✔ What does she struggle with?
- ✔ Is there a way you could give them more of what they're good at and less of what they struggle with?
- ✔ Have you told them exactly what you need from them?
- ✔ Have you told them how they're not measuring up? And did you tell them this in a way that they could hear it—and not just feel attacked?
- ✔ Do they know that you want them to bring ideas as well as problems to the table? Have you told them that? And even more important, how have you reacted when they have brought ideas? If you responded, "Oh that won't work," are you surprised they've never tried this again?

✓ What do they need to succeed?

✓ Are you meeting with them regularly so you have a relationship that includes consistent two-way conversations?

It does little good to focus on what you don't have, unless you have tried to make it work and have truly determined that the employee is not able to do the work. If you have thoughtfully evaluated the employee and the needs of the job, only then can you move on and go find the more perfect employee. As long as the employee in front of you is your employee, and you are not ready to fire them, then do what you can to help them succeed.

Dreaming of perfect simply gets in the way of seeing what is in front of you. When you try to hold on to the perfect employee that was (or might be), then you are missing (and perhaps driving away) the actual employee in front of you. It's much easier to be a good supervisor to the perfect employee. Being a good supervisor to actual people takes a little more attention. The imaginary ones may be perfect, but they are not very effective at getting the real work done!

Coaching Corner

- What or who do you compare your staff to? How does this get in the way?

- What or who do you compare yourself to? How does this get in the way?

- What does the person standing in front of you need to succeed? Have you talked to them about that? Do they know what is expected and/or what is missing?

- What does your perfect employee look like? How big of a gap is there between this imaginary person and your actual staff? Is that gap tolerable or problematic?

THE PROBLEM WITH COMMON SENSE

When I was an HR director, one of the programs in my organization was a Head Start preschool. One day a supervising teacher in that program came to me for help with her assistant. She told me that this assistant teacher often stood near the phone in the classroom as it rang and rang. The teacher would often wait, she said, expecting the assistant to answer the phone. But every time, she would eventually have to run across the classroom and pick up the phone. She was frustrated with the assistant and wanted to know what she should do.

The supervisor was exasperated. "She just stands there! It's happened three or four times in the past month. I don't know what to do!"

"Have you told her to answer the phone when it rings?" I asked.

"No. I shouldn't have to do that. It's common sense that you answer the phone when you're standing right next to it."

"Is it?" I asked. "I hear that it is common sense for you, but it may not be for your assistant. You need to tell her what your expectation is. In this instance, you need to tell her not only that you expect her to answer the phone when it rings, but what she should say and how to say it, and how to handle the likely callers."

"I shouldn't have to do that," the teacher complained.

"It isn't a should or shouldn't. It just is. You need her to answer the phone. She's not doing that. Let her know what you need. And take the judgment out of it. You don't know what she's thinking until you talk to her about it."

The teacher knew me well and was able to hear my advice. She nodded her head when I told her to take the judgment out of it. "You're right," she said. "I have a lot of judgment about this. It's hard for me to imagine why she doesn't do something so obvious but you're right. I need to talk to her. It's just hard for me to be so bossy."

We talked about the difference between being bossy and being clear. "Start with a question," I told her. "Ask her why she doesn't answer the phone and then tell her what you need her to do."

It turned out that the assistant thought it would be disrespectful for her to answer the phone. She assumed that it was the supervisor's right, and her job, to answer the phone. Once she understood the expectation then she performed the task just fine.

The problem with common sense is that it stems from an egocentric place. It assumes that my common sense is everyone's common sense. It assumes that my cultural norms are the norms. It assumes that logic, reason, perspective, and understanding are the same for everyone. Furthermore, it assumes that my way is obvious and anyone who doesn't see it that way is stupid or lazy or at least uninformed. There is judgment and privilege in the claims about "common sense."

Common sense denies the reality that we all have different ways of understanding and interpreting rules and traditions. It denies that different views are not better or worse, but just different. It denies that we all know lots of things but sometimes what we know in common is not as much as we think.

If something seems obvious to you, notice it and then consider that it may or may not be obvious to your staff. If necessary, explain your expectation in a calm, neutral voice, and give them a chance to change their behavior.

You could also acknowledge your assumption and ask them about theirs. "I realize I've been assuming that you would answer the phone when you're closer to it than I am. Is there a reason that you don't?" Make sure your tone is neutral or your judgment will come through.

In any case, remember that what is common sense to you may not be so obvious to anyone else. And vice versa!

Coaching Corner

- Think of a time when you thought something was common sense. Now think of at least three reasons it might not have been common sense to other people.

- Put yourself on the other side of a common sense comment. Imagine someone comes to you at work and says, "I can't imagine why you haven't done this. It's simply common sense!" Would you feel engaged and excited to perform the task? How would you feel about the person who approached you in this manner?
- Are there any activities or responsibilities that you have been assuming that someone on your staff knew they should be doing? If they haven't been doing them, how could you explain your expectations in a calm, neutral, and respectful voice?

WHAT DO YOU BELIEVE?

My niece, Casi, worked for a trucking company. When her daughter was eighteen months old, she posted the following update on Facebook:

> This morning I told my boss I'd be checking out early this afternoon to go the county fair with my family and she came back from lunch with tickets and a parking pass for us. I love that I get to do what I love and put my family first.

Compare that to this story, shared by Robert Reich that same day also on Facebook:

> A manager at a large insurance company was asked by top management to dictate the following terms to my employees: for restroom breaks you should average less than seven minutes per day or 1.5 % of your total work day; this should be approximately nine minutes per day if you work a ten-hour day.

What can we glean about these managers based on these two posts? It is clear that they act very differently toward their employees, and also harbor some fundamental beliefs about how workers work.

Casi's boss must believe that if Casi feels supported and appreciated, she will produce more for the organization. And indeed, in her post she communicates the loyalty to and excitement about her work that she feels in part because of the support and trust they give her. The management in example two is showing their belief that people must be strictly controlled in order not to waste time and money, and that the employees are not to be fully trusted. How do you think the employees felt in response to these minute-management rules, and how do you think that showed up in their long-term productivity? Who would you rather work for?

Coaching Corner

- Two beliefs about employees are demonstrated in this section. One is focused on rewarding and encouraging employees and the other is focused on monitoring and restricting employees. Which way is most closely aligned with your beliefs? Can you state in a sentence what you believe about how people act at work?
- Can you state three examples of how your beliefs show up in actions?
- Do you have any fears or doubts about your own beliefs? Looking at the "what-ifs" can help you test your own theory as well as look for responses to your concerns.

CHAPTER 5:

How You Lead

HIKING TOGETHER

I was hiking with my family at Multnomah Falls in Oregon when I noticed another family hiking in tandem with us. We were a group of five: my husband and I, our son, his wife, and their young son. The other group was a family of three: a mom, a dad, and a teenager. Our hiking speed was similar so we took turns passing each other and taking breaks. First we'd pass the father, then the son, then the mom. Then we'd take a break and they would each pass us. I was struck by the fact that the members of this other family were heading to the same place but they were not traveling together. They were each walking by themselves and they were not talking to each other. At all. I never once witnessed them take more than a step or two together, and the only time I saw them exchange words was when the father reprimanded the young boy for kicking rocks.

I thought about how I like to hike with my family. There are definitely times when we are not all together; we flow into different configurations of twos or threes or solitary time, but in general we are within shouting distance and we share the experience. "Look at that lichen!" "How far do you think we've hiked?" "How about if we all head off on this side path for a bit?" If someone gets too far out, the person in the front waits for all of us to catch up and regroup, then we're off and hiking again.

Admittedly, I don't know this family or how they usually relate to each other. They could have gotten in a fight in the car that might have tainted their experience that day. Or maybe they were doing a challenge of taking quiet time. However, it led me to think about how some families—and by extension some work groups—act in a disconnected manner. Other families and work groups act in a more connected manner and actively develop a plan to ensure the connected process. As supervisors, we need to look at how our team hikes together—not literally (although that would be fun too), but as a team going toward a destination. You are both the leader of the team and a member of the team.

To ensure that your team is hiking together, ask yourself the following questions:

- ✔ Is everyone absolutely clear of the destination and the route?
- ✔ Does everyone know what they are expected to contribute as well as the responsibilities of every other member?
- ✔ Are you traveling within shouting distance of each other?
- ✔ Can you make adjustments to the route if you need to?
- ✔ Can you show each other new insights or learning along the way?
- ✔ Can you back each other up if someone gets hurt or finds themselves out of their capacity?

✔ Can you stop to appreciate the beauty of the trip
and enjoy the others' company?

So many times managers assume that their team knows all they
need to know. They forget to share updates. They forget to listen
to the people who are on the journey alongside them. They forget
to stop and look around to make sure the team is connected and
everyone is doing their part.

Keeping in touch with everyone is one of the reasons you need
to have regular time to meet with each member of your team one-
on-one, as well as a time to meet all together. You, as the leader,
need to make sure the destination and the route are clear. Then you
need to make sure that your team has what they need to do their
work. You need to listen to them and see how their hike is going. It is
essential to make sure your team is all headed on the same route to
the same destination and that the whole team is traveling together.

Coaching Corner

- Take a minute and quietly think about this hiking
  metaphor. What comes up for you? (You might have
  some new ideas, thoughts, analogies, clarification, or
  questions about your destination. Or you might be
  motivated to action, or feel the urge to go for an actual
  hike . . . Pay attention to whatever comes.) If you're
  not a hiker, what metaphor works for you? What new
  understanding does thinking about it this way bring you?
- What do you do to encourage your team, including
  yourself, to travel together?
- Who supports you in your leadership role? What do you
  need from them at this time?

BUILD A VISION FOR YOUR TEAM

If you want to build a ship, don't drum up the men to gather wood, divide the work and give orders. Instead, teach them to yearn for the vast and endless sea!
—Antoine Saint Exupery, author of *The Little Prince*

It happens to all of us at one time or another. We wake up one morning and realize that we don't want to go to work. We're tired, we're frustrated, we're bored, we're overwhelmed. We realize that we've been simply getting by at work for a while. We are just putting one foot in front of the other and doing tasks. There are a variety of ways we reach this point, but one of the most common ways is that we've lost sight of **why** we are doing what we are doing.

One of the underlying reasons we get bored at work is because we've become separated from the outcome of our work. We have fallen asleep to the power of our work. This is where a compelling vision can wake us up and reconnect us with the purpose of our work. Just as Antoine Saint Exupery illustrates in the quote above, it is by reconnecting to a powerful vision of your work that you, and your team, can become motivated and reenergized. Depending on your mission, can you create a compelling vision? What would your team be yearning for?

Here are a few examples:

- ✓ Teach them to yearn for peace and justice, and they will remember why they work so hard for social justice in their nonprofit.
- ✓ Teach them to yearn for extraordinary customer service, and they will remember why it matters how they answer the phone.
- ✓ Teach them to yearn for the best wine in California, and they will remember why it matters how they work together in the winemaking process.

✔ Teach them to yearn for the best widget on the
market, and they will remember why their individual
part of the widget-making process matters.

What is the vision of your work team? By necessity, much of our day-to-day work gets focused on what is in front of us. I know that when I worked in an organization, I sometimes felt like I was bouncing from one imminent crisis to the next with no sense of direction or control. This is not an effective model for business, or for life.

We must build a vision about where we are going, and only from that point can we form an effective plan to implement that vision. Does your team have a common vision of what they are working toward? It is important to take time to make sure everyone on the team knows and can imagine the vision. From that vision, make a plan and visit it regularly to make sure you're all still headed in the right direction. Don't let the vision be a document that languishes in a file until it's time for the next visioning process. **Use** the vision to inspire people. Use the vision to wake people up from automatic pilot. The vision can get people focused, even when the way to the vision seems cluttered with day-to-day details.

We start with our vision. What do we try to accomplish? What do we yearn for? As individuals, as teams, as organizations? And then we back up to where we are now and fill in the gaps. We make goals that will move us closer to our vision. If we don't have a vision and remember what we are yearning for, then the work will always be too much. On the other hand, if we can hold on to a vision while making progress toward it through concrete goals, we will be more focused and more effective in our work and with each other. When we share the scent of the ocean, we can build better boats.

Coaching Corner

- How do you keep your organization's vision alive for you and your team?

- What "wakes you up" about the work you do and how does that affect your performance?
- What part of you is asleep to your work and your life and how does that affect you?

LAUGH A LOT

I led a small organization through a two-day, off-site retreat. When the retreat ended, I reflected on the amazing work that the group had accomplished in two days. Besides their obvious commitment to the work of the retreat, I was struck by how much laughter there was. Good-hearted bantering, gentle teasing, silly jokes, and raucous, almost-wetting-your-pants laughter. It was delightful. It was a fun and productive two days, and I especially noticed how focused everyone would become after a random bout of laughter.

This organization's mission was to develop leadership within a specific working class community for economic, gender, and racial equality. This was no frivolous group of employees. Their work mattered and they knew it. And they knew that laughing together would help them work better together.

It reminded me of my work with an AIDS organization at the height of the epidemic. We laughed a lot. We also cried a lot. But the laughter was essential. It was part of the culture that helped us do the hard work of that time. I know that if we could laugh then and there, any workplace can laugh.

There is something powerful about a group that laughs and plays together. In these organizations—the one I led the retreat for and the one I used to work for—the groups were also successful at working together. There's a synergistic alchemy that makes us all more than the sum of our parts—and the laughter is both a symbol and a key ingredient of that.

I was struck by the familiarity and fun of the laughter at the retreat. In my experience most work groups don't laugh and play like that. Most workplaces focus on the seriousness of the work they do. They may tolerate an occasional joke or gentle tease, but for many organizations the culture demands that frivolity be left at the door. In doing so, we leave part of who we are at the door.

The two organizations I mentioned do intense work. And precisely because of this, there's an attitude that "We better have fun too!" It's a counterintuitive logic that works. I am reminded of the quote I heard about a very successful surgeon who was known to remind his staff, "Everybody slow down—we're in a hurry here!" It's the same kind of nonlinear thinking that produces dramatic results. This work matters and we better have fun while we're doing it.

Having fun and laughing together breaks tensions, relieves stress, and builds connections. It opens us up to do our best work. It connects us in a direct way. These connections carry on and weave through the work we do together.

And you know what? The **Great Place to Work® Institute thinks laughter is important too.** This is a national group that has been listening to employees and evaluating employers since 1980 in order to understand what makes a workplace great. In one of their reports, I read that one consistent distinction that separates the top companies on that list from the rest was that employees expressed agreement to the statement, "I have fun at work."

So laugh a little. Laugh a lot. Play together and it will improve your work together.

Coaching Corner

- Do you feel guilty if you take five minutes to play or laugh at work? What do you need to give yourself permission to lighten up?
- Think about a time when you shared a good hearty laugh with someone—at work or away from work. How

did you feel after the laughter? How could that feeling impact your work?

- How would your team respond to the statement "I have fun at work." As a supervisor, how do you (or would you) react to laughter during work?

GPS AND MENTORING

My husband and I were going to visit his mother. We hadn't been to her place lately, so we entered the address into the GPS at the start of the trip. Three hours later, it told us to get off on our designated exit. After several turns, we found ourselves driving on a small bumpy country lane that was one step removed from a dirt road. We slowly drove through turn after turn and ended up where we were going but it took a while. On our way back we found that the next exit on the freeway would have been a straight shot to where we were going.

"I wish we could teach the GPS to more carefully consider its options before directing us where to go," I thought. I laughed at myself as I realized that I wanted to mentor the GPS into making more effective decisions.

In many cases, this is what you strive to do with your employees. Mentoring takes more time than just telling them what to do, but in the long run it will save you from having to make all the decisions yourself, and you will be fostering an environment that values strategic thinking and independent working.

When you move into a mentorship role, you are doing more coaching than directing. That means you need to ask more questions. The point of questions is not to make your employee guess what you are thinking, but rather to get them to think about their actions. Using open-ended questions gets people to try out some different ideas, perhaps to see a different way of doing things or to consider alternative actions and their potential consequences.

Consider the following questions to help your staff think through their options:

✓ "So, how many different ways do you see to get from here to there?" (This is not an open-ended question, but it sets the stage for the next ones.)
✓ "What do you see as the pros and cons of each?"
✓ "Given what you know about our mission and purpose, which route would best suit our needs?"
✓ And after the project is completed, ask them to consider: "How do you think it went?"

Through a questioning process, you can guide your employees to be more thoughtful in their decision-making. This is not a one-time process, however. You cannot simply say, "Be more thoughtful," and expect their behavior to change. Questions set you up as a guide, helping your staff to think through their choices. Ask them to outline their options and bring you a recommendation. This step of helping them articulate their choices and make a recommendation might go quickly, or it might take a year or more, depending on the complexity of the project. Through this process, in incremental steps, you are helping mentor the employee into independent thinking. Eventually, when they have made several good recommendations, they might be authorized to make the next decision on their own.

Our GPS gave us technically correct advice. It did get us where we were going. The advice did not suit our purpose, however, of wanting a direct route. When you mentor your employees, you can help them consider all the variables they need to weigh into their eventual decision so that you can both be comfortable with the outcome. Your employees will feel more confident to act on their own without second-guessing their choices. And you will be able to trust them to think strategically and act independently. And you will both get to where you're going.

Coaching Corner

- On a scale of 1 to 5, how comfortable are you asking questions of your employees? If you rate yourself as uncomfortable, what do you tell yourself about the kind of person who asks questions? Do you have a belief that a supervisor must know what to do and should not look like he or she doesn't?
- How could you practice asking open-ended questions?
- Do you believe that people can learn how to make better decisions, or do you think people either make good decisions or they don't? How does either belief affect your mentorship of your employees?
- If you supervise employees who don't have to make a lot of decisions in their work, how else can you apply mentorship skills? Is there a new skill they could learn? Is there a soft skill, like dependability, where you could use questions to help your employees consider their impact?

THE POWER OF THE PAUSE

> *Between stimulus and response there is a space. In that space is our power to choose our response. In our response lies our growth and our freedom.*
>
> —Viktor E. Frankl

When we practice the art of the pause, we gain freedom to be the kind of supervisor (and the kind of person) that we want to be. As supervisors, reacting impulsively often gets us in trouble or makes matters worse. And almost all of us have personal examples of this. When I am coaching supervisors, I sometimes ask a manager, "What happened?" and they often answer with something like, "Before I knew it, I had suspended her." Or, "I was just so mad, I told him he was being stupid." Yikes! If these managers had paused, and then chosen their response, they would not have gotten themselves or the organization in such a mess.

The pause may be a few seconds, or it may be a few days, but the pause matters. In a few seconds you can remind yourself, "They are seeing this differently than I am. What do I want to do about that?" In two seconds you can ask yourself, "How do I want to respond?" That pause can change the world!

Here are a few examples of when a pause is called for in your work as a supervisor:

✓ **An employee does something that you don't understand.** They may ask a question that was fine to begin with but now that they've asked it eight times, it sounds pretty stupid. Or they made a mistake. Or they are acting in a way that seems unreasonable given the situation. You simply don't know what they are thinking or doing. Good time to pause . . . and choose how to respond.

✓ **You feel your buttons being pushed.** We all have our triggers. Some of them are pretty firmly entrenched, and we can react in a situation before we even realize what's happening. Usually when we are irritated by something in this way, we are reacting to old stories. One of my strongest triggers is the simple word "relax." If someone tells me to relax because they assume I'm getting upset, it sends me through the roof. I have learned to step back and take a deep breath as I remind myself that this is a trigger for me.

✓ **When you apologize.** A client told me about a tricky situation when she double-booked an appointment with her employee the week after she had severely criticized that very employee for double-booking an appointment. And now she had done it to her. She told me she had addressed it directly and told her employee, "I'm sorry; I know I just talked to you about this and I shouldn't have done it but when can we reschedule?" She was confused and upset that the employee did not accept her apology and acted all huffy at her. I suggested she try a few pauses in that sentence. "I'm sorry. (Pause.) I know I just talked to you about this. (Pause.) I shouldn't have done it. (Pause.) Can we reschedule?" When an apology is followed immediately by an excuse, the excuse eats up the apology. Apologizing and letting that stand alone for even a few seconds, gives time for the offended person to feel the apology as well as to hear it. In that pause, you can also erase the word "but" because that word effectively erases an apology.

✓ **When you need more information to make a decision.** This is a fairly obvious one, but often people think they have to make decisions on the spot. Sometimes they even forget that there may be more to the story. This can lead to more big trouble. Pause. Think. Do I have all the information I need? Have I spoken to everyone involved in this incident? Am I ready to make a decision? Wait until the answer to all those questions is yes.

✓ **In the midst of ambiguity.** There are times in an organization when things are changing and it is uncomfortable. You may have announced a decision that people don't like, you may be doing things in a new way, or maybe someone was just fired. It is uncomfortable. People may be unhappy. People may be unsure. And as a leader, you want to fix it. You want to do something, anything, to make things feel more secure. Sometimes, you just need to tolerate the ambiguity and discomfort. Pause and decide. Wait.

The pause can be powerful. Breathe through it and choose your next action. We can choose to respond intentionally instead of reacting unconsciously. In that pause, we can also find our better selves.

Coaching Corner

- Looking back, can you recognize times when a pause would have helped you respond more appropriately in a certain situation?
- Find something to do to build the practice of the pause. I have developed the practice of literally taking a step backward. This is not a big deal to anyone observing me but it is a physical reminder to me to slow down. It gives me time to ask myself, "What do you want to do next?"
- Practice saying a few things out loud so you are ready when you need them for a pause. "Give me a minute to think about that." "Mmmm, I'll get back to you about this."

TRIPLE VISION REQUIRED

When I was on vacation in Hawaii, I hiked through a lush rainforest. It was a spectacular hike through an awe-inspiring landscape, passing several waterfalls on the way and traveling through a bamboo forest. When the wind rustled it was like being inside a wind chime! It was magical. While hiking I found I had to continuously shift my vision to take in everything I needed, and wanted, to see.

I had to use triple vision: First, I had to watch the ground to confirm each step—through thick mud, convoluted root systems, steep terrain, and rushing streams of water. Second, I had to keep glancing ahead to see where I was going and to make sure I knew how the path wound through the forest. And third, every once in a while, I had to stop. The stops allowed me to catch my breath and to take it all in—to get my bearings and to savor the experience. After all, that's why I was out there.

Supervision requires similar skills in terms of taking in multiple views while moving forward. First, a supervisor must be aware of the immediate circumstances. Second, he or she must see the path ahead, and third, the supervisor has to keep the big picture of the entire organization in mind. Keeping all three concerns in focus requires an ability to shift attention and to see different perspectives, and a commitment to doing this while in the midst of daily tasks and struggles.

The first perspective focuses on the immediate surroundings. A supervisor must always be aware of the current circumstances of the workplace: staffing, projects, problems, threats, successes, deadlines, and priorities. In order to know all this, not only must the supervisor keep his or her eyes open, but also speak and listen to all members of the team—with the understanding that each person has their own view of the terrain underfoot. In other words, supervisors have to keep a view of the ground and make sure their staff is also on firm footing in the day-to-day work.

Second, a supervisor must keep the goals and the plan to get to the destination in mind at all times. This includes work trajectories for each team member, cumulative objectives, and adjustments. It is essential that you look up from the daily commotion and make sure you're on track to reach your goals. If you lose sight of the path, those daily steps, even if stable, can end up leading you off course. The path is defined by the mission, vision, and values that keep you on track as you move forward toward your goals.

And finally a supervisor must stop occasionally. I know that this feels nearly impossible in the midst of the enormous amount of work that you face. It is, however, an essential skill for survival and success. If you do not stop to catch your breath, you will burn out and become ineffective or mean, or both. Stopping means claiming weekends as time off, taking vacations, getting enough sleep, and taking care of yourself in other ways. It also means stepping back for reflection, which is necessary in order to survey the big picture. Take time to stop and say, "Look at what we've accomplished." The big picture also includes seeing the entire organization as well as the organization's place in the community and perhaps also within larger society. The knowledge of the landscape and the organization's place in it helps you to position your team for maximum effectiveness and it allows you to be a member of the leadership team for the entire organization. You cannot lead in a vacuum.

When you are able to integrate these three views, you are able to keep the whole process on track. As you hike through the forest, you can also take in the smells of everything around you, notice the numerous shades of green, pace your steps with your hiking partners, and feel the sunlight on your skin.

Triple vision is required to be an effective supervisor. Being aware of the immediate terrain, the path ahead, and the entire environment allows you to be a true leader. It also lets you enjoy the hike along the way.

Coaching Corner

- Where is your vision usually focused as a supervisor?
- What practices do you do to ensure that you alternate your vision on a regular basis?
- Do you have beliefs, spoken or hidden, that get in your way of stopping occasionally?
- What do you bring to the leadership of the organization that would be lost if you allowed yourself to burn out?

DON'T JUST ADVISE, OFFER SUPPORT

Joan's e-mail program was messing up. She mentioned to her boss that this was the holdup in getting him the report he was waiting for.

"Did you close all your other programs?" he asked. "Have you tried restarting your computer?" Her boss didn't wait for any answers; he just marched over to Joan's desk and started trying to fix the computer for her. Joan decided it was time for a break and left the office. She spent her break complaining to her friend about how frustrating it was to work for her boss. "He doesn't listen to me. He just takes over. I hate it."

The problem wasn't that her boss had tried to fix Joan's computer, but rather that he did so when Joan hadn't asked him to help her. She was simply telling him about a glitch she'd encountered. She expected to troubleshoot the problem on her own, and was only letting him know that the report was held up. Maybe her boss was eager to save her from frustration and that's why he offered his help. But he didn't in fact offer his help; he just "helped."

And therein lies the critical difference. Unsolicited advice or action is rarely seen as helpful. Rather than alleviating frustrations it often adds to them.

In a supervisory relationship there is an implied understanding that the supervisor knows more or better than the supervisee. There is a period when an employee is new to a job or learning new skills when the supervisor is in a de facto training role. Once that training is completed, though, the exchange of advice should be handled in a more thoughtful manner. The supervisor needs to honor their employees' capacity to take care of their own problems.

Here's another example: Tom goes to his supervisor and says, "I've been working on the project and I've hit a snag. I'm not sure what I should do." Many supervisors assume that employees come to them at these junctures because they want to know what to do. In this case, Tom may want help, but we don't know yet. Too many supervisors assume that whenever a staff member talks to them, they want advice or clear directives. If, however, a supervisor wants to build a more effective relationship wherein you work in partnership with your staff, then there are other ways to respond to Tom's concern:

EXAMPLES OF A TAKE-CHARGE RESPONSE	EXAMPLES OF A PARTNER RESPONSE
"Follow these steps and you'll be fine."	"What are your options?
"It's your job to know what to do."	"What are you considering?"
"I'll take care of it."	"How can I help?"

The responses in the first column tell the staff member that the supervisor will take over. They tell the staff member that the supervisor does not care about the staff member's learning process or ideas. The only thing that apparently matters to the supervisor is the outcome. When you reply with take-charge responses, the staff member will generally stop bringing you ideas. The staff member might also stop caring about his or her own ideas or growth.

The responses in the second column, on the other hand, tell the staff member that the supervisor is available to help but trusts that the staff member has ideas and thoughts about the situation. Most of all, these responses tell the staff member that the supervisor will listen to them, a principle practice of partnership.

A supervisor who wants to keep his or her staff engaged will build a practice of listening first and then asking if they want help. Often the employee simply wants to see if they're thinking in the right direction. They may want to keep you in the loop or vent their frustration with you. Listen and ask.

After asking what the staff member is thinking, the supervisor can offer help in the following ways:

- ✔ "Can I give you a few ideas?"
- ✔ "I have a couple thoughts. Would you like to hear them?"
- ✔ "Do you want advice or are you just thinking out loud?"

In this kind of advanced relationship, you are acting as a mentor and helping your employee try out ideas and think through problems while also acknowledging that you are there to support, guide, and help them when necessary. It also shows respect and recognition of their own process to ask questions before just taking over.

Consider the difference if Joan's supervisor had responded to her e-mail troubles with the following: "That sounds frustrating. Want some help?" "Not yet but thanks for offering. I'll let you know."

When you have staff who are well-trained and skilled in their work, you don't want them to simply fly solo nor to stop using or being confident in their skills. Keep connected to them and build a practice of having them talk things through with you. This will give you an opportunity to see how they're doing, offer advice, and guide them when necessary. It starts with listening and then asking what they need. It can really be that simple.

Coaching Corner

- Have you ever received unwanted advice? How did it feel?
- What is your automatic response when staff members come to you with a problem?
- Find some words that feel comfortable for you to say in response to a staff member bringing a problem to you. Commit to trying it the next time that happens and see how it goes.

MOMENTS OF WONDER

1. In the average adult, the skin covers twelve to twenty square feet and accounts for 12 percent of body weight.
2. A raccoon can run at speeds of up to fifteen miles per hour.
3. Every day the average person loses sixty to one hundred strands of hair.
4. A fish called anthias, a member of the bass family, swims in the Red Sea. Each male of this species keeps a harem of up to a dozen female fish. When the male dies, one of the females undergoes a sex change and takes over the harem as a fully functioning male!
5. The largest internal organ is the small intestine. Despite being called the smaller of the two intestines, your small intestine is actually four times as long as the average adult is tall.
6. The colossal squid has the largest eyes of any animal. Each one of the colossal squid's eyes can be bigger than a dinner plate and has a lens the size of an orange. Each eye has a built-in "headlight," an organ known as a photophore that can produce light so that whenever the colossal squid focuses its eyes to the front, the photophores produce enough light for the squid to see in the dark.
7. You get a new stomach lining every three to four days.
8. There are two thousand species of fireflies.
9. When babies are born, they have 300 bones. Adults have 206. Bones fuse together during growth to come up with the new number. The last bones generally fuse together in our twenties.
10. Sneezes regularly exceed one hundred miles per hour. Coughs clock in at about sixty miles per hour.

These random facts are listed here to encourage you to step back from the work in front of you for a moment and simply feel the "wow" of a moment of wonder. Creating brief moments of wonder can help you be more curious, more grateful, and more open. Bringing those feelings into the workplace, even for seconds at a time, can enliven the environment. When people are curious, they are more likely to ask questions and not make assumptions. When people are grateful, they bring appreciation to their work with each other. And when they are open, they tend to be less reactive.

Dr. Robert Emmons, a professor of psychology at the University of California, Davis, has done extensive studies about the impact of gratitude on people's lives. He found that gratitude improves emotional and physical health, and it can strengthen relationships and communities. It also increases energy levels and helps people to deal with tragedy and crisis.

So take a moment or two to feel awe. Find random facts such as those listed above and share them with your team. During staff meetings, pause to notice what is working (maybe you'll even see some small wondrous accomplishments!) instead of focusing only on problem-solving. And when there are successes, celebrate. Celebration might include bonuses or parties but it can also be a simple pause to openly acknowledge and appreciate the work that led to the success.

One client described moments of wonder as little desserts that she looked forward to after a work task. Consider inviting your staff to bring one amazing fact to each team meeting and see what happens.

The Research Project on Gratitude and Thankfulness http://gratitudepower.net/science.htm
Retrieved 1/22/16

Coaching Corner

- Can you remember the last time you felt awe and wonder? What was the situation and how did it impact you?
- When you think of bringing moments of wonder to

your team, what's your reaction? If it really was a
transformative practice, would it be worth a minute of
time every week? What's the worst that could happen?

• Think of the last big or small success your team had.
Was the moment acknowledged or did the team
just look at the next problem in front of them? When
could you plan a time to acknowledge the work and
successes of your team?

CHAPTER 6:
How You Communicate Expectations

AVOID THE JUDGES' TABLE

The contestants had all cooked their hearts out. Most contestants were sure they had done a great job. A few were downright cocky: "I'm going to win this one. She can take her knives and go home!"

After they perform the challenge of the day, the contestants on *Top Chef* are summoned to some form of the dreaded "judges' table." This is when they learn how they did. The experts tell them who did well and who did poorly.

The pronouncements at the judges' table are often a surprise for the contestants. The ones who were sure they had done well are often the ones at the bottom of the ranking, and sometimes the rare contestant who admitted he or she had not done their best work will be declared the winner. Bottom line is that the contestants don't know how they've done until the judges tell them. Until they hear the external evaluation, their own opinion is suspect. Even if they have a sense of their own performance, it doesn't matter until it is validated, or invalidated, by the official judges. It makes for interesting TV, but it makes a horrible model for evaluation.

This is **not** how you want to offer feedback as a supervisor. It is a golden rule of human resources that there should be no surprises in an evaluation. You should be giving your staff information throughout the year about how they're doing and any areas they need to improve. By the time you get to an employee's official evaluation, he or she should be able to give it to him or herself. In order to get to that point, you need to take three steps throughout the year to ensure there will be no surprises at the "judges' table."

✓ **Be clear about your expectations.** Be explicitly clear about what is required of the employee. In fact, this should start before day one on the job. During the hiring process, let the candidate know what the job is, what the priorities are, what kind of skills are needed to succeed in the job, and what it will be like to work with you. Then, from day one on, explain to each employee what his or her job is and how to do the job. Avoid just saying to them, "We expect you to offer excellent customer service." Instead say, "We expect you to greet each client with a smile and a personal greeting. We expect you to solve their problem within two minutes or take them to someone who can." Go through their job description, show them procedures, explain to them the organization's mission and values, and tell them everything they need to know to succeed in their job. And make sure they understand everything you explain to them. Just because you've said it doesn't mean you've said it clearly, or that they have understood it all. There are many components of a job and it can be hard to retain all the expectations at once. For this reason, revisit the expectations until you're sure your employee is clear about what they're expected to do.

✓ **Give prompt and specific feedback.** Let your employees know when things come up along the way what they are doing right and what they're not. Take the judgment out of it. This is important information that each employee needs to know to succeed. Let them know what's working and what isn't working—and why. Explain the expectation again, making sure it is understood, and then tell them how their performance matches and does not match the expectation. Be specific. "I see you're working hard to solve a customer's problem within two minutes but I don't see a smile or hear a greeting. That is just as important."

✓ **Train employees to evaluate their own performance.** Once an employee understands the expectations of the job, and you have given them clear feedback about where they've hit the mark and where they've missed it, then work with them to use the criteria to evaluate their own work. Coach them. Ask questions. "What are the two main components of successful customer service for your job?" (If they don't know, go back to step number one!) "How did you do with the two-minute mark for complaint resolution this week?" "How did you do with greeting each customer with a smile and a personal hello?" "What percentage of the time would you estimate you met both criteria?" "How could you do even better next week?" In this way, you are helping them learn an essential skill for success: self-evaluation.

The drama of *Top Chef* is seeing how the judges' table plays out. If the contestants on reality TV shows were asked to do effective self-evaluations instead of relying on the external evaluation from the judges, it would make for boring TV. But in our workplaces, we want successful results—not dramatic entertainment!

Coaching Corner

- Rate your own performance in terms of giving clear expectations. Do you simply assume that people know how to do their work? Are you afraid your employees will think you're being "bossy"?
- How does it change your approach to giving feedback if you think of it as information needed for success instead of judgment?
- Is there a part of you that values the "judges' table" approach to supervision? What is that about? And how does it affect your feedback?

THE TRANSPARENT SUPERVISOR

Transparency is an important value in many organizations. Transparency implies openness, being "see-through." It denotes an organization that is striving to include staff in decisions that affect them and to avoid having unnecessary secrets. In supervision, perhaps most of all, your staff want to know that "what you see is what you get"—meaning they are not going to be surprised by unknown problems or ambushed by information that they should have known previously.

A key part of transparency in supervision is clarity about expectations, right from the start. When a supervisor is clear, people know what is expected of them, and they can understand ahead of time what they need to do and how they are expected to do it. Clear expectations prevent surprises and problems. When there is transparent communication, your staff can understand what success looks like and know what they are aiming for in their work. They know what you're thinking and what you're looking for.

Most supervisors value the idea of transparency—at least in general terms—but most employees don't feel the effects of that value. This is often a matter of taking time to figure out what your expectations are and then taking time to tell them to your staff. It takes time to be transparent and most workplaces are running on empty when it comes to using time in a proactive manner. It takes time for a supervisor, and an organization, to identify what their expectations are so they can then be transparent about them. Too often, supervisors aren't clear about their expectations until something goes wrong, then it is imperative that they take time to say, "No, that's not how we do things here." But wouldn't it be better, and more time efficient for everyone, to explain "how we do things" ahead of time so the employees are set up for success?

Here's a list of fifteen questions to help you be transparent by thinking through your expectations and explaining what they are to your staff ahead of time:

1. How do you see your role as a supervisor?
2. How do you see their role as supervisee?
3. How do you expect people to prepare for their one-on-one meetings with you? How often will those meetings be held? What's the format?
4. What are your expectations in terms of staff members doing their work, both individually and together?
5. What does teamwork look like to you? How do you expect team members to treat each other?
6. What do you expect people to do when they have ideas for areas outside their own job area?
7. How do you expect people to handle conflict?

8. What should employees bring directly to you?
9. What should people do if they make a mistake?
10. What information do you expect people to share? When and how?
11. What are your deal-breakers? (What actions will not be tolerated?)
12. How/when do you expect employees to learn new skills or take on new projects? What's the process?
13. What are the values of the organization—and how do they apply to their job?
14. What are your personal values in terms of the work—and how do they show up?
15. What do you see as the bottom line of the work of this organization?

Take a week or a month or a year to go through this list. Think it through and then have a series of conversations with your employees. Be transparent about what you need from them. Let them know: this is how to be successful here.

Coaching Corner

- Have you ever had the experience of doing something and finding out after the fact that you shouldn't have done it? Or that you shouldn't have done it that way? What did it feel like when that happened? Did you feel set up?
- Do you have a strong reaction to any of the fifteen questions listed? What does that tell you about yourself or your work? What values or assumptions prompt your reaction?
- Make a plan about how you will share your answers to these questions. It might be that you share one answer a week in a team meeting or three a month in your one-

on-one meetings. Write your plan down. Put it on your
calendar. Commit to being more transparent about your
expectations.

- Do you know these answers in regard to your own
work? Are there any questions you want to discuss with
your boss?

GIVE THEM A MAP

My grandson used to love Dora the Explorer books. In them, a
bilingual girl solves mysteries and problems by going on adventures. She brings her sidekick, a talking monkey named Boots, and
a magical backpack with her on every adventure. The backpack has
whatever she needs for the particular adventure, including a map.
There is **always** a map so they can double check where they are
going and how to get there.

Good supervisors will make sure their staff members always
have a map so they too can double check where they are going and
how to get there. Good supervisors will also be available to answer
questions, tackle roadblocks, or solve unexpected problems.

Some supervisors don't understand the importance of this
map. Others seem to like the power of being the only one who
knows how to navigate the terrain. Still others believe that it's up
to their staff to build their own maps, and if they don't then that's
their problem! However, if you are focused on the organization's
mission, each person must be clear about how to accomplish the
priorities of his or her job. And maps are essential for moving effectively through each priority.

Supervision entails ensuring that every employee has access
to up-to-date maps. A good supervisor will recognize when their
employees could benefit from having a map. Many times maps will
be given during initial training about the job, but sometimes addi-

tional maps must be given once the employee is proficient enough in a set of skills or when the supervisor notices one is missing. The next time there is an opportunity to learn a new procedure, the supervisor will point it out. "Now we're going to be closing out the fiscal year. As we tackle each step, keep notes so you can document the entire procedure step-by-step and be ready to do it again when you need to."

The maps I refer to are concrete ways to capture the critical processes of certain jobs or projects. Often these are written policies or procedures. They might also be flow charts, handwritten notes, or recorded conversations. The map building helps staff identify the steps to get from A to Z. It sets staff members up to be independent in completing a process or a project once they have developed the skills and completed all the sections of the task or project. It frees them to proceed through the steps without having to check in at every point.

Once your staff members have the map, the next step, if necessary, is to remind them to look at it. Some employees get used to asking for help at every juncture and think they need permission to proceed. It can be tempting to be the supervisor with all the answers. It can feel good (even when it feels annoying) to know that you can save people when they get stuck. But before defaulting to this mode, remind your staff: "Have you checked the process list you created last time?" Or encourage them: "Go over your notes and see if you can figure out the next step. If it doesn't seem clear, check back in."

Don't abandon your staff, but help them work independently through routine and expected processes. The map you provide your staff may not lead to as much fun as Dora the Explorer finds on her adventures, but it is just as magical!

Coaching Corner

- Do you give your staff maps to follow? When is it part of your practice to help staff learn how to work independently through a process? Have you been clear about when they can proceed on their own?
- When you have given your staff the map and authority to proceed, have they understood the danger signs that might require consultation? Have you discussed the changes in conditions or detours that would render the map ineffective?
- Do you have the maps you need to do your routine and expected work? If not, what do you need to do to talk to your boss about your need for a map and clarity about the terrain?

UNMET EXPECTATIONS

Traveling is a great way to recognize some of your unspoken, and sometimes unrealized, expectations. During a recent trip, I had to pause and recognize that just because my expectations weren't met didn't mean it was anyone's fault. My expectations were mine alone, and it was not up to the citizens of Florida to meet my expectations.

Flying home, I thought about the moments when I bumped up against my expectations and realized they were related to three types of expectations:

✓ **Unrecognized Expectations.** These were my un-spoken assumptions about how things should work. It started on the plane when a few people pushed their way up the aisle and out, without waiting for people to exit orderly row-by-row. In my mind, it's a rule of travel that you wait your turn. Then I found myself frustrated about road signs. I held an expectation that freeways should have clear signage identifying the roads (including the one you're on) and how far it is to the next major city. **Those are the rules!** But of course, they're not really rules. They were my unrecognized expectations.

✓ **Values.** Okay, I'm from Northern California, so recycling is ubiquitous here. It is also a shared value. While I'm sure that many people in Florida personally recycle, I did not see any public receptacles for recycling. It was almost painful for me to throw away plastic bottles and paper cups. I had to stop and see this for what it was: my value. And while I think people should share my values (because of course we all think we are right), I am not queen of the world.

✓ **Confusion.** While driving or walking around someplace unfamiliar, I experienced confusion fairly often. I inadvertently drove around three major airports— one of them several times. My GPS was dying, which I didn't yet know, so in retrospect I can see how that added to the problem. I was frustrated, but part of this stemmed from my expectation that I should not be confused.

So let's look at how our expectations are connected to supervision. Using my experience traveling, I can apply these three areas of unmet expectations to supervision.

✓ **Unrecognized Expectations.** Think about what you consider to be obvious, if unspoken, rules. You may be assuming that there are rules about things that everyone just knows. They don't. Based on their culture or their personal experience, they may not have the same rules as you do. It is up to you as a supervisor to spell out any expectations that are not being met.

Some common office-related, unrealized expectations might include:

- Not leaving your originals in the copy machine.
- Showing initiative.
- Following up on projects and tasks.
- Getting along with coworkers.
- Leaving your personal issues at home.

✓ **Values.** Many workplaces have values that are clearly stated and lived. Other workplaces have unarticulated but strongly respected values. And other workplaces don't think about values at all. The unmet expectation would most likely show up in the second kind of workplace, where there are strong but unarticulated values. Workers assume that people just know "how we do things here." If there is a new employee, we assume they'll catch on. That's setting a trap for someone. If there are strong values, the organization will be best served by articulating those values and training on those values. If the organization doesn't do that, then you, as a supervisor who wants to help your staff succeed, should. Name the value and show your new hires how it is lived in the organization.

Examples:

- "We value honesty here. If there is ever an incident where you are tempted to tell a white lie or use subterfuge, don't do it. It will be more than a mistake, it will be a major mistake because this value is so important here."

- "Teamwork is the way we function together. Let me tell you what that means: We help each other out. We do what needs to be done. We interact with each other in a friendly and cooperative manner. We don't compete with each other. We work together for the good of the organization."

✓ **Confusion.** Most supervisors tell their staff, "If you have any questions, let me know." But this is not enough. When employees feel like they should know something, it is hard to ask for help. They may feel like they just have to muddle through. Or they may not even know they don't know.

Make a clear expectation about what you want them to do when they are confused. "There may be times when you're not sure what to do. You may feel confused about your next step or how much autonomy you should show, or even realize that you don't know a critical fact that you think you should know. When you face any kind of confusion, I expect you to ask me for help. That is part of my job. I want you to feel confident doing your work."

Especially with a new employee, it is critical to be that clear about your approach to questions. With a long-term employee, there will certainly be times when you think they should know the answer to the thing they're asking about. That's another issue that must also be addressed directly. You might say something like, "I'm glad you're checking in with me. I am, however, a little surprised that you don't know this. Let's go over it again, but before I

do, let's talk about how you can retain this information for next time." Or, "Let's talk about where
your decision-making authority is and how you can
recognize it."

Being clear about expectations is a critical skill for any supervisor. Watch out for those hidden areas where expectations can
sneak up on you. If you do encounter some unmet expectations,
pause and remember it is not up to your employees to meet your
unspoken expectations. Connect your expectations to the work and
make them clear. Then you and your staff can travel together more
confidently.

Coaching Corner

- What unrealized expectations have come up in your
  own life? How have you reacted?
- Do you recognize any unspoken expectations you have
  with your employees? When and how will you discuss
  these issues with your employee?
- What are the values of your workplace? Are they
  articulated or unspoken? How can you best convey
  them to your employees to make sure everyone is on
  the same page?

DELEGATION MADE SIMPLE

Two managers find themselves talking about how overwhelmed
they feel in trying to keep up with their work. Their bosses give
them the appropriate, but not particularly helpful, advice that they
"need to delegate more."

The two managers roll their eyes at the familiar but unrealistic directive. Then they decide they better try it. They each decide to assign a project to their top performer.

Micromanaging Mary tells her assistant, "My whole career is riding on this project, but I just can't carry it all. I'm counting on you. I will be meeting with you daily to make sure you're taking all the appropriate steps and that you deal with any problems that come up. It's going to be more work than just doing it myself, but my boss says I've got to delegate more. So, let's go!"

Hands-off Hal tells his staff member, "This is a really important project. I've got to move some stuff off my plate so I need you to step up and run this project from beginning to end. I'm going to be out of the office quite a bit in the next month, but if you have any questions, give me a call. I'll get back to you when I can. Don't screw this up!"

How do you think their projects went? How do you think their staff felt? While the concept of delegating is straightforward—authorizing one of your employees to do work for which you are ultimately responsible—it is often tricky in practice. I often see supervisors, like Mary and Hal, veering too far in one direction or the other; they either dole out the project in bite-size pieces and micromanage every step of the way, or they assign the task and then leave the person on their own to figure it out without any support or guidance.

Luckily, there is a wide swath of territory in between these extremes in which a supervisor can delegate in a manner that employees feel confident to proceed while not feeling like they are tethered to the supervisor for every step. Delegating in this way also lets the supervisor trust that the employee knows what they are doing and that they will be successful in delivering the expected results.

Like many steps of supervision, doing it right takes an investment of time up front, but it will save tremendous time and worry in the future. Here's the four-step process:

1. State the Process

Don't be coy about what you're doing. Tell the employee that you are starting a process in which you will be delegating a task, responsibility, or project to them. Explain how the process will work and that your expectation is that they will give serious attention to each step in the process, ask questions to ensure their understanding, and ultimately accept responsibility for the assignment.

2. Show

Next it's time to show the employee what you want them to do. You take the lead. For a simple task, this may be a five-minute demonstration. For a responsibility, this may be a multifaceted process that happens over a period of time until you have broken the responsibility into bite-sized pieces so they understand the scope of the work. For a complicated, time-tiered project, this could happen over the course of an entire project.

3. Share

During this step, you share the work as you start to let go but you don't set the employee loose just yet. You listen to them answer a call, give them tips, perhaps even point out the answer if they forget something. Again, with a simple task this may be a quick one-time step. With a complicated or time-dependent process, this will be more complicated. If you are training them to do a report, the share step might mean you ask them to gather the raw data and then you sit with them while they enter it into the system. All along the way, you continue to highlight that you're in a process. You remind them that you're sharing the work this time and that next time they will be expected to take the lead.

4. Support

In this stage you let the employee take the lead but you don't abandon them. You let them answer calls for an hour and then check in with them. You ask them to plan the curriculum for the training and you review it. You ask them to come prepared to your meetings with a list of questions and a plan for the next step of the process. You remind them that they are taking the lead now but you are there to support them. Tell them that if they run into anything that they're not prepared for to let you know. You assure them that you will help them problem-solve. And when they have completed this round, acknowledge that they have stepped up to the task and that you feel confident that they can handle the responsibility.

You're still the supervisor, though; you stay in support mode even if it's rarely necessary for you to actively help out.

Through this four-step process you and the employee can both be confident that nothing will fall through the cracks. That together you are a strong team and can count on each other to move the work forward. Learn from the mistakes of Micromanaging Mary and Hands-off Hal. When it's time to delegate, do so with the skill and the confidence-building style of a Successful Supervisor.

Coaching Corner

- Looking at the micromanage to hands-off spectrum, where do you fall as a manager? How would your employees rate you? Are you where you want to be on the spectrum?
- Think of a time when you were successfully trained to do a new task or assume a new responsibility. What worked about the training and what did not work?
- Have a conversation with your employees to identify their best learning style. Ask them what's working with the delegating process now and how it could work better for them. Give them time to think about it and then follow up. Really listen to what they have to say. Even if it doesn't fit your perspective of what works, listen and consider their perspective.

PREVENTING CONFUSION

A friend needed to update his professional license and went online to take a course. He started at his professional membership page and clicked through a few links until he found the class he wanted to take. He registered and paid $199 via credit card. The transaction went through and then he was ready to take the class. He couldn't find it. He looked on the site, he looked in his e-mail, he read through the FAQ section. He could not find the link to the class he had paid for. Eventually he backtracked three sites to his professional membership page and logged into his licensing account and found a highlighted 13-digit number. Although he was hesitant to click on an unknown link, he was desperate so he clicked on it. And finally found his class.

Admittedly, my friend is not the most technically sophisticated guy in the world but he was simply trying to take a class on a reporting procedure and shouldn't have needed to waste 45 minutes finding his class. There could have been a way to lead him through the steps without so much frustration and confusion.

In contrast, when I went with a friend to the Chihuly Museum in Seattle, a docent approached us soon after we entered the first room and said, "Let me tell you what you're looking at and how the museum is set up." He proceeded to tell us about the exhibit in that room and how the next rooms were set up, what to look for in each room, and a brief history of the museum. This took just two to three minutes, but it felt so welcoming. He ended with a general offer: "If you have any questions or need anything, feel free to ask any of us wearing a jacket like this." Perfect!

Think about what you can tell your employees, new and old, about what is going to happen and what they can expect. Take a few minutes to fill them in. It may be about something that is so obvious or familiar to you that you might not even think of talking about it, but it can make a world of difference to an employee. People tend to feel nervous when they don't know what's going on or what's going to happen next. They might feel like they don't matter, or that they don't know how to be effective in their work during these times. When this happens, employees are certainly not doing their best work.

To help your employees do their best, therefore, tell them what to expect. I'm thinking specifically about processes that are not immediate or urgent, but that are places where unease can set in if no one knows what's going to happen.

Here's a list of things to consider:

- ✓ How will evaluations happen?
- ✓ What is the process to follow if they have a suggestion or a problem? Do they need to bring everything to you first?
- ✓ How do you celebrate birthdays/holidays here? Or do you not do that at all?
- ✓ When there is a change coming, when will it happen? How will it happen? How will it impact them in their job?
- ✓ How will you deal with concerns about their work?
- ✓ What are deal-breakers for you and what will happen if they do one of those?
- ✓ Is there anything they need to know about you? (e.g., "I'm not a morning person so please don't be offended when I'm not chatty first thing in the morning.")
- ✓ What should they know about how you work? (e.g., "I try not to micromanage but when we are going to publish a statement from this office, I will be involved in every draft and edit. It is a priority for me and it is one area where I know I do tend to micromanage.")
- ✓ Are there any office politics or history that will impact their job? (e.g., "You need to know that our

work with the contract department is sometimes strained. We're working with them on this but if someone is abrupt with you, try not to take it personally. If it interferes with your work, let me know." This is different than "Fiscal hates us. Don't worry about it.")

✓ What can they expect from you as a supervisor?

Make these explanations a practice as a supervisor. It is especially important for new employees, but it's helpful to periodically recap for all employees.

We can't know everything, but sharing what we do know shows that you support employees and recognize them as valuable. A simple statement of "Here's what you can expect . . ." can help build the relationship and clarify expectations. It can also save people from feeling confused while they spend time and energy wondering, "What's going on?!"

Coaching Corner

- Have you had the experience of not knowing what to expect? What did it feel like? What were your concerns?

- Have you found yourself telling a staff member, "Oh no, that's not how we do it here." How did that work? Looking back, is there a way you could have set it up so they didn't have to do it the wrong way in order to learn the right way?

- What practical step can you take to build a practice of looking through your employees' eyes to see what they need to know? Can you add a question to consider their perspective to your one-on-one meetings?

WHO DOES WHAT?

Too many times while working with organizations (both large and small) people tell me, "I wish I had a better idea of how her work intersects with mine," or "I don't know what he does all day."

Often it's just assumed that staff knows each other's jobs. Sometimes they do, but they still may not know how their coworkers' tasks affect their own work. And once again, from a supervisor's perspective, it is easy to assume that everyone knows what you know. But you usually have the big picture and staff may need help to see what you see. The following note from a colleague is a great example of how a lack of understanding about someone else's job can get in the way of the work. This note was written after someone commented that they were afraid to bring a mistake to the fiscal department.

> *It's always been my thought that education/information about the importance of fiscal and why they are so "scary" would make it easier to work with staff. We are driven by strict accounting standards that require a certain level of integrity and do all that we can to protect the organization. Yes, there are some fiscal folks who take it to the level of dictatorship though it need not be that way. It would be so helpful to tell a new employee why fiscal has to be so serious—standards, deadlines—and to explain to them that we are there to uphold the integrity of the organization.*

In response to this note, this colleague and I set up joint meetings with the intention of helping the fiscal and the HR staff know and understand what we each did and how the departments related. And it was a success for all involved.

Take time during one or more staff meetings to give people a chance to explain to each other what they do. Not in a boring review of their job way, but as an inside peek into their world.

Take this in bite-sized pieces if necessary, breaking it up into more than one meeting. Give each person three to five minutes to answer a list of predetermined questions. Or pass out a list giving each person the opportunity to sign up to share at a future staff meeting. If you have time, allow a little Q&A after each person shares, but don't let it become an interrogation or justification for their work.

Here are some questions you might use as a template if you want to encourage your employees to share with one another about what they do.

1. What are the top three priorities of your job?
2. How does your job support our mission?
3. What do you spend most of your time doing?
4. What do you enjoy most about your job? What are the favorite parts?
5. What are the least favorite parts of your job?
6. What do you need from your coworkers in order to be most effective in your job?

This sharing exercise will help people understand each other and also provide an excellent opportunity for you, as the leader, to publicly appreciate the work that each staff member does to support the whole team. You can also reinforce the synergy that comes from all of you putting your collaborative efforts together to support the whole. When staff feels appreciated and understood, everyone, including the supervisor, feels better and works better. Win-win!

Coaching Corner

- What have you done to ensure that your team understands the work that each of them does? How can you check in on your staff's understanding of the big picture of the work you do together?

- You have a certain understanding of the work of your team from your perspective as supervisor. This may or may not match your staff's perspective. How can your perspective differ from that of your staff?
- Answer the six questions from the template about your own job so you can feel what it's like to do this exercise. How does it feel to answer the questions? Do you feel proud or excited or overwhelmed? (You might even share at a staff meeting that you did the exercise yourself, or share some of your answers, to emphasize that you are one part of the team.)

CHAPTER 7:

How You Give (and Get) Feedback

IT'S SIMPLY INFORMATION

On a recent excursion to the grocery store, I tried to slide my new chip-enhanced credit card through the machine at checkout the way I always have. "That doesn't work for these cards," the store clerk told me. "You have to slide it in down here and leave it there while I process your purchase." She pointed to where I should insert my card and spoke in a calm voice. Now I knew how to do it. It was easy. She didn't use an annoyed or impatient tone, and I didn't feel stupid or defensive.

This simple interaction serves as a great example of what feedback should be like. The clerk told me something I needed to know to complete my purchase. Feedback at work should be just as routine: here's information you need to do your job.

One of your roles as a supervisor is to give feedback to your staff members. This is a difficult process for many people. Feedback is often associated with a negative process where someone tells you what's wrong with you. But feedback is really just information. Feedback can be positive, negative, or constructive. It can be supportive or it can be critical. It can be helpful or it can be irrelevant. As a supervisor, you want to give feedback that is meaningful and helpful. It is not easy for most of us to give honest feedback but it is a critical skill for a supervisor. As a supervisor, feedback is simply information for your staff about how they are doing: what's working and what's not working.

The feedback about what is working is usually easy to give. Name what they did that worked well. "Your report was on time and formatted in a way that made it easy to read. Good job." It is important to recognize what is working and not just focus on what is not working.

Supervisors are sometimes afraid to give feedback about what is not working. They are worried that people will get defensive or get their feelings hurt. And they might, if you offer the feedback in a condescending or disrespectful way. If the clerk at the store had said in an exasperated tone, "Those are the new chip cards. You don't slide it anymore!" then I would have had a different reaction to her feedback.

Giving feedback needs to be handled in a direct and neutral manner. When feedback is given in a tone laden with judgment, it doesn't feel like information. When the feedback is about something that is not working, it is easy for feedback to be taken as a criticism of the person—rather than a task or action—and that makes it an inherently difficult process.

Feedback is information that you have and that your employees need. Most people want to do a good job and they want to know if they're doing something wrong. When you approach the conversation with the assumption that the information you're giving is something the staff member needs and wants, then it is simply an exchange of knowledge.

One of the benefits of conducting regular one-on-one meetings is that it normalizes feedback. In my own check-in meetings with my staff, I aimed to cover three things:

1. What's working?
2. What's not working?
3. What's next? (What are our top priorities going forward?)

If this is the basic agenda for regular meetings, then no one is surprised to hear talk of things that are not working. Having regular constructive conversations makes it easier to give quick informational feedback: "Hey, I want to talk about how you handled that incident with your coworker yesterday. I have some ideas about how it could have gone better." It isn't heavy-handed; it's just a regular meeting with an exchange of information focused on building mutual success.

When you approach feedback as important, success-oriented information, it is likely to be received that way. Your staff will respond as I did to the clerk in the store: "Okay, now I know."

Coaching Corner

- Think of a time when you were given feedback that did not lead to any change in your behavior. How was it given and how did you respond to it?
- Now think of a time when you received feedback that impacted your actions. How was that feedback given? What was it that led you to change how you were doing things?
- Practice saying the following phrase (out loud) in three different ways. "I know how you can do this in a better way." The first time, say it with the emphasis on **I,** emphasizing that you know better than they do. The second time, say it in a tone that suggests impatience and exasperation. The third time, say it with

the enthusiasm of offering someone a good idea to think about. Do you hear the difference that your tone brings to the same words? Can you sense how it feels different to use those different tones, for you and your staff members?

A COACHING STYLE OF SUPERVISION: WORKING TOGETHER FOR A COMMON GOAL

A supervisor with a coaching style works to help his or her people learn about and develop their skills. This supervisor works in partnership with his or her staff to fulfill the mission. A supervisor with a coaching style invites ideas and suggestions about the work because he or she does not have to have all the answers all the time. All of these practices describe part of a coaching approach to supervision.

Some people mistakenly think a coaching style of supervision means warm and fuzzy and coddling. These people might even try being supportive and like how it works but as soon as problems come up, they revert to an authoritarian style of supervision. In truth, a coaching style of supervision can help you be a more effective supervisor from the day you hire someone right on through to termination, if that becomes necessary.

Adopting a coaching style can help you be more connected to the people you supervise. However, if you focus only on the positive aspects of the work that is being done, you have only succeeded in becoming more human and more humane—a good thing, no doubt, but you have not understood or embraced the concept and power of coaching in a supervision relationship.

To truly adopt a coaching approach to supervision, you need to learn how to help your staff through difficult choices, challenges, and even failures. Helping them through these difficulties does not mean simply supporting them, it also means helping them to understand what didn't work, why it didn't work, and how the work could have gone better with some planning or a different approach. It means helping them think through the choices they face. And it means giving them clear and effective feedback that they can learn from. A coaching approach to supervision means helping your staff learn and supporting them to be successful.

Traditional supervision is focused on a "boss" and a "subordinate." The boss knows more and knows best. The subordinate is there to get the work done, and if they can't or won't do it, the boss will find someone who will. This model has never worked very well and it certainly doesn't work well now. The difference between an authoritative approach to supervision and a coaching approach to supervision is the difference between a bossy director and a knowledgeable collaborator.

People want to be respected in their work. In supervision with a coaching style, the supervisor and the employee are partners in getting the work done. They work together, in different ways and tasks, to reach a common goal. The employee knows what the end result is and the supervisor respects the work that the employee does. The supervisor also respects the **person** doing the work— as an individual as well as an employee. And the employee gets to respect—rather than fear—the supervisor. Respect and partnership are foundations to a coaching style of supervision.

Working as partners, the supervisor and the employee both understand their roles, goals, and responsibilities. There are no hidden agendas, surprises, or "gotchas!" There may be an unexpected turn of events or problems that arise, but there are no manipulative games going on—from either the supervisor or the employee. If there are, they are addressed. There is a clear and mutual understanding of the work that needs to be done and why it needs to be done.

Working as partners with mutual understanding, the supervisor and employee create agreements. The agreements may be explicit or implicit but they are mutually understood. Both participants agree what the priorities are, what the time lines are, and what the consequences will be if the agreements are not kept.

If something is not working, either in work projects, job behaviors, or team interactions, it is up to the supervisor to address the specific issues in a timely and clear manner. This is where a coaching style of supervision can build upon what is already in place to address the problem in a consistent and clear manner. The supervisor acts with respect and in partnership, seeking understanding, and making agreements about how to proceed. Making an agreement does not mean that the employee has the power to approve or disapprove of any action; the supervisor must direct the conversation and the action. It is a conversation, however, not a monologue.

A coaching style of supervision can guide you through hard conversations about what is not working so well. You do not need to abandon coaching when there are problems. You can use the values and skills of coaching in supervision to reinforce the team and the partnerships while still addressing the issues and prioritizing the work outcomes. Bringing a coaching style to your supervision builds stronger teams, clearer communication, and better outcomes. Keep the values of respect, partnership, understanding, and agreements in mind and you will be more than a warm and fuzzy supervisor: you will be a more effective supervisor.

Coaching Corner

- How do you deal with problems that come up with the staff that you supervise? Do you avoid them or try to convince someone to do something different, make gentle suggestions, or come down hard?
- What comes up for you internally when you must deal with problem behaviors as a supervisor?
- Are there fears or concerns that come up for you when you consider coaching your staff?
- Does your concern about being a supportive supervisor ever get in the way of you being an effective supervisor?

A Sample Coaching Conversation

Jonathan is responsible for producing a monthly printed news-letter. The newsletter was late last month because of a prob-lem with an external print shop. That problem was addressed with the vendor. Now it is a week before the newsletter should go out and you have not seen the newsletter draft that you are supposed to proofread ten days before it goes out. As a supervisor, how do you proceed using a coaching style?

You call Jonathan into your office. After checking in with him about how he's doing, you ask a direct question: "What's going on with the newsletter?"

"Oh, everything is fine," Jonathan replies. "I'm just run-ning a bit behind because Sharon didn't get her article to me on time. I should be able to get it to you tomorrow for proofing and still get it out on time."

You're tempted to let it go. Why make trouble if there is no trouble? But you know you need to address the sit-uation. "Jonathan, we had an agreement that you would get the newsletter to me for proofreading at least ten days before launch date. That time line still gives Edith and I time to proofread it and then you time to pull it all together for the final version. When our established time line is delayed, sev-eral of us have to rearrange our schedules and our priorities to work around the delay. I clear my calendar every month to be available to be a part of this process. I want to work with you to make a plan so this will not happen again. What do you suggest?" (Note that here you are respecting his input and his ownership of the issue while still being clear that you expect your agreements to be kept. You are also not just berating him—the conversation is about explaining why this delay matters and about finding a solution to prevent this in the future.)

continued ⇨

Jonathan tries to wiggle: "I don't think there's any problem. I think Sharon just hit writer's block and she'll get her articles to me on time from now on. The newsletter won't be late."

Again, it would be easy to just accept this wiggle, maybe even wiggle along with him, but that would not be respecting your agreement or the process of addressing problems directly and in a timely manner.

"This isn't about Sharon," you state calmly. "I expect you to work with Sharon about your time line with her. This is about our agreement. How can we make sure this doesn't happen again?" (Note that there is no anger or animosity here. This is simply you stating the way it is. Your tone is respectful and neutral at all times. You maintain your partnership with Jonathan at all times, using "we" and "our" to underline the common problem here.)

"Well," says Jonathan. "I guess I could work with the team to have some backup plans for when we run into deadline glitches. And maybe I could review the time line with them to make sure everyone understands their part and the consequences of delays on everyone else."

"That sounds great, Jonathan. Anything else?"

Jonathan is quiet and shrugs his shoulders. You resist the urge to suggest something or wrap it up. You wait. Silently. You keep waiting for another full minute if necessary.

"How about if I build some kind of celebration for every issue that goes out? That might be fun?" he asks in a hesitating manner.

"That would be great." You commend him for his creative idea and then go back to the important part—the work outcome and the importance of keeping agreements. "And we're on the same page about the importance of the deadline and our agreements?"

"I get it," he says. "I will keep the schedule and my agreements in front of me and let you know immediately if there are any problems."

In this conversation, you helped Jonathan problem-solve the missed deadline. In addition, the team will be in a stronger position to face future problems because you've helped Jonathan become a better leader of his team. You've also modeled how to address problems with a coaching style. You have been an effective supervisor!

THE SPACE BETWEEN

I've seen it happen many times. A supervisor needs to discuss an issue or concern with an employee. Their intention is to convey something clean, like, "I need to see you at your desk at nine, ready to work, every day." But instead they say something like, "You've disappointed me again. I can't believe you thought it was okay to show up a half hour late." Instead of talking about actions, the supervisor is criticizing the person. Their comments are personal and judgmental.

In moments when you feel yourself reacting emotionally to someone's actions, it can be helpful to separate the actions from yourself and from the other person. I think of the space between us. By that I mean that the conversation is not about you as an individual and it's not about me as an individual, it is about actions that happened "out there." This is an image that helps me to make my feedback neutral. It's a way to picture the actions happening at arm's length. It isn't about what was done to me or how your actions affected me; it's about the work and the work is external to both of us.

When I need to give difficult feedback to someone, I consider this space, the neutral zone between us. Then I keep it nonjudgmental and nonpersonal. It is as if I were showing you a videotape of what happened. Whatever actions I am addressing, we are both looking at them and it is separate from both of us. The feedback is not personal about you or me; the feedback is about specific actions that happened out there. These actions need to change. Yes, it was you who took the actions and you who need to take different actions next time, but it is not about who you are as a person. This image helps me not to conflate the actions and the person. The person is not bad, flawed, or wrong; they simply need to change how they handle particular situations because of the way these actions are affecting the work.

When you criticize the **person**, he or she is almost guaranteed to become defensive. So think about the space between and use it to keep your comments neutral. It will be much more likely then that the person can hear your feedback and make a decision how to proceed.

Coaching Corner

- How does imagining the space between shift the conversation for you, if at all?
- Have you ever felt attacked by someone criticizing something you've done? Can you imagine how it would have been different if the person had simply shown you a videotape of what you did without the personal blame?
- What value is there in framing feedback in a way that diffuses defensiveness?
- Is there a conversation you can prepare for by imagining the space between?

ACCIDENTS HAPPEN

Let's say you work in a kitchen, and while you're planning the menu for the next day, you suddenly hear a loud crash. You turn to see that the dishwasher has dropped a stack of a dozen plates and every one of them is broken. He did not intentionally set out to break the plates; it just happened. It was an accident. Sometimes accidents just happen, right?

Employees don't usually intend to cause trouble. Sometimes though, a customer becomes infuriated, a coworker feels harassed, or a project ends up collated incorrectly, leading to a waste of thousands of pages of paper. In all of these incidents, an employee might proclaim that it just happened. "It was an accident," they say.

Accidents do happen, but as we all know, there are also accidents waiting to happen. I used to tell my kids about the difference between two kinds of accidents: the first type truly just happens, with no warning or contribution on your part; the second type could be anticipated with a little foresight. In other words, some accidents are preventable. An example of the first type might be that an employee slips and falls, breaking a dozen plates—accident. But what if the employee slipped on a wet floor because he had spilled water an hour ago and didn't bother to clean it up? This is an example of an accident waiting to happen. The person should have thought about the consequences of his prior actions, and therefore could have avoided what later turned into an "accident."

If you're working with an employee who has a lot of preventable "accidents," there is an opportunity for some feedback and some training. If you notice that their accidents are mostly of the type that a bit of foresight could have prevented, then it's an opportunity for you to coach your employee about how to think ahead and how to accept responsibility. Some employees have never learned the difference between true accidents and accidents waiting to happen. Coaching could be a breakthrough for them.

Of course, it would be quicker to simply tell the employee what the specific problem is and that if it happens again, she is going to be disciplined. That is a viable option. However, the employee will likely not learn anything if you take this approach. You will have reinforced her idea that bad things just happen to her.

By taking a few minutes to help her think through the situation, you can help her understand how she contributed to the "accident." By asking her how she could have thought ahead and prevented the accident, you give her an opportunity to learn. Most of us learn better when we are a part of the process instead of just being told the answer. You can help her recognize how she could have foreseen the possible outcome and how she could try to think ahead next time to take actions to prevent accidents from happening.

If the employee tells you that this was a one-time thing and it will never happen again, have your list of examples ready to remind her of the several times something like this has already happened. Stay firm in your plan to help her learn through this process. If she does not see how she might have been able to prevent the accidents, you can use seatbelts as an example. None of us ever thinks we are actually going to have an accident on any given day, but we wear our seatbelts every day, just in case. The same is true with the process of thinking ahead: we need to take time to think about what might happen as a result of our actions (or inactions) in any given situation. Then, based on foresight, we can usually prevent accidents, or keep them from being catastrophic. Conveying this information to your employee is a process, and you might need to have several conversations to coach them through why and how you believe their accidents, at times, might have been preventable.

Here's a practice I've developed to help people practice the act of anticipating potential accidents. I teach them to think ahead by using the acronym BAD.

B   **Block.** Block yourself from acting impulsively or reactively. Take a moment to think through the situation.

A   **Assess.** Assess the big picture and consider your choices and the potential outcomes of each action.

D   **Decide.** Decide and take the best course of action.

Using the BAD technique can happen in a matter of minutes, even seconds, once you're used to the process. A lot of people do the BAD process automatically, but for those employees who speak too fast, or react before they think, this can be a valuable lesson. As their supervisor, you can coach these employees to learn this valuable practice, which will serve them, and your organization. Helping them learn to slow down and practice BAD in action can lead to many fewer accidents.

Coaching Corner

- Can you think of a time that you were responsible for an accident, when, had you done something differently, the outcome would have been different?
- What judgment do you make about people (including yourself) who make mistakes or cause accidents?
- Consider finding an example of a preventable accident in the news to use as a teaching moment with your staff. Using a news story prevents anyone from taking the example personally while you still help your staff do some retroactive BAD analysis.

A FORMULA FOR GIVING FEEDBACK

Using a simple framework to provide feedback to your employees keeps your comments succinct and focused. This formula can be helpful for supervisors who tend to ramble on or move into lecture mode. Rarely is lecturing helpful. You always want to give feedback that is specific, quick, and clean. It often takes time and attention to think through the exact feedback you want to give someone.

Here's a four-step process to clarify your feedback and prepare a concise statement for your staff. I use the acronym NOIR to help remember the steps. This formula can be used to give any specific feedback, whether positive or negative. Because negative feedback is usually harder to formulate, I am using an example of a staff member who has been rude to her teammates, which has caused her coworkers to start to avoid her. The acronym NOIR stands for Need, Observation, Impact, and Request.

> **Step 1. NEED.** This statement recognizes a common need or want that you and your staff member share or a need that you know is motivating your staff member. By starting with a statement of a need, you are joining with your staff member instead of acting in opposition to him or her.
>
> Example: "I know we both want this program to be successful."
>
> A statement of your staff member's need might be "I know you need to meet the deadline and you're focused on that right now."
>
> **Step 2. OBSERVATION.** This statement is where you clearly and objectively name the actions that happened. The challenge here is to make your feedback absolutely objective without interpretation or judgment. Imagine you are showing the person a videotape of their actions.

Example: "I saw you brush past one of your team members and then raise your voice to another coworker." (NOT: "You were angry and disrespectful today." That's interpreting the action, not reporting your observation.)

Step 3. IMPACT. Why does this matter? How did the actions you saw impact the person's work? This describes why and how the actions matter. This step is where you also might mention your interpretation of what you saw. If you do include any interpretation, make sure you specifically phrase it as **your** interpretation or guess. And still make sure neither your tone nor word choice are about judging the employee.

Example: "When you treat your coworkers this way, I see them hesitate to interact with you and that impedes the flow of communication that we need in order to work successfully together. It also makes me wonder if you are respecting their contributions to the team."

Step 4. REQUEST. What are you asking them to do differently? What does the solution to this behavior look like?

Example: "I'd like to see you recognize the personal space of your coworkers and speak to everyone in this workspace in a calm and neutral voice. For me, these are important parts of being a respectful employee here. Respectful interactions are something I value and expect from each employee."

When you put all these statements together, you have a succinct statement that invites a conversation about next steps:

"I know you're focused on the deadline now. I just saw you brush past one of your team members and then raise your voice to another coworker. I see your coworkers hesitate to interact with you and that impedes the flow of communication we need to work successfully together. I'd like to see you interacting respectfully with your coworkers, which includes making room for each other in our workspace as well as speaking to each other in a calm and neutral voice."

And here's an example of NOIR feedback to address positive behavior:

"I know that you have many competing priorities that you need to juggle. During the last hour, I saw you talking to representatives from three different departments about three separate projects. You spoke in a calm voice, you answered their questions quickly, and you took time to smile and chat while you looked up the status of their particular project on your computer. This is a great example of flexibility, which is highly valued in your work. All three departments will not hesitate to ask for help or status updates in the future. Keep up the great work."

Using this NOIR acronym can help you prepare for feedback conversations, especially when the feedback is negative. The feedback you give will be clear and actionable.

Coaching Corner

- Are you someone who tends to ramble or lecture your staff? If so, what would you gain by using this formula to help you be more concise? And what might you lose?

- Try the formula out in a couple of imagined scenarios and then try it out in a specific situation you need to address. (Possible imagined scenarios: someone does not meet their deadlines and someone is consistently late to work.)

- If you are using this formula to prepare for a feedback conversation, and find that it is difficult to name the impact of the actions about which you are giving feedback, then consider that the behavior might simply be a different style of work and that the style does not

really impact the work and therefore the feedback is
not relevant or necessary.

EVALUATION TIME

You and your staff have had a great year. As you write up one staff
member's annual performance evaluation, it's almost all positive
feedback on a job well done. There is only one area where this person could be a little stronger. You are disappointed when you discuss the evaluation with your staff member that she focuses only
on the one area where you did not rate her highly. This is not an
anomaly. This is the human brain on feedback.

Research shows that people hate to get feedback and that they
hear negative feedback much more strongly than positive! It is normal to react strongly to perceived criticism, even if it is delivered
in the best possible manner. If it is delivered in a less-than-ideal
manner, then the delivery can become the focus of the response
instead of the content.

In addition, our brains are conditioned to feel threatened when
we feel like we're not looking good in the eyes of someone important. We fear being excluded from the "tribe" and our primitive
brains may therefore interpret any negative feedback as a threat to
survival. When we hear what we perceive to be criticism, our hearts
race, our muscles tense, blood pressure rises; we move into fight or
flight response. A team of neuroscientists from Ohio State University conducted a research study that showed that electrical activity
in the brain spikes more strongly in test subjects in response to negative stimuli than to equally potent positive stimuli. In addition, our
brains respond to "rejection" in the same manner that they respond
to being poked with a hot stick!

With all this brain reaction going on, how can the process of
giving feedback in general, and performance evaluations in par-

ticular, be an effective process? Most organizations have a process of giving regular written performance evaluations. And most staff members dread the process. There are several things you can do, as a supervisor, to make the entire performance evaluation process less threatening and more collaborative.

1. **Make the evaluation a joint process.** Ask your staff member to do a self-evaluation as part of the process. When you meet, focus on the conversation (not the form) and make the discussion a mutual conversation focused on the mission. Prevent the process from being you against them by bringing your staff member into the conversation early so it is not just you lecturing them. Sit next to them instead of across a desk from them. These actions will all signal to the brain that the person is not being excluded.

2. **Keep everything job-related.** How does their performance match the requirements of the job description? The job description is the criteria. This means no comments about how nice they are unless you can tie that virtue to their job. (For example, having a pleasant voice and a friendly conversational tone is a key characteristic of a customer service representative but not relevant to a data-entry clerk who works alone for most of her job.) Tie every comment to their job performance, which will mean things are less likely to be taken as feedback about who they are as a person.

3. **No surprises.** Always address all issues as they come up throughout the year. Don't wait for the evaluation to make the point. If there are surprises in the evaluation, then you did not do your job as a supervisor along the way.

4. Watch out for loaded words and hidden bias.
Edit your language so you're not using loaded words
that will trigger defensiveness, like "attitude." Watch
out also for signs of unintended bias—e.g., referring
to "common sense" or "everyone knows." Those words
betray a view of the world that focuses on style rather
than work. If something affects the outcome of a person's work or interferes with others' work, then address
it. If it is just different, then how does it matter?

5. Make the entire process fair and objective.
Make sure the criteria are clear for each job and consistent throughout the organization. Watch for sub-
jectivity in measures and in "grading." Pay attention
to the process and the outcomes to ensure fairness.
Participants should have faith in the evaluation process as well as the outcomes.

6. Focus on the future. Work together to build goals
for the next evaluation process. Goals should address
any problems identified in the evaluation process as
well as developmental goals to help a staff member
build skills and prepare for future opportunities.
Frame the goals as what success looks like instead of
what failure looks like.

References include:
Tiffany A. Ito, Jeff T. Larsen, N. Kyle Smith, and John T. Cacioppo, Ohio State
University (1998); Naomi Eisenberger, PhD, at the University of California,
Los Angeles, Kipling Williams, PhD, at Purdue University, and colleagues
found that social rejection activates many of the same brain regions involved
in physical pain (*Science*, 2003). *Coaching and the Brain* by David Rock and
Linda J. Page (2009).

Coaching Corner

- How does the brain research cited in this section help you prepare to give or receive feedback?
- Think of a time when you felt that feedback or a performance evaluation you received was not fair. How does that experience impact your responsibility to give feedback and conduct performance evaluations?
- How does the experience of giving a performance evaluation change for you if the focus is primarily on the conversation and the form is simply a way to document the conversation?

"YOU'VE GOT A BAD ATTITUDE"

These words must be among the least helpful words spoken in the workplace. I understand the frustration that causes people to utter these words, but if you ever feel the temptation to say them, bite your tongue!

Someone who has a bad attitude already sees work, and thereby you, their supervisor, as an adversary. Telling them that they've got a bad attitude and had better straighten out only reinforces their belief that you're out to get them and that the job is stupid, a waste of time, beneath them, too hard, ridiculous . . . So you can think it, but don't ever say it.

This is not to say you should ignore a bad attitude in the workplace, however. After all, it can be contagious and infect others. Ignoring it tells the other employees that you don't care about how people act or the tone or words that people use. Why should they bother to work hard and remain positive if it doesn't matter? Therefore you must address it in a way that allows the possibility for change, and if change is not forthcoming, then you have a clear path to release that employee to find more satisfying employment.

So how do you do that?

First, identify what exactly it is that an employee is doing that you are interpreting as a "bad attitude." An attitude is an internal construct, so while you can't know what someone is actually thinking, you can identify what they do. What do they do, exactly, that you identify as having a bad attitude? Write it down.

✓ He rolls his eyes every time I approach his desk or try to talk to him.

✓ She gossips with other employees about clients and about me.

✓ He has something negative to say about every idea that is presented in a staff meeting.

✓ He does the least amount of work possible.   .

Now, review the list and tease out any assumptions you've made, anything that is not work-related, and anything that is not concrete observable actions.

✓ He rolls his eyes every time I approach his desk or try to talk to him. (Okay, as long as you really mean "every" and not just "sometimes." If it's not every time, use "sometimes.")

✓ She has been heard talking about her coworkers behind their backs and does not bring issues directly to the person she has issues with. (Gossiping is a vague word that has connotations of personal information that could get confused with restricting free speech. How do you know what she is talking about? If you've heard specific comments about clients and you, then you can address this in terms of teamwork and customer service.)

✓ He has something negative to say about every idea that is presented in a staff meeting. (Probably not

"every idea," but otherwise this is a clear action;
think of a few specifics to refer to as examples.)

✓ He does the least amount of work possible.
(How do you know? Is he working hard and not
producing as much as others, or is he goofing off?
Does he know how much work you expect him to
complete? Maybe this becomes "reads a personal
book at his desk when he is finished with the
immediate assignment instead of looking for more
work or offering to help his coworkers.")

Now, you've done your homework. You have work-related,
observable behaviors that are possible to change. Only after you've
done these steps are you ready to address the issues associated with
the bad attitude, without saying anything about anyone having a
"bad attitude." You will be ready to address work performance issues
rather than your interpretations of how someone thinks and feels
about their work. Attitude is a mind-set and as a supervisor you
are concerned with external actions and outcomes. Keep focused
on their actions and outcomes so you're equipped to approach the
conversation from a productive angle.

Coaching Corner

- What have you seen happen when someone is told
  they have a "bad attitude"? How effective was it in
  changing anyone's behavior?
- When in your life have you experienced a negative
  reaction to some situation? How did it feel and where
  did it lead?
- What other words or phrases like "bad attitude" have
  you used—either with yourself or with others—that
  close down conversations instead of opening them up?

Confronting a Bad Attitude

You've done your homework. You've identified exactly what behaviors and actions an employee takes that exhibit his or her bad attitude. Now it's time to meet with the employee about his or her work performance.

"Jane, I asked to meet with you today to address some concerns I have with your work performance. I want to tell you my concerns straight through and then I'll give you a chance to respond. Are you ready to listen?"

Wait for agreement—even if it is a mumbled "whatever."

"I have heard statements you've made, on several occasions, that are disrespectful to clients and that encourage your coworkers to act against the best interests of this team, such as when you asked a coworker to clock in for you." (Be prepared to give specific examples.)

"In meetings you have consistently expressed negativity toward ideas that are brought up. While I welcome thoughtful disagreements, immediate negativity isn't helpful to the team. Your objections do not relate to the content of any idea but are expressed in response to any suggestion that I make regarding teamwork. Teamwork is a value of this organization and a value of mine as a leader.

"And finally, I need to let you know that your productivity is not meeting our expectations. You are spending too much time making personal phone calls, visiting staff in other departments, and visiting non-work-related websites. I had IT pull up your computer history and it showed you had spent an average of an hour a day visiting shopping and job-hunting sites. All of this results in reduced client hours."

Give the employee a chance to reply. Again, you want to make sure he or she has every opportunity to explain him

continued ⇨

or herself. You want them to feel heard. You don't want it to come back later that you didn't give them a chance to explain themselves.

Maybe Jane responds that she was just kidding about the clients and when she told her coworker to clock in for her. She might say she doesn't think she really spends that much time on the Internet. And the negativity, well, she can't help it if she thinks team building is stupid. Every place she's worked does some stupid team-building stuff and it never changes anything.

In your response to Jane, you will give specific measures for what Jane needs to do if she wants to keep her job. You will detail these out, one-by-one, and then ask her: "Are you interested in making these changes?"

Now, Jane can make any number of responses. The most likely ones are:

1. "Okay, I'll try."
2. "You're crazy. I'm not doing anything different than anyone else. I don't know who's been messing with my computer but I didn't visit all those sites."
3. "I don't have to change. What are you going to do, fire me?"

Your responses for each numbered response might be:

1. Thank her and proceed. (She may or may not make the changes, but at this point you need to take her at her word and give her a chance to show you that she can change.)
2. Tell her you're sorry to hear that she doesn't accept responsibility for her

actions. Ask her to take a day off (or a weekend) to consider what you're saying and to decide if she wants to continue to work here. If she doesn't, that's fine. You can prepare a check for her and she can start to look for another job. If she does decide to come back, you tell her you will expect her to make the changes necessary to improve her work performance.

3. You say that you will indeed fire her if her actions don't change, but it's not your preference. (Then repeat the part of #2 about taking time to think about the job and decide if she wants it.)

Write a memo to Jane to document your meeting with her. This can be a simple note to document an oral warning or it can be an actual written warning. In any case, make sure you note the date and topics of discussion.

Follow through to see what Jane chooses. If she chooses #1 or if she returns to work ready to give it a try, set up a series of meetings with her to review the expectations and her actions in regard to each one. This meeting should happen on a regular basis (weekly would be best). The primary responsibility at this point for you as her supervisor is to follow up and make sure you hold Jane accountable for the issues you brought to her attention. It does no one any good if you address these issues and then don't follow up. Why bother? If she is showing effort and making some changes, yet it's still not meeting the expectations you have discussed, these meetings give you a chance to support her improvement and reinforce the remaining issues and expectations for change.

If she improves her work performance, acknowledge the

⇨

changes and thank her. Let her be successful; do not hold her past actions against her if she's working to change her behavior. If she does not change her performance, document the misses and follow your organization's discipline policy. After an appropriate period of time, let her go if she has shown little or no improvement.

The whole process is done with respect. There is no need to get punitive or condescending. Your job is to present your expectations and the clear consequences of not following them. And then to follow up and follow through. All of this is done without ever using the words "bad attitude."

GETTING FEEDBACK

A friend recently told me about an important lesson she learned at work. Her boss said something she found offensive. My friend politely told her boss, "I found the way you said that to be a little offensive." Her boss got up, left the room, and slammed the door. Lesson learned: don't offer any feedback to your boss.

While the employee perhaps could have offered the feedback in a more thoughtful manner, given the positional power in this situation, the supervisor needed to look past the form and respond to the content first, then later she could have addressed the form of the feedback. Any time a staff member offers feedback to a supervisor, it takes courage. The supervisor needs to recognize that.

The boss later apologized for her reaction and told my friend that she didn't like the way she'd given her the feedback. The boss acknowledged that she shouldn't have slammed the door. And then she walked away.

It's good that the boss apologized but bad that she stopped there. That one sentence of apology ended the conversation. There was no further conversation about what didn't work in the way my friend had given her information, nor were there any hints about a better way to say something in the future. Lesson relearned: don't offer any feedback to your boss.

A good practice for any supervisor is to open the door to feedback. As with any relationship, a supervisor-employee relationship needs to be two-way to be authentic and effective. In order to help your staff do their best work, you need to hear from them about what is working and not working with your supervision. Hearing feedback does not mean that the supervisor must then change everything or anything. For example, if the employee said, "Well, I'd like you to just leave me alone," the appropriate response might be, "That's not going to happen. I'm going to be overseeing your work and checking in with you. Is there anything in particular, within those parameters, that you'd like me to consider changing?"

Hearing the feedback gives the supervisor a chance to consider changing some practices or approaches that might work better for the employee. In addition, this process can serve as a model for how to hear and respond to feedback.

Here's the thing, however: very few employees are going to give unsolicited feedback to their supervisors. If you want to get feedback, you need to build a process to receive it. The best processes are organization-wide, but if there is no structured process in your organization, then you can institute your own process.

Schedule a time to meet that gives the employee time to prepare, perhaps a week out. Let the employee know that you'd like to hear how things are working for them with your supervision. You can let them know up front that you might not be able to make all the changes that they might ask for, but that you'd like to hear their concerns and their ideas. One simple and effective model is: Stop/Start/Keep. What do you want me to stop doing? What do you want me to start doing? And what do you want me to keep doing?

And then, and this is critical: **listen**. Listen to what they say and don't respond immediately. Listen and ask questions to understand. If they say something that sounds confusing or even crazy to you, simply say, "Tell me more." Or, "How would that help you be more successful in your work?" And **listen** some more. When they are done, thank them. It is brave for any employee to give feedback to their supervisor. Tell them you'll consider their ideas and let them know what you can do when you meet next time. Then take a break so you can separate any reactions you may have from the actual content of the feedback. Come back soon (the next day maybe) and let them know what you heard and what you're going to do about it. If you can't make the changes they suggested, let them know why. And thank them again for their ideas.

Inviting feedback and listening to it can help you be a better supervisor to that particular employee and maybe to other employees too. It can help to build your working relationship, and it can show them a mature and effective manner in which to receive feedback.

If my friend had experienced a process like this, the lesson learned would have been different. The lesson learned could have been: giving feedback can be powerful and productive for everyone.

Coaching Corner

- What lessons have your staff learned in their interactions with you, particularly when the lesson was unintended?
- What opportunities or structure currently exist in your organization for employees to give feedback to you or other supervisors?
- Imagine someone has just told you that something you said was offensive. Try on the idea of simply asking them, "Really? Tell me more." What comes up for you, in your mind and your body, when you imagine that response?
- Respond to the following Peter Bregman quote: "Feedback exposes you to yourself, which is why it is both tremendously unsettling and exceptionally valuable. It can be an incredible gift, a field guide for acting with impact in the world."

CHAPTER 8:
How You Act When
Things Aren't Working

LOOK FOR THE GRAY

Some people see things as black or white. From this point of view, there is no gray. There is no middle ground. Even people who don't normally see the world in this way sometimes fall into this two-shade thinking when faced with a complicated situation in which there is no clear path. The discomfort of not knowing what to do or how things will turn out can be so strong that people start looking for a quick fix. It seems easier to just categorize things (and people) into positive or negative groups rather than to deal with the nuances.

I see this kind of categorizing showing up fairly often when supervisors are faced with problem behaviors from an employee. Instead of trusting their skills to address the issue, they panic. They try to oversimplify the situation, either by making it all about a bad apple ("This is a bad employee. I must get rid of him!"), or by choosing to pretend that everything is fine by ignoring the behaviors and hoping it will go away on its own.

Often this right/wrong way of thinking leads supervisors to make a decision too early in the game. Perhaps an employee has had some performance issues. Let's imagine that last year Sally was promoted by her boss, Fred, who thought she was going to be a star. Now she's made some bad judgment calls in her job. Now Fred is frustrated and disappointed in her performance. He's not sure how to work with her so he decides he must have made a mistake. Sally didn't have what he thought she did. It's time for her to go. She is now a "bad employee" on her way out.

Once she is labeled a "bad employee" in his eyes, then several unfortunate things happen. Fred gives up on her. He is now just waiting to get through the process so he can hire someone to replace her. In Fred's mind, Sally is now essentially a lame duck, so why give her any more projects or help her to see how she could make better decisions? Since Sally has been labeled "bad" there is a drop in trust, and because he feels he can't trust her, he pretty much stops working with her, let alone trying to train her in new responsibilities. There are no more casual conversations. There are no more check-ins. There are no more problem-solving sessions. When Fred does talk to Sally, he documents every conversation. Now every meeting they have is characterized as "discipline meetings." Sally is being shunned.

This scenario is problematic for several reasons. First of all, it's not fair. Unless the employee is being investigated for a serious violation that could lead to immediate termination, then she deserves a chance to turn her performance around. How is there any opportunity for Sally to correct her performance if all support and conversation have been withdrawn? Additionally it's problematic because every other employee notices what is happening. Even if Fred doesn't directly tell any of them that Sally is a "bad employee," they see the change in the way she is being treated and involved in the team. They get the message: if an employee has a problem or does something wrong, they will be treated badly. There is no room for mistakes, no room for risk, no room for innovation, no room for improvement, no room for true teamwork.

As a supervisor, avoid this mistake at all costs. As with so many aspects of supervision, it begins with you. Watch out for black or white thinking. Allow more room for gray. Most employees, as well as most situations, are more complicated than simply good or bad. There are good employees who make mistakes. There are employees who make poor choices. There are employees who don't know what is expected of them. If you begin to label someone as a "bad employee," check your own actions first. Have you explained clearly what is expected of them? Does this person have the skills to do the job? And even if you have given them every opportunity to improve and they haven't, what is compelling you to shut them out? That is not necessary.

Sometimes a decision must be made to put an employee on a discipline plan or to terminate them. When that decision has been made, it is possible and preferable to treat the employee with respect. During the discipline process, explain what the problem is and what changes are needed for the person to keep their job. Stay in the relationship. Do not shun them. Even if they are not right for the job, be clear, direct, and reasonable. Respect the person even if you do not appreciate their actions. If nothing else, this will decrease your liability for a lawsuit.

Keep your interactions neutral. Watch your tone and your body language. State the facts and the consequences. Remember that people are complicated. There is a lot of gray in the world. And while the complicated situations may not be as easy to move through, we need to remember to look for the gray. It's more honest and more human to do so.

Coaching Corner

- When people do not live up to your expectations, how do you respond?

- Is there a situation in which you tend to label people as good or bad? How does that impact your relationship with them?
- When faced with a situation in which you don't know what to do or how it will turn out, do you tend to move right into action? What happens if you let yourself stay in "not knowing" for a period of time?

MAKE DISCIPLINE REAL OR DON'T GO THERE

Consider the following problematic scenario: an employee does something that is outside of accepted protocol. Let's say he starts coming to work a few minutes late. At first, his supervisor ignores it, assuming something came up and the situation will correct itself. It doesn't. So the supervisor speaks to the employee and reminds him that the job starts at eight and he needs to correct his tardiness.

Nothing changes. In fact, the employee who was arriving five to ten minutes late starts slipping in fifteen to twenty minutes late. Eventually the supervisor is forced to deal with the situation and issues an official verbal warning. Later there is a written letter of warning. For two days the employee arrives on time. Then it starts up again; he starts coming in later and later until he is back to his previous level of arriving fifteen to twenty minutes late. The supervisor talks to him, asks what's going on, maybe even threatens to fire him. Still he arrives late. But the supervisor does nothing other than complain about what's now become a habit. The employee's performance does not improve and there are no consequences for his actions.

What's going on here? Why is there no follow-through on the discipline process? Perhaps it's the case that the supervisor realizes, belatedly, that this is not a battle she wants to fight. The employee is a wonderful employee in all other ways. I've heard supervisors say in situations like these, "I'm not going to fire him for being a few minutes late. I'd be shooting myself in the foot. He's great at the rest of his job. Who knows what I would get if I had to start all over?"

Unfortunately, however, because the supervisor has reprimanded the employee, and even threatened to fire him, she's set up a problematic dynamic. When a policy is broken or a performance is unacceptable, she starts the discipline process. But if along the way that discipline process fizzles out, not only does this send the wrong message to the affected employee, but to all other employees who see it happening. It tells employees that management does not follow through. It tells them that supervisors don't mean what they say. And it tells them that it's okay to break policies and that inappropriate actions will be tolerated.

When a discipline process is started but not followed through, it sends a powerful message that you do not want to send—that the organization tolerates substandard performance. It is also then difficult to differentiate when there will be follow-through with **real** discipline issues. The staff sees that discipline is arbitrary, and that some employees get away with things and others get busted. In the worst-case scenario, this could lead to discrimination charges and other grievances.

I am not saying that you must terminate a good employee for being late. Nor am I saying that you should never terminate an employee for being late. I am saying that you need to know **whether** you will terminate for being late or not. You must decide ahead of time what your actual deal-breakers are. What will you terminate for? You must know this before you make any threats. Never threaten actions that you will not follow through to their conclusion, if necessary. Talking to an employee about what's not working involves acknowledging that the action is a problem and that you want to see changes. You can offer to be flexible, by changing their workday so that they start a half hour later and leave a half hour later. Consider changing their job responsibilities if you are not going to hold them accountable for certain tasks. Or change the policy or procedure that no one ever follows.

Before you make any of these adaptations, however, make sure you are willing to live with the changes. Not just for this person but for **every** person in that job. You need to be prepared that others will ask for the same kind of allowances if you grant them to one person. And if you're not going to grant the same kind of allowances, you better have a good objective reason why not.

Use the discipline process when it is appropriate and when you are ready to see it through if necessary. When an organization starts a discipline process and does not follow through, it sends a message to every employee that the discipline process is a farce. This is a disincentive for every employee trying to follow procedures and do good work. Make the discipline process real, or don't even go there.

Coaching Corner

- What beliefs do you have about the kind of boss who fires people? Do these beliefs get in the way of being an effective supervisor?
- Are there any performance problems that you are tolerating simply because you don't want to deal with the interpersonal messiness of having to confront the person?
- Are you being consistent about policy and procedure enforcement with your employees?
- Are you sending messages that act as a disincentive for employees? What are the costs of this and how can you address the situation?

FAIR DISCIPLINE IN FOUR STEPS

Having to discipline an employee is a part of supervision that many supervisors dread. Some people even decline a promotion because they don't want to deal with it. While many organizations consider themselves at-will employers and retain the right to terminate employees at any time for any reason, it's important to consider the value of fairness. In most circumstances, it is fair to give employees a chance to correct any problems that might arise. This is an overview of what the steps of a fair discipline process might look like. I am assuming here that the discipline process is in response to a performance problem and not an egregious action that could require immediate termination.

Before implementing this discipline process, it is important to ask yourself a few questions. Only when the answer to these questions is yes is it appropriate to move into a discipline process. If the answer to any of these questions is no, then you, as a supervisor, need to address your own role and responsibilities. These are the first steps you must take to help your staff member improve their performance.

- ✔ Does this employee know what is expected of them?
- ✔ Does she understand what the job requires and the outcomes you are looking for?
- ✔ Does the employee know how to do the work and have the tools needed to do the work?
- ✔ Is the problem an issue of performance (rather than training)?

If you are clear that the employee can do the work and knows what is expected of them and it's still not happening, then the following four steps outline a progressive discipline process wherein an employee is given notice and time to improve their performance before being fired.

1. Let the employee know what the problem is and how it needs to change. This would involve a conversation that would take place one-on-one. You should make sure the employee understands what needs to be done and then make an informal note of the conversation in your supervisor's file (not the official personnel file at this point).

2. After the initial notification, observe the employee and see if the change is happening. You will have regular meetings with the employee to see how things are progressing, and to ask if they have any questions. If the required change is not happening, you want to ask what's going on. "What is standing in the way of this change happening?" might be an appropriate question to ask.

   If, after an appropriate period of time, the change still has not taken place, then you will issue a verbal warning. This warning would state clearly that the requested change did not happen as directed. You will need to reiterate what the problem is, what needs to happen, and when it needs to happen by, and then add what the consequence will be if the change is not made. Be clear here that this is a serious concern. You might say something like, "You need to know that your job is in jeopardy if this change does not happen." Follow up the verbal warning with an e-mail to document the conversation. "This e-mail will confirm that we met today to discuss my concerns about your performance in the area of punctuality. If change does not happen immediately and continue, then you will be subject to further disciplinary action, up to and including termination." (That's the official HR language, but make sure you verbally issue the warning in a clear and direct manner so it is not just seen as technical language.) You might want to cc HR on this e-mail so they are in the loop about where you are in the four-step process.

3. If the change still does not happen after a fair period of time, you will issue a written warning detailing the information contained in the verbal warning noted above. This written warning is given to the employee and a copy is sent to HR to be placed in the official personnel file.

4. If the change has still not been made within a reasonable time period, you can move to termination. If you've witnessed some effort to change on the part of the employee, but the actions they're taking are inconsistent, then you might issue a "last chance" warning. **All supervisors should talk to Human Resources, their boss, or an attorney before they fire anyone.**

In none of these steps should conversations or documentation be delivered in a manner that is denigrating. All verbal and written communication and correspondence should be handled as a clarification of expectations and an identification of clear consequences. At each step, you want to document what is happening, noting dates, conversations, and the employee's response. Taking these steps not only ensures a fair process, but will also help you prove that you did what you needed to do if there is ever any question about the discipline process. Documentation of each step is required to ensure a clean and thorough process. Work with your HR department at each step from #2 on so they are aware of what is happening. HR will be watching for consistency throughout the organization as well as legal and liability concerns.

Discipline is something that most supervisors dread. It is part of your job, however, and avoiding it when it is necessary makes you less effective and can impact the entire organization. Be calm, clear, and direct in your feedback and you might find that the result is overall improved performance. That is the hoped-for response. In any case, this kind of a process assures your staff that you are fair and follow through on problems. Learning how to effectively discipline makes you and your organization stronger and safer.

Coaching Corner

- What reactions do you have to the word "discipline"? How might those reactions make it hard for you to take appropriate steps with the people you supervise?
- Are there actions or situations that you have been ignoring in order to avoid having to confront someone? How can you address those problems without being punitive?
- Can you stay in a relationship with someone and still move through a discipline process? If not, what gets in the way?

What Is a "Fair Period of Time"?

Not surprisingly, the answer is a vague "It depends." It depends on many factors, including:

- ✔ Is your organization an at-will employer?
- ✔ Is there a collective bargaining agreement in place?
- ✔ How long has the person been an employee?
- ✔ What is their job?
- ✔ How long have they been in their current position?
- ✔ How serious are the actions that are leading to their termination?
- ✔ Are there any complicating factors that make the potential termination messy?
- ✔ How long have the performance problems been tolerated with no feedback or correction plan?
- ✔ What has been done so far to document the problems?

For these and many other reasons, there is no clear answer to the question of how long it takes to fire someone. These questions also underline the importance of involving someone with HR knowledge in the discipline process and the termination decision. In some circumstances termination can be immediate, while in many circumstances it would be expected that you give the person a few weeks or months to see if they can make the requested changes. Occasionally it will take longer.

Never terminate someone in anger or in reaction to a situation you just heard about. If necessary, suspend the person while you find out what happened and how your organization wants to proceed. **Work with HR. HR is your friend in this difficult process.**

TOUGH TIMES CALL FOR TOUGH TRUTHS

There are times when entire organizations find themselves in financial trouble. When that happens, organizations look at layoffs and furloughs and other cost-cutting measures. Employees feel scared and morale is low. As a supervisor, you may feel powerless to help your employees, but you are probably the most important link for your staff during tough economic times.

Studies have repeatedly shown that the number one reason people leave their jobs is because of their supervisor. The corollary to that, which is also important to remember, is that a good supervisor can make a bad situation bearable. So whether your organization is facing layoffs or just cutting costs, when times are tough remember that the people you supervise are nervous and waiting for bad news. They know times are tough and they are worried about whether it might affect them and their livelihood. Even if your employees just survived layoffs or your organization does not project any, know that people are afraid. They are hearing bad news around them. And they are looking to you to tell them the truth.

Tell the truth. If there are possible layoffs ahead, admit it. Promise them that as soon as any specific decisions are made, you will let them know. (Don't let the time between that conversation and its follow-up be too long because people will be anxious about their fate. The alternative choice is not to say anything until you know the exact decisions, but this can lead to someone making a big purchase, like a new car, because they assumed they had money coming in. It's better to let people know what might be in store as soon as you know that's a possibility.) If tough cuts are being made, acknowledge that they're tough. Acknowledge that these are scary times. If you don't know whether there will be cuts, say so. If you are asked whether you made the decision about who was laid off, tell the truth. And if you did make those decisions, make sure there was an objective rationale for the choices you made. The more transparent you are, the more trust you build.

Be kind. During tough economic times, more than ever, people need to know that you recognize them as individual people and not cogs in a machine. This does not mean anything goes, but it does mean you need to check in with people, and that you need to try to be compassionate. A simple "How you doing?" can be enough to let your employee know you care about them.

Be available. Don't hide in your office. Walk around and check in with people. You can keep your talk work-specific, but do engage your team. If people feel overwhelmed with too much work from shifting projects or downsized coworkers, help them determine what the top priorities need to be. This will let them know they are not alone.

During layoffs, some people may feel depressed and others may feel angry. If possible, have a focus group or a staff meeting to let people express their feelings. Then help them get back to work. Perhaps use your EAP (Employee Assistance Program), or hire a consultant to facilitate a group and then take the team out to lunch or coffee together. This doesn't have to be a big expense. Just allow time for people to be together and process what's happening. It's good to have set-aside time to acknowledge the feelings that are coming up, but that doesn't mean that work becomes a therapy group. You are there to work and you need to be the one who brings the focus back to the work. Remind the group about the vision behind the work you all do. Remind them that the work matters. And then help them get back to it.

Your job as a supervisor is to be a leader, and this can be extra hard during complex times, especially when you are most likely feeling all the same feelings as your employees. The bottom line is this: tell the truth. It may be the most important thing you can do.

Coaching Corner

- Is there anything you are avoiding talking to your team about? What gets in your way of telling the truth?

- Do you think that it's your job to protect your employees from bad news? How can you show leadership in the midst of a difficult situation?
- What personal preparation do you need to do to be able to tell the truth to your team?

PAUSE. BREATHE. DECIDE.

I pulled into the hotel valet parking at 8:32 A.M. I had hit unexpected traffic that ate up the extra forty minutes I'd allowed before my 8:30 start time for a training I was presenting. I was glad to be through the traffic and figured a couple minutes would be forgiven. After I handed over my car keys in the parking lot, I went into the hotel lobby and asked for directions to the Cambridge Room. They said they didn't have a Cambridge Room! They directed me to another hotel four blocks away. I took a deep breath. "Okay, I'll run!" I thought. I knew it would take me longer to get the car back and to try to weave through traffic to get to the other hotel. Then the scene was repeated at the next hotel! I couldn't believe that there were three different Marriotts within a few blocks! By the time I ran another four blocks away, I ended up being over a half hour late for my own training. I paused very briefly outside the room and reminded myself of the important practice that helps me stay present: pause-breathe-decide.

First, I paused. I literally stopped in the hall before I opened the door. Even though I was late, I knew a few seconds spent composing myself before I walked in would be worth the time. Next, I took three deep breaths to get in my body and be present. I reminded myself that I couldn't change the fact that I was late. Finally, I made a decision about how to proceed. "Okay," I told myself. "How can you make this work? I can walk in and give them a good training that will help them become better supervisors. To do that, I need to let go of my stress and be present. Here I go!" Then I entered the Cambridge Room, apologized for my delay, and explained the traffic situation as I set up and got started on the job I was there to do.

It was a stressful start but this profound practice of pause-breathe-decide served me well. Once I entered the room, I was able to dive into my training feeling calm and focused. While I don't wish this experience of being late upon you, I do recommend practicing and using pause-breathe-decide. You can use it when you run into something unexpected, when you're running late, when you're walking into a difficult meeting or expecting a difficult conversation. It is a good practice to keep yourself present and bring your best self to the task at hand.

Pause, breathe, decide is founded on the simple truths that:

- ✓ It does not help, in a stressful moment, to focus on what went wrong or what might go wrong, but instead focus on moving forward.
- ✓ Staying connected to your body is one of the most powerful proven ways to combat stress.
- ✓ Making thoughtful, purposeful decisions, even in the midst of stress or upset, will help you be present and do what you need to do.

Pause. Pausing can be a momentary stop that takes literally a few seconds but it is a conscious reminder to your brain and your body that you will proceed with purpose and choice and not simply react to external circumstances. This pause can help you remember that relationships matter, that you can't change the past, that you can only control what you do, and that people see things in different ways. It is a momentary pause that can save untold time by not making a bad situation worse. In that moment I sometimes take a step back by rocking back on one foot to let my body know that I am stopping for a moment. When I first started this practice I would use that physical action to prompt the question, "What am I trying to do here?" Now that question does not have to be stated out loud; the pause itself asks that question.

Breathe. Literally. I take at least one deep full-gut breath. Sometimes I take three. (Three deep breaths have been proven to reduce blood pressure.) With this deep breath, I answer my question and settle into it. In the first parking lot, during my quick breath, I reminded myself, "I can't change this situation. I am late and I'm in the wrong place. What's my next best move?" In the hall outside the Cambridge Room, when I finally got to the right place, my thought as I breathed in was, "I'm going to go in and do my training in the best way I can. I am going to be present and authentic and share what I know to be true." In other situations, the thought with the breath might be, "This relationship is more important to me than winning a minor argument." Or "I don't understand what just happened. I need more information." Or "Clearly this employee sees things differently than I do. What do I want to do about that?"

Decide. This is the moment before you step forward. What am I going to do? How do I want to proceed? The power of this moment is that you are choosing and not simply reacting.

This entire process can happen in ten seconds. Most of us remember to pause and consider when we're facing big hairy decisions, ones that might take much more deliberation than ten seconds, but sometimes we forget the moment-by-moment choices we make every day.

The pause-breathe-decide practice underlines that you can

choose how to act in any given moment. There are choices in every interaction with an employee, in every interaction with your partner or your kids. There are choices when your buttons are pushed and when you're in a hurry. This three-step practice can help you remember that you always have a choice about your actions. You may be tempted to simply react but you can choose to choose. Practice it and use it. Pause. Breathe. Decide. It's a practice that will help you be present and be the supervisor you intend to be.

Coaching Corner

- Have there been times when you have reacted to a person or a situation in the moment only to regret it later? Consider one of these situations and imagine what you might have done differently if you had paused.
- If you imagine this practice will somehow just hold you up when you're in a hurry, get out a stopwatch and time ten seconds. Take a deep breath as you watch the seconds tick by. How do you feel?
- What could you do to remind yourself to pause (like my practice of literally falling back on one foot)? Practice this action until it feels comfortable and commit to trying it once in the next week and then assessing how it changed the situation, either internally or externally.

CONTAIN THE COMPLAINING

I was working with a group I knew well. We were supposed to be discussing supervision situations but people were not participating the way they usually did. I could feel the discontent. They were restless and grouchy and not present. The energy of the group was stopping us from doing the work they were there to do. I stopped the process. "Okay, time to let it out," I said. "Here's the deal: you've got two minutes to complain. Say everything and anything that's bothering you." I set the timer and told them, "Go!"

Someone asked, "Who's starting?"

I explained, "We're not taking turns. Just go. Say it, everyone at once." As soon as a few people started talking and the group understood that they were all supposed to join in and talk all at once, it all came out! I did it too. A big free-form complaint session! By the end of the two minutes most of the group was laughing. And then we could all move on! Sometimes you just have to let it out.

Complaining has its place. When things are seriously wrong or dangerous, it is important to complain, to get things fixed. And sometimes work (and life) is not fair, we have way too much to do, and things break or people don't show up or you feel sick. And on and on. It's okay when routine troubles strike us to take a few minutes and dip into the lake of "It's Not Fair!" But then we have to get out of there!

Too often work groups wallow in the lake and keep each other there. It's hard to get out of that mucky lake when everyone around you is complaining. As a leader, it's important for you to recognize when the complaints need attention and follow-up and when the complaining is disconnected and unproductive. When people are stuck complaining about things that do not directly impact their work and there is really nothing to be done, then it might be time for another tactic. There is a need to occasionally let complaints out but also to set parameters around complaining so that it's short and therapeutic, and not the status quo of the workspace.

Here are three practices you can build to set up healthy parameters for containing the negativity that unfettered complaining can generate.

✓ **Limit venting time.** If you notice that most of your staff meetings and/or your regular check-ins with

staff are spent complaining about irrelevant concerns, then stop and figure it out. Is everyone complaining or is it one or two particular employees?
Complaining that helps people understand and then
solve a problem can be useful. If the complaining
is not followed up with actions to fix the problems,
then it is time to contain the complaining. Unlim-
ited complaining is not helpful. As in my silly (and
effective) practice above, give people a little time to
complain and then make it clear that it is time to
move on.

✓ **One-time venting rule.** As an HR director, my
office became complaint central for a while. It was
important to give people a safe place to complain and
it was important that people knew that they could tell
me what was going on. But at some point I realized
that some people were coming back time after time to
complain about the same things; problems that they
could address but they were not taking responsibility
for fixing. That's when I instituted a one-time venting
rule. People could complain about something and
do nothing about it—once. But if they came back a
second time and complained about the same thing,
I asked them, "What are you going to do about it?"
I would then help them make a plan, but they had
to either take action or let it go. (For example, June
complaining that Sarah hurt her feelings by not listening to her talk about her problems with her boy-
friend. June needs to talk directly to Sarah.)

✓ **Reframe the conversation to face the future.**
Along with the one-time rule, I focused on helping
the complainant face forward. It's okay to look back

and see what happened and how that impacted you, but when it is time to solve problems, we must look ahead. Ask them, "Where do we go from here? What do you need to be different going forward? What can you do?" Help people to think about solutions instead of blame.

Let people feel what they're feeling, and then hear what you need to hear from the complaining. Sometimes the complaints point to real and important issues that must be handled. When you realize, however, that people are simply hanging out in the muck, contain the complaining and help your team move forward.

Coaching Corner

- Think of a time when you fell into a habit of complaining. How did you feel? How did it affect people around you?
- Think about something that is not fair in your work or life. Write down short phrases that come to mind when you think about this event while looking at the past— even if the past was five minutes ago. After a couple minutes note how you feel. Now, start a new sheet of paper and write down what comes to mind when you think about where you go from here, facing forward. How do you feel now?
- Is there a particular complainer on your team? How can you practice deep listening to ensure that you hear their concerns and that they feel heard and then help them move to action?

DON'T JUST COMPLAIN ABOUT YOUR STAFF

Sometimes when I'm coaching a supervisor, they'll express their frustration about a particular employee through complaining. That's okay. As discussed previously, we all need to vent. Listening is an important part of coaching, so I will listen and ask questions to make sure I get the gist of the situation, then I'll generally say something like, "So are you ready to try something new?" Usually the supervisor says yes, but then often within a few minutes, they'll fall right back into complaining. Or they'll go negative: "Oh, that will never work." "This person won't change."

I try to bring them back to a solution focus, but they've already decided that it's the individual's fault and they just want to complain. They aren't ready to try new strategies or consider changing the structure of how they do things. They have decided that the person is the problem. The supervisor in these cases is taking the employee's actions personally. Once things have gotten to the place where the supervisor thinks the situation is unworkable, their negative perception often becomes a self-fulfilling prophecy. Even if the employee tries to make the changes the supervisor has asked for, it may not be enough, because once the supervisor has decided that the employee is the problem, they often don't see anything but a problem.

Here are some options to consider when you find yourself frustrated with a particular employee:

✓ **Have you been clear?** Have you been absolutely clear about what the employee needs to do? About the mission, responsibilities, tasks, the level of initiative required, the whole terrain of "how" to do the job as well as what to do? About what is not working? Have you given the employee clear feedback with clear steps needed to turn the performance around?

✓ **Have you had critical two-way conversations?** Have you listened to the employee? Did you ask what the problem is? Have you seriously considered their answers and not just blown them off? Have you asked them to bring you a plan to turn their job around?

✓ **Have you offered appropriate support?** Have you let the employee know that you want to figure this out? Have you supported them in learning the job? Have you given the employee enough time to learn and put it all together? Has there been enough relevant training?

✓ **Have you considered the system?** Have you considered the structure of the job? Have you considered the job flow around the employee? Are other employees connected to this job doing what they need to be doing? Does the job structure make sense? Make sure you are not asking for opposite skills in one job and then being repeatedly surprised that one person can't do it all (i.e., attention to detail and big-picture thinking).

One study I read said that 85 percent of the time, performance problems are caused by the system. Too often supervisors jump to the termination solution before considering options for success. Then a new person will come in and there will soon be trouble again. Or another team member will become the new problem employee, because the system is at fault and not the person causing the problems.

Sometimes system-based solutions can be complicated and take time. But other times, once it's recognized as a system problem, the solution can be surprising simple and happen quickly. The "fly in the urinal" story is a great (and funny) example of changing the system to support the behavior you want. Over twenty years ago, a maintenance man at the Amsterdam Airport came up with a solution to reduce urinal splash. His solution consisted of putting a picture of a fly onto each urinal. Suddenly men had something tangible to aim at and "spillage rates" dropped 80 percent! That translates into major savings in maintenance costs.

Ask yourself the question, "What can you do to help this person succeed?" Is there a solution, like the fly in the urinal, that can help them do the right thing?

Again, this is not to say that you should never fire people. Sometimes things just aren't working and you need to take that step. But be sure it's not your first choice. Is there a way to move beyond your own complaining to solutions? To support success? What is the equivalent of the fly in the urinal for your situation?

Coaching Corner

- Have you ever fallen into the mind-set of making an individual "bad" because of their performance issues? How did it feel and what did you do as a result of that mind-set? How would it have been different if you'd focused on the behavior instead of making it personal?

- Set aside three minutes. Take the first minute to make a list: If there were a system issue here, what would it be? For the next two minutes, do a brainstorm to find the possible fly in the urinal solutions for these system issues. Make it fun and just see what you come up with.

- Schedule specific one-on-one time to meet with each person you supervise to have a two-way conversation about what success in that job looks like and what might be getting in the way. Listen at least as much as you talk.

DO YOU AVOID OR APPROACH CONFLICT?

Everyone is so nice at Organization XYZ! They smile, chat with each other, and seem to do good work. Meetings are quick and calm. People seem focused on their work and everyone knows how things are done. There aren't many changes and there are certainly no conflicts. It seems like a good place to work.

But wait, when you look a little closer, you notice that in addition to the smiles, there is a lot of eye rolling happening. Sometimes the chatter between employees is about other employees. And in those quick meetings, not much happens.

Most decisions are made outside of meetings so the meetings are used simply to formalize the decisions, or to announce the decisions to those who weren't part of the behind-the-scene discussions. When new employees dare to ask questions or raise concerns about how things are done, they are quickly labeled troublemakers. "They're not team players," their supervisors will explain. And when they are let go within the first year, they will be told, "It's just not a good fit." And that will be true.

Those employees that don't fit in resist the underlying culture of conflict-avoidance at Organization XYZ. Individuals avoid it, meetings avoid it, and the organization as a whole avoids it. The leadership in particular is not at all comfortable with conflict. It is confusing for new employees because often the leadership will say all the right things: bring your concerns to us, we're open to new ideas, we want to be the best we can be. There is probably a grievance policy in the handbook and there may even be a conflict-resolution policy. But those are just for show.

It's not that anyone ever intended for those policies to be in name only; it's simply that the leadership does not know how to handle conflict, so they go through the motions and when new staff members actually want to air any grievances or talk about disagreements, it looks like they are troublemakers.

If a particular employee tries to question or change a policy or practice, he or she is viewed as a complainer. The organization has a veneer of niceness that covers a culture of passive-aggressiveness, backroom decision-making, and a firm commitment to the idea that "we're fine the way we are and we're not going to change."

Conflict exists wherever life exists. The conflict-avoidant organization is not free of conflict. It simply pushes the conflict underground where it poisons relationships, undermines the system, and disrupts effective work.

At the other end of the spectrum would be Organization ABC, where people yell at each other, belittle each other, and fight for the win at any cost. This is clearly an unhealthy culture where there is too much conflict.

Consider Organization LMN as the healthy organization that falls in the middle of the spectrum. People smile here too, but people also frown and might even occasionally raise their voice a little. People chat and discuss and engage with each other. The work done here is not just good, it is also innovative, and employees are eager to come to work.

It's not that Organization LMN instigates conflict. But if conflict arises, leaders know how to encourage conflict about the right things. The leaders not only understand that conflict is part of life, but that it is necessary for good decisions and strong innovative work. So they watch for conflict and when they sense that it might be lurking, they surface it. "It looks like you might disagree with this idea, Wendy. What are you thinking?"

The meetings here are active and even boisterous sometimes. Ideas are bounced around and people actively disagree with each other. When decisions need to be made, everyone puts their ideas on the table and talks them through—in one or more meetings. They understand how the decision will be made—whether it's going to be voted on by everyone, the supervisor will decide, or the executive committee is going to decide. They know how the decision will be made and why it is being decided in that way, and once it is made, they respect and support it—whether it was their initial choice or not. Everyone understands that the decision was made for the good of the organization. No one takes it personally that their particular idea was not championed.

When interpersonal conflict arises, employees utilize the active conflict-resolution process if the conflict is impacting the work. If the conflict is not affecting the employees' work, they set it aside. Employees at Organization LMN recognize that they may not like everyone they work with, but they are expected to respect everyone. And they do.

Every employee is trained in conflict resolution and the training is updated regularly. There are designated mediators who have received additional training and these individuals are available to help resolve work-related conflict when individuals need help.

Organization LMN has intentionally built this culture of healthy conflict. It is not that employees are fighting with each other, but that they say what they think (relevant to the work) and they tolerate other employees having a different way of looking at things. They understand what healthy conflict is and how it can improve their work and their relationships. They don't go looking for conflict, but when it comes up, every employee knows what to do with it. New employees are encouraged to rock the boat. They are often promoted after they have questioned and improved a redundant policy or practice.

Employees at Organization LMN feel safe to be who they are. They feel valued for their unique ideas and contributions. They bring their whole selves to work.

This organization has a core value that recognizes conflict as part of life at work. Conflict is surfaced and addressed. Decisions are made out in the open with everyone understanding when they're part of the decision. Organization LMN is committed to fulfilling its mission in the best way possible, which also allows room for change and growth and innovation.

Organization XYZ and Organization ABC are extreme ends of a spectrum. Too much conflict and not enough conflict are both problems for an organization. There's room in the middle of this spectrum for various responses to conflict. The point is to acknowledge conflict as part of an organization and make a healthy plan to work through it in a way that serves the work and the culture.

Coaching Corner

- Where on the spectrum does your organization fall? And as a leader, how do you contribute to the culture of conflict?
- When you were growing up, how did you see people handling (or not handling) conflict? In your home, at school, in the community, on TV? Consider what you grew up with and compare it to your current attitudes and practices.
- When you consider the description of Organization LMN, does it sound exciting or scary to you? What would you need to thrive in an organization with that culture?

Approaching Conflict*: Ten Steps

*Conflict is NOT the Same as Fighting or Addressing Performance Problems.

1. **Take time to prepare.** You want to make sure that you have clearly identified the problem area and separated the actual problem from your immediate reaction to the problem. What is the problem you are trying to address? How is this impacting your work? What is your bottom-line request that you want to ask of the other person?

2. **Understand and consider the other perspective.** Remember that any person you are approaching sees the world differently from you. Be prepared to hear about their view of reality. If you know they are worried about their workload, your consideration of that will help them to hear you.

3. **Don't broadside them.** Your coworkers will be much more likely to hear your concern if you don't throw it at them on the fly. Make an appointment. Give some context for what you want to talk about, and time to consider the topic. "I'd like to talk to you about my ideas for the new reporting requirements. Would it work if we meet on Tuesday to discuss it and then plan a follow-up meeting in a week to discuss any concerns you might have?"

4. **Start with your common interest.** Remind your colleague that you both want the same thing (i.e., to meet our deadline for the joint report we have to write) and that you understand you each have different jobs to help you succeed in doing that.

5. **Be specific and open at the same time.** Make a clear request and remember that your suggested solution is only one way to reach your desired outcomes. Try to reach agreement about the next step. Don't let the discussion flounder indefinitely in possibilities that never grow up to be anything! Use I-statements and focus on what you need to solve. Focus on the underlying issue and be open to finding a way to solve the problem that works for both of you. Ultimately, know your bottom line and state it more than once. "I need to know that you will get me the data I need for the report in a timely manner."

6. **Watch how you say what you say.** What you say is only a small part of your communication message. Make sure your tone and your body language don't undermine you. Be in alignment.

7. **Let others talk.** Listen carefully to understand the perspective of the person you're talking to. Ask questions. Show respect. Use active listening skills. Make sure that they feel heard. Don't let yourself attack or get defensive. Try not to be reactive or blaming.

8. **Come back to your common purpose**. Use your common purpose like a broken record if necessary. "I know we both want our clients to be served and our teammates to feel appreciated." Build from this common interest and know that even if you think your idea is the best way forward, there are other ways that could work. Try on any other ideas presented.

9. **It's not the end of the world if someone disagrees with you.** Disagreements and conflicts can build relationships.

continued ⇨

Stay respectful and keep that broken record of your common purpose in mind and present in the interaction. Remember that disagreements can actually produce stronger results if handled correctly. Remember also that in the workplace, position and power matter. Workplaces are not democracies. As the supervisor, you may have to make the final decision. If working with a peer, you may have to come back to it another day when you both have more information. And if you are working with your supervisor, you may have to concede.

10. **Do not take things personally and don't make things personal.** Keep the whole discussion about the work. Even if someone says to you, "That's never going to work!" consider that maybe it's their low blood sugar talking! Rejecting your idea is not rejecting you, and letting it become about you (or your program) will only make the next proposal more difficult. If you end up having to pull rank, make it objective and focused on the work and the mission. Don't hold on to the conflict (even after it's settled) and make them the bad guy for challenging ideas.

CHAPTER 9:

How You Work with Your Team

ARE YOU A FAMILY OR A TEAM?

I get nervous every time I hear someone say, "We're like a family here." Many work groups pride themselves on being like a family. They care about each other, rely on each other, and build real connections. That's what they mean by being a family.

And while a family model emphasizes the warmth and caring between staff members that keeps people connected and going through intense periods of work and growth, it also has its drawbacks. The metaphor can have unanticipated consequences for the work group. Consider the fact that many people have less-than-perfect families. Although people who use the metaphor usually intend it to convey the Norman Rockwell image of a family, that is not everyone's experience of family. Nor is Norman Rockwell the ideal of family for everyone. Differences in perception can disenfranchise an employee from the well-intentioned group.

The image of family can lead to some inappropriate behaviors as well. If we're a family, then it might seem okay for one employee to clock in for his "sister," for example, or to cover up for a "brother" if there are mistakes or problems. It can also lead to a lack of boundaries, especially between you as a supervisor and your staff, that can blur the lines of communication and responsibility. Are you their friend, their family, or their supervisor? Even if the distinctions are clear to you, they might be confusing to your staff.

Unfortunately, in many families there are habits of inclusion and exclusion, and in the workplace this can lead to alliances and cliques that include some employees and exclude others. This can disrupt communication and work habits. If a supervisor is involved in any of these favored groups, then there is at least the appearance of a conflict of interest and perhaps an actual conflict of interest.

In many ways the most dangerous component of a family model for the workplace is that it sets the supervisor up as a parent. If the group is a family, then you as the leader must be the parent. And if you are the parent, then your staff are children. This makes you the one who has the answers, the one who sets the limits, the one who offers rewards and punishments, and the one who takes care of everyone. The children may start vying for your parental attention and often there is one "child" who will act out. If any of this leads to a situation where you must let someone go, then what? No one gets "fired" from his or her family! The whole group can feel betrayed.

I find it much more powerful—and healthy—to use a team model. Think of a soccer team. First of all, everyone on the team is explicitly clear about what the point of the game is: to score goals and win the game. Each player has an assigned position and knows their job. They back each other up during the game. The players respond within their position on the field to make the best use of their own skills and the skills and opportunities of their teammates. And there is a captain. This person sets strategies and assigns jobs, but the captain does not make every decision about how to move down the field. Every team member supports and communicates with each other to make the best out of everyone's skills for the success of the whole team. This creates a synergy that makes the team stronger than the sum of its individual parts.

As a supervisor, you act as the captain of the team, not the mom or dad. The team model can prevent some problematic behaviors. If any of the above problematic behaviors are present—such as employees breaking rules to look out for each other, or parent-child dynamics—then introducing the team model can create a catalyst to change the behaviors—for the good of the team.

The family model can affect a work group in a complex manner. A work group is not a family, and pretending it is can lead to inadvertent, and sometimes damaging, behaviors. You can care about each other without needing to evoke family dynamics. Instead, build your team model to work together for a common goal, each person using their best skills in combination with their teammates' skills, for mutual success.

Coaching Corner

- Are there ways in which you have held yourself as a parent for your group? How has that affected your work?
- If you hold yourself as a captain of your team, how does that affect your power in, and over, the group?
- If you've used the family model, what steps could you take to begin a conversation about yourselves as a team?

ARE YOU PLAYING THE SAME GAME?

On vacations, my family and I often play games. One of the games we like to play is double, triple, and quadruple solitaire. Despite the apparent oxymoron of playing solitaire with other people, it's a game that can be high energy and offers a fun way for people to be together. (For those unfamiliar with group solitaire, it is just like basic solitaire except that everyone puts their aces in the middle and all players play off all the aces. As with solitary solitaire, the aim is to get the most cards into the middle.)

After playing several four-person games, I pondered the strategy that we each brought to the game. My husband and my daughter-in-law had dominated the game. They took turns winning each hand. They both played fast and aggressively, rushing to get every possible play onto the aces before anyone else could, sometimes even knocking another player's card out of the way. My daughter and I, on the other hand, played in a slow and deliberate manner; occasionally we would even back off of a play if someone else seemed to need the play more than we did.

As it turns out, we were actually playing two very different games. We were all playing to win, but the definition of winning was different. The fast players were playing to win as individuals; the slower players were playing for all of us to win (to get all four sets of fifty-two cards up into the middle).

Confusion could have arisen if the faster players thought they went out first because they were better/smarter/faster than the others without recognizing that we were playing a different game. They **may** have been better/smarter/faster than us, but that wasn't the only factor at play in this game. On the flip side, from the perspective of the slower players, the "real win" might have been sabotaged by those not taking time to look at the big picture. The major factor in this game of cards was that we were playing for fun. If we had been focused on outcomes, it mattered that we were playing for different goals.

Looking at individual styles is a critical factor for your team at work as well. Is everyone playing for the same goal? Some workers play for the individual win over the team win. This might show up in gossiping, blaming, and working at cross-purposes or outright sabotage. How would you know? If you watched my family playing quadruple solitaire, it would look like we were all playing for the same goal. It would, in fact, look like the slower ones were trying to win but just were not very good at it. It is only by talking explicitly about it that the difference would be discovered.

It is important that you, as the leader of your team, talk about your goals and strategies with your team to ensure that everyone is on the same page. "This is the point of our work in this department and this is how we do it." When I was a director of HR, I wrote a statement about the purpose, focus, and values of the HR department. I would review it with new hires and annually with the whole staff. It made explicit my view of what the work of the department was and how I expected the work to be done—both in manner and by tasks (e.g., with a smile and returning calls within twenty-four hours). It was a focus of conversation and feedback for my staff. Without explicit discussion about **how** we're going to work together, how can a leader hold an employee accountable for anything more than specific tasks?

With a purpose statement and conversation I could say, "Tell me how you showed our commitment to customer service this week." Most importantly, with a clear direction established by the leader, every member of the team knows that everyone else is working for the same goals; there will be less confusion or cross-purposes in their work. And if there is confusion, it gives you and the team members a place to start a conversation. "We're all working to support the employees, right? So, I'm concerned about how we responded to that call about a leave of absence. Can we talk about how we could do that better, as a department?"

While playing quadruple solitaire is fun, there were no consequences of "winning the least"; we were playing for different goals, yes, but we were really playing to have fun together. The difference for your team, however, is that playing for different goals can be devastating for your team and the organization. Make sure that every player on your team is working for the same goal and has the same definition of winning.

Coaching Corner

- Are you clear about the goals of your department and how you want them to be reached?
- Are there areas in your work or your life where you wonder if you're working for the same goal as those around you?
- Are you comfortable with how you're playing the game? Are you doing anything that is out of alignment with your values?

UNDERVALUED TEAM MEMBERS: INTROVERTS AT WORK

Our society and our workplaces idolize extroverts. We see leaders as the charismatic people who inspire others to follow them. We see movie stars and sports heroes as ultimate success stories. We expect successful people to be gregarious and outgoing and quick thinking.

At meetings, when decisions need to be made, we usually throw open the discussion for ten to fifteen minutes, during which time people often talk over each other, and if disagreements arise, then the participants speak louder and try to convince the other side why their solution is superior. At the end, either the leader will make a decision on what they've heard, or it will be put to a vote.

All the while, there are probably one or two quiet people in the room who are not speaking up. No one pays any attention to them. Those quiet people are the introverts who are listening intently to the exchange. If given a few minutes of quiet, they could most likely concisely and clearly lay out the pros and cons of the decision in a thoughtful summary and tell everyone their considered opinion on the best decision. Too often, however, there is no room for this kind of listening and analysis.

In her book *Quiet: The Power of Introverts in a World That Can't Stop Talking*, Susan Cain describes how some businesses actively hire for extroverted qualities, and as a result, over time, there is no one left to say, "Wait a minute, let's think about this."

Every organization needs a mix of personality and thinking styles to ensure that decisions and processes are not rushed or one-sided. Too many staffing problems happen when managers overlook concerns or act too quickly. They overlook concerns because they don't have time for them; they don't hear the quietly stated problem or they have intentionally or unintentionally trained people to not bring up issues. They act too quickly when they simply react in the moment without having the whole story or thinking about the consequences of their actions.

One of the main differences between introverts and extroverts is how we focus. In general, introverts have a stronger internal focus and therefore they are more likely to think before they speak. They process information in a more time-consuming deliberate fashion, act calmly, and are comfortable alone, taking time to connect and warm up to people, preferably in small group settings. When they have expended energy, introverts seek quiet (often alone) time to recharge, whereas extroverts often seek activity with others to recharge.

Introverts at work are more likely to:

- ✓ ask thoughtful questions
- ✓ recognize what's not working
- ✓ think in a complex, nuanced fashion
- ✓ show empathy and strong listening skills
- ✓ stick with difficult problems

As leaders, introverts have been shown to be better supervisors for engaged employees because they invite participation and support innovation and healthy risk-taking. In addition, they don't jump to conclusions without considering the facts. They go for the win-win solutions, consider the impact of their words and actions on others, and stay focused on the mission, vision, and values instead of jumping on the next big fad.

All of these traits can add value to a work group. This is not to say that extroverts don't also add value to a team. Everyone knows the values of extroverts. It is not that introverts are better or worse than extroverts or vice versa. Rather, workplaces benefit from a balance and diversity of thinking and interaction styles. Yet typically, workplaces are more prone to hire, support, encourage, and promote extroverts, while often losing sight of the value of introverts.

I want to remind you, as supervisors, that there is an important place in any work group for people who might process information differently, who make connections in a nondominant manner, and who don't talk loud or fast but still have important ideas to contribute.

Don't overlook the quiet members of your staff. And if you are a quiet one, know that you are not alone and that you bring value to your work in your own quiet, thoughtful way.

Coaching Corner

- Do you consider yourself to be more of an introvert or an extrovert? How have you noticed this working for you or against you?
- How do you tend to act when you work with someone who focuses and acts differently than you do? Have you noticed how they react to you? Make a note to notice this kind of interaction in your next meeting.
- How are decisions made in your organization? Do you feel confident that every voice is considered when group decisions are made?

MAKING ROOM FOR INTROVERTS

Some of the most cherished work standards don't work for introverts. Expectations of consistent, immediate responses, an emphasis
on group work, and decision-making processes in which the loudest
and most persistent people "win" are some common practices that
play to an extroverted style. As a supervisor, I encourage you to look
beyond standard practices and consider how to make room for different kinds of thinking and being in your work group. I want to
offer a few ideas about how to make room for the voice and qualities
of the quiet ones. Here are some practices that can build a culture
and managers who are welcoming to introverts—and extroverts too.

- ✓ **Give interview candidates a peek at the questions.** Introverts perform better when they have some
  idea of what to expect. Giving every candidate the interview questions five minutes before the interview starts
  will give them the same advantage but will help even
  the playing field for introverts who can be more present
  and thoughtful as a result of having been given time to
  digest the questions. It's not that introverts can't think
  on their feet, they just do it differently than extroverts.

- ✓ **Give people time to ponder.** Send out meeting
  agendas a day ahead of time if there are going to be
  discussion items. The introverts in the group will
  have time to think about the topic and will be more
  likely to come prepared to discuss options and ideas.
  Practice this with individuals too: "I'd like to
  hear some ideas from you about how we could
  improve our customer service. Let's discuss this at
  our next one-on-one meeting." Or "Think about how
  this could have gone better. Let's meet tomorrow at
  two o'clock to discuss it."

✓ **Build in solitary work time as well as group time.** Group work is fine but give people some solitary work time also. The whole team will function better. Brainstorms are exponentially better when people come together to share ideas after generating lists on their own. Use this practice to play to everyone's strengths. Introverts don't need to be left alone all the time, but they do need some alone time to think and process their ideas and feelings.

✓ **Build a culture that supports downtime.** Many work cultures now are 24/7. Make it clear that it is not only okay to take breaks and vacations but that it is expected. Model that expectation. Don't be the workplace that gives lip service to downtime but then sends e-mails at three in the morning and then another one at six saying, "I haven't heard back from you yet."

Your workplace will function better when people have real time off, on a regular basis. People work better when they can shut off their work brains for hours at a time. It's important to note here that a recent study showed that happy employees were 31 percent more productive at work.

✓ **Train people to facilitate meetings.** Introverts often have a hard time being heard in meetings. This can be addressed by training people to facilitate the meetings. You may normally run the staff meetings but that is different from actively facilitating. Find a way to train some (or all) staff in basic facilitation skills, like how to stop cross-talking and how to ask for input without putting people on the spot. The facilitation role can be something you do or it can be rotated on a regular (e.g., weekly) basis among the meeting participants. Then everyone will be more thoughtful about how to include others in the discussion.

✓ **Create policies that give clear guidance about problem-solving.** Don't wait to hear about problems until they become large problems. Build clear policies and practices that tell people what kinds of things you want to hear about, when you want to hear about them, and how you want to hear about them. Who should and can they report to? It is especially important to let staff know who they should talk to if their supervisor is the one acting inappropriately. Without clear policies, introverts might not bring up concerns until they are big and problematic.

Also, train everyone in healthy conflict and basic conflict resolution skills. This will save countless hours lost to interpersonal conflicts. It would also be great to train people about personality styles, too, so they know that a different style doesn't mean worse, just different. When people understand how to work through differences in a productive manner, misunderstandings don't fester into problems that impact every member of the team.

✓ **Expand the vision of what a leader looks like.** Talk about quiet leaders. Acknowledge the employees who offer quiet and effective solutions or ideas. Work with the organization to recognize quiet leaders and mentor them as well as the extroverted ones. Open leadership trainings for anyone who is interested in applying.

Dr. Seuss once said, "I love writing for children but en masse they terrify me." He was an introvert—can you tell? Make room for introverts to offer their skills, ideas, and practices to the workplace. The reward of having all voices at the table will be well worth the effort.

Coaching Corner

- Whether you are more of an introvert or an extrovert, what is your image of a leader? Which of the qualities that occur to you are associated with extroversion and which ones relate to introversion?
- If you are an introvert, is there a way you can claim your seat at the table in a strong and assertive manner while still being true to your type? How can you embody your own approach and skills of leadership? If you are going to meetings led by others, can you request that meeting agendas be sent out early or that meetings have a facilitator? Can you plan breaks in meetings so there is downtime in between productivity sessions?
- If you are an extrovert, what can you do to actively include introverts in discussions, whether in groups or in one-on-one meetings?

The 31 percent more productive quote is adapted from The Happiness Choice (Wiley 2013), by Marilyn Tam, Ph.D. https://www.linkedin.com/pulse/20140121000342-1291685-productivity-hacks-happy-people-are-productive-people retrieved 1/17/16

WORKING AND PLAYING FOR THE TEAM

As a baseball fan, I am often struck by the way that individual players defer to the decision of the team's manager. When I became an active fan and started watching more games, I would watch San

Francisco Giant's manager Bruce Bochy go out to the mound to tell the pitcher he was finished for the day. I could sometimes see the disappointment on the pitcher's face. I saw one guy shake his head, another mouth the word "no," and yet another say, "What are you doing here?"—but they would all hand the ball over and leave the field without further comment.

This demonstration of putting the team first is one that any manager can work toward. The point isn't that the players obeyed Bochy simply because he was the boss. They submitted their own glory, judgment, and will to his decisions because they knew it was for the good of the team. This was possible because Bochy had built a unified team that understood and joined forces for the common good, thus becoming bigger than one player's skills or limits. You could see the emphasis on the team's well-being in all the players, but what happened on the pitcher's mound was most obvious to those of us watching at home.

This kind of alignment behind the mission, vision, and goals of any work group does not happen by accident, nor does it happen through coercion. It happens through intentional focus and consistent talk and action. It cannot just appear in time for the playoffs, or the latest crisis in any given work group. It is built over time and it is a process led by the manager.

The priority of the team's goal over individual aims ensures that every player is aligned with the mission of the team. This alignment is evident when every person stands behind the group's decisions and their common goals, even if it may be difficult or even counterintuitive at times. Sometimes the manager has to bench the best player, discipline someone who was successful but broke the rules getting there, or even fire a popular team member who is unwilling to contribute to the greater good.

To align the various members of a team requires talking about your mission, vision, and values frequently, not just when people are hired. It means making these vague ideals real. Every person on your team should be able to draw a clear line connecting their job and the organization's mission, without hesitation. Talking pro-actively about what teamwork looks like for your team, and what it doesn't look like, is another important practice in building the team-focused identity.

Just like Bruce Bochy leading the Giants, you want to be the supervisor who leads your team in a way that promotes every staff member playing their best game for the good of the team.

Coaching Corner

* When did you last experience the feeling of all-hands-on-deck teamwork? (Whether it was at work or somewhere else.) How did you feel during the experience? After the experience?
* When did you last talk about your organization's mission with your team? What can you do to actively emphasize mission, vision, and team goals for the entire team?
* Are there any actions you are rewarding that actually recognize individual success **over** team cooperation? (e.g., Giving a raise to someone who ignores policies, or praising the person who intimidates team members.)

Lessons from Baseball

1. **"All Together; Stronger Together."** Baseball is a team sport: batting alone won't win the game and neither will pitching or fielding. It takes all the players all doing their best to get the job done. It takes the players, coaches, trainers, managers, fans, and all the behind-the-scenes people to build a successful team. And when every component of that equation works together, it is synergistic: the whole is much more than the sum of its parts. The entire team is stronger together, which is the Giant's tagline.

   Underlining this unified approach often can help a team build cohesion and appreciation for every aspect of the organization's work. Too often, administration is treated like a distant relative who must be tolerated. Make sure every team member knows the importance of their own work as part of the whole, as well as how every other position supports the whole.

2. **Mission First.** Baseball jerseys have the team name on the front and the individual player's name on the back. One of the Giants team slogans was: "Play for the front of the jersey, not the back," meaning that they were playing for the team, not themselves.

   This slogan is a great quick reminder that it's all about the mission—the mission of the team and the mission of the organization. Each participant must put their ego aside and offer their individual accomplishments in service to the mission.

3. **Mindfulness.** Many people complain that baseball is boring—and it can be; but it is also a great example

continued ⇨

of every player on the field practicing mindfulness whether they know it or not. Each player has to be relaxed, attentive, and present at all times. They may go for innings without being involved in a play but at any moment a ball going 120 miles per hour could come flying at them and they better be ready. Their safety, career, and the success of the team depend on it. And they have to be aware of all that's going on all over the field: how many outs, how many strikes, who's on base, what might happen, and how might it impact them. They have to keep all the rules in mind so if a ball does come their way, they know exactly what they have to do with it—with no time to think about it. And they have to know their teammates and communicate with them across the field.

This is what training and practice does. You want your team to know their jobs so well that they will respond appropriately. The more people can be relaxed, attentive, and present, the better work everyone will do.

4. **Multiple Viewpoints.** When there is a close call in baseball, one team or the other has the option to call for a replay review. They call a central office in New York City and the experts review the play, from multiple camera angles, to determine what happened and whether the call the umpire made was correct.

It is important for every supervisor, and every organization, to remember that no one person can possibly hold the entire truth. Sometimes it takes multiple angles, visions, views, and perspectives to make sure you've got it right. Slow down and consider what others may see that you aren't seeing, and when you need to be willing to ask for help from other points of view.

5. **Have Fun.** One season the Giants had an "All Brandon Weekend" promotion in honor of the three Brandons on the team. That's just silly and fun. Plus, when you watch the team they seem to have fun together. When they won the World Series in 2012, one of the players said, "Hey, I get to play for my job. How great is that?" That's a great attitude to bring to work every day.

Having fun together is not a workplace requirement, but it sure helps. I'm not talking about goofing off and wasting time; I'm talking about a culture that appreciates fun and connection and laughter. That kind of culture makes people feel good about coming to work and that good feeling shows up in the quality of the work.

RAUCOUS GEESE

We heard the geese before we saw them. I was walking with a friend near my home one fall when we heard a flock squawking in the sky. They were still quite far away but we spotted them heading toward us. As they got closer we looked into the sky and saw that they were a fairly messy V. The left side of the V was four times longer than the right side. As they passed over us, the end of the long left side suddenly "sprinted" forward. It looked like twenty geese sped forward to take over the front of the V, while also turning the whole formation to the left. At the same time, other birds from the long left line split off and flew over to the right line, which met them halfway because the whole formation was now taking a hard left. By then, the squawking had stopped. It was as if they had communicated the plan, executed the plan, and now there was nothing urgent to talk about.

What we witnessed that day was much more than a dance where the leader fell back and was replaced by another goose. In fact, there is no clear leader or supervisor in this scene. So what can we learn from a hundred geese flying in a shifting formation?

✓ **Sometimes it's important to change directions.** Whether we're talking about an organization, a team, or an individual, there comes a time when we wonder if we're moving in the right direction. As soon as that wondering begins, pay attention. Ask questions. Tune into what is not working. Know what your criteria are for success and decide if you need to make adjustments to your plan.

✓ **It is necessary to make a plan.** You can't plan for every eventuality, but if you don't look ahead and make a plan, you and your team will simply keep doing the same thing over and over, even when it is no longer working. Talk to each other about how things are going (as individual members of the team and the team as a whole) and make a plan to adjust as necessary.

✓ **Everyone has his or her part in any change.** About 90 percent of those geese were ready and active in their change in direction and leadership. Could the same be said of your team and your organization? Is every employee clear what their role is during routine times and during change efforts?

✓ **Communication is critical.** When people don't know what's going on in an organization, they either make things up or put their heads in the sand. Communicate clearly with your staff so they know what's happening now, what's coming, and what you expect from them.

What struck me most about the geese I saw on my walk was their agility and their communication. Working as a team to accomplish a goal is a lot trickier than flying in a stable formation. In a work environment, there are constantly moving pieces and players. There has to be someone who is attentive to the bigger picture of goals, strategy, and implementation. There has to be someone ensuring team communication happens and that the team remains agile to respond to whatever needs arise. That someone is you!

Coaching Corner

- Think about a change you've made in the past—whether for yourself or your team. How did you know it was time? What were the initial signs that it might be time for a change and what made you sure enough to act?
- How and when do you take time to plan strategically for your team? Too often we're just doing what's in front of us. Set aside a time to look ahead and make a plan to guide you and your team over the next transition.
- Who on your team is thirsty for information and how can you communicate with them?

WORKING TOGETHER

One day I needed an incentive to do my strength training so I turned on the TV to distract me through my weights. I flipped to an old episode of *Project Runway*. The reality show is focused on clothing designers and this episode was a team challenge. You could tell immediately which team was going to win and which was going to lose. The winning team actually worked as a team, playing to each other's strengths and trusting one another. The other team couldn't even agree on how to divide the work. Their process was chaotic and ungainly. I started thinking about all the ways that team blew it in terms of the group process.

Here are three basic rules for group process that might come in handy—either when you find yourself on a reality show or during your next staff process:

✓ **Ground Rules.** Make them and use them. Ground rules are intended to build a structure for a group process so everyone can contribute. It is important to cover the basic ground rules like confidentiality and respect, but also consider ground rules about how you want to work together.

One helpful ground rule is to focus on how the group can move forward rather than backward. On reality TV shows, groups spend a lot of time looking at what happened in the past and blaming each other for the outcomes. When they do that they are not able to focus on the task at hand.

Another helpful ground rule is to clearly determine how decisions will be made. Discussing this ahead of time gives the group power before there are vested interests in any particular decision. Will the decision be made by majority? By the leader? By consensus? Plan for it.

Making ground rules can help any group build safety and process guidelines that help each person and the group be more effective together.

✓ **Leadership.** Groups need leadership, whether that leadership is claimed by one designated leader or a method of shared leadership. In work groups there is usually a designated person in charge, but that person may or may not be the actual leader for that group. The leader is the one who helps keep the group focused and functioning. The leader may be elected, designated, ad-hoc, or rotating, but without some kind of leadership, the group is most likely to function like a loose coalition rather than a focused constructive team.

✓ **Clear Purpose.** Without a clearly identified purpose, many groups flounder. Without a clear purpose people end up working at cross-purposes, or drifting in unnecessary directions with their work. It is quite common for people working together to have a different understanding about what they are doing and how they are going to accomplish it. A group needs a clearly identified and commonly understood purpose.

One of the teams participating in the team challenge on *Project Runway* didn't spend much time talking about their group process but they did spend time facing forward, following their leader, and reminding each other of their clear purpose. And then they spend time together celebrating their win.

Coaching Corner

- What do you see as your role in facilitating group processes for your team? Did you decide on that role or did it just happen?
- How would you state the purpose of your team's work? Are you confident that everyone knows that?
- Have you ever jumped into a situation only to realize that you had no plan and limited resources? Reflecting on that situation now, what could you have done differently to set yourself up for a better process?

CHAPTER 10:

How You Meet

MEETING STRUCTURE

There are three cement sculptures in my front yard created by my husband. To create them, he first made a metal framework (an armature) as the basic shape, over which he applied the cement. I was struck by the magic of the completed artwork; the rough metal armature he started with was no longer visible but you knew it was there holding the shape. It took work to turn the armature into artwork, and yet even as a non-sculptor, I could see that if you just built onto that foundational structure, you would arrive at some version of the finished form.

Historically, I have resisted structure in my life. When I have tried to set up an exercise program, when I have tried to establish a time management system to get my work done more efficiently, and even when I have tried to schedule regular meetings with the people I supervise, I always ran into resistance—from me! As soon as I told myself to do something, I rebelled as if I were thirteen years old and facing a homework assignment.

After my husband created the sculptures, I made the connection that designing effective frameworks was the beginning of creating finished products. I could see more clearly the power and purpose of structure. If I established the structure and built on it, I would have the final product I wanted in the same way my husband had ended up with a beautiful sculpture. Using this metaphor as a new approach to examine my resistance and relationship to structure, I was able to uncover assumptions, counteract old beliefs, and anchor new practices. I befriended structure.

Structure can be a powerful support to supervision. Often in supervision, as in life, days and schedules become so full we rarely accomplish all the goals we intend to. Crafting a solid "armature" to which your tasks cohere can support you to more efficiently arrive at those goals.

One of the important foundations of good supervision is to have regularly scheduled meetings with each person you supervise. This ensures that you take time to check in with everyone on your team. In this meeting, you can give each other updates on projects, talk about upcoming events and assignments, clarify expectations, and give timely feedback on work performance.

You can also listen. This is a crucial part of the structure. When the people you supervise know that they have a regular time to meet with you, they can save questions and concerns that are not urgent. They can talk through problems with you, and get direction and support to move forward. Once these meetings are regular, they will typically decrease unscheduled interruptions in your day, and will reduce confusion and mistakes. Employees will be able to do their own work with more efficiency and effectiveness. Even though you must invest time up front, once this basic structure of your supervision is in place, it will save you time in the long run.

Ideally this is structured as a weekly meeting time. Depending on the person and the job, less frequent—but still regular—time periods might work (monthly is the least often I would recommend for any job). The most essential component about these meetings is consistency. It is important that these meetings are scheduled and not just spur of the moment when you have a few extra minutes. When you schedule the meetings it underlines their importance and it gives both you and your staff time to prepare for the meeting.

You can also enact structure for yourself with respect to the content of the meetings. Use a standard list of questions to remind yourself about the topics that are important to cover. Ask what's working, what's not working, and what's next? "What's next" covers what is coming up in their next week as well as their top priorities moving forward.

After your specific questions, always ask, "Anything else?" If the person brings something up, ask the final question again, "Anything else?" This keeps the door open and lets each person you're meeting with know that you want to hear whatever is on his or her mind. Remember that these are two-way conversations so during the "what's working" section, be sure to acknowledge any specific successes since the last time you met. During the "what's next" section, take time to review any expectations or procedures that are necessary for the priorities they are facing.

Remembering the armatures underpinning the sculptures gave me a way to befriend and integrate a stronger, clearer structure into my own work. Having regular and dependable meetings with those you supervise is an important part of achieving the best outcomes for your organization. It takes motivation and time to initially form this framework, especially if it's a change from the way you normally approach your work. However, it will make all the difference in how you and your team work together to create beautiful work!

Coaching Corner

- How have you historically responded to structure? Does this response work for you or against you?

- How can you use structure to ensure that you spend your time on the important issues and not only the urgent issues?
- What are some things you always intend to do but never get around to because work and life get in the way? Is there a way that a structure could help make those things happen?

STATE OF THE TEAM

Every January the president delivers a State of the Union address. Every once in a while, consider doing the same. Step back and have a discussion with your team about how you're doing. This might happen at the start of the year, the end of a project, or your anniversary date. Pick a date and use it to do an informal assessment about how your work is progressing. Think about it as an annual checkup.

Are you and your team on the same page? Are you all rowing in the same direction? Your team may be just one person you supervise, a department, or an entire organization. However you define your team, are you working toward the same goals? Do you have the same priorities? Are you staying clear about the mission and how the daily work connects to it?

Here's an exercise to generate conversation in this area. Meet with each person individually and have them write down their top three to five priorities. At the same time, you write down your list of their top three to five priorities. Then compare notes (in a calm, curious, nonjudgmental way). Talk about each of your answers. Are you on the same page?

People who've tried this exercise reported that they and their staff did not always have the same lists, and when they did, they were often not in the same order. Ideally you would come up with the same lists, which would indicate that you are both clear about the purpose and priorities of that job. But if you don't, it's still important information. What does that tell you? Does it mean you are out of synch, or has something changed and one of you didn't realize it? Does it mean that day-to-day reality does not match theoretical priorities? Or does it mean that the employee does not understand the most important aspects of her job? Whatever answers are revealed, the important thing is to talk about them. The conversation that follows the exercise is more important than the exercise itself.

Suppose your employee reports that customer service is the number one priority and you write that it's number three. First of all, it's great that it is on both of your lists. So then talk about it. What do you consider to be more important and why? What does the employee think is the most important priority? Maybe a task that you put as number one is really the number one priority for your own job and not theirs. Again, the conversation is what matters.

Make this a conversation that opens things up. It's not about getting the right answer, but about what the answers tell you about your work together. Let this be a conversation that builds the relationship and moves your work forward.

This is a chance to clarify and correct course if in fact someone you supervise is focusing on the wrong goals or priorities. Acknowledge them for the priorities and goals they listed, and then talk about what needs to change. Give room to talk about challenges and also about what strengths each of you brings to the work.

Make this annual conversation something that matters. If you haven't already established a regular ongoing meeting time with every person you supervise, make this the first and then keep it going.

Establishing a set time to have this big-picture conversation can help keep yourself and your team on track. Make it fun. Make it special. Bring snacks. Highlight it on the calendar. It's not an evaluation; it's a checkup. The health of your team may depend on it.

Coaching Corner

- Can you clearly articulate the top three priorities for your team and the work of each member of the team? If you can't, it's not fair to expect your team to hold or execute those priorities.
- How can you structure conversations to ensure that the emphasis is on what you need to discuss and not on "getting the right answer"?
- What time of year would make the most sense for you to do your team's state of the team discussion? How can you make sure it happens?

MAKE TIME FOR WHAT YOU VALUE

I once had a friend, let's call her Betty, who said all the right friendship things when we were together. At the end of each visit, she would profess her love and appreciation for our friendship and vow that we "must not wait so long to get together next time" as she rushed off to her next appointment.

A few months later I would realize that I hadn't heard from Betty. So I would call up and after another month or so we would meet for lunch. This cycle played out many, many times before I realized that Betty never called me. Once I noticed this, I also saw that when we got together the entire conversation focused on Betty. She told me what she was doing, who she was dating, how her work was, and what trips she was planning. I noticed that she literally did not once ask me how I was doing. Except for the last few minutes of every visit when she expressed her intense interest in our friendship, it did not seem to matter to her that I was there. When I tried to talk to her about this she apologized, but nothing changed.

Betty did not act like she valued our friendship even though she said she did, and probably even thought she did. Eventually, I let her and the friendship go, in part to make time for what I valued, and in part because I could see that she did not actually honor our friendship despite her words.

We've all heard that time is money but even more directly time is value. We make time for what we value. In our hectic, overwhelmed, nonstop days, if we don't intentionally plan for quality time with our staff or our children, partners, and friends, it doesn't happen. Periodically, we must stop and look at our priorities in order to live the lives we intend to live and to do the work we intend to do. The line between time, values, and intentionality is a clear one.

Making time for what we value is hard to do in the workplace. I hear about people feeling overwhelmed and overworked in every organization I visit. "More work, less time" is the constant refrain. With that as the default, it is hard to be the one voice calling for time out. Yet, in the long run, this is the voice that speaks most directly to leadership.

Taking time to identify the values of the organization and your department is also important work. Without recognizing what guides your work, you cannot be effective in it. You cannot make time for what you do not recognize. Values are what distinguish the important from the unimportant tasks. Values can be our touchstones when we are making decisions. Which decision is most aligned with my value of quality, for example? Or teamwork? Or efficiency?

As a leader, you must consciously set aside time to spend on the non-immediate but important concerns that reflect your values. Otherwise, you will find yourself just reacting to whatever situations arise. It is only through intentionally making time for what you value, such as developing relationships, reflecting on your own actions, refocusing yourself (and the team) on the mission, and attending to supervision, that you can be the leader who demonstrates values and therefore stands apart. Your organization may be successfully completing tasks and producing results—for now. Without attention to what matters most, however, you might lose focus and get swept off course.

Every organization and team has a core set of values. Sometimes those values are identified in a handbook or on a plaque on the wall but even if they are not, you can identify them by how people act and what they give their time and attention to. And sometimes, as was the case with Betty, those operating values do not match up with the spoken values of the organization. It might be a written value that teamwork is a value but in reality individual actions are recognized and rewarded. In this case, employees aren't supported to take the time for teamwork and they're taught indirectly that it's not really important in this organization's culture.

It's essential to build in systems that hold the space for values. Without a system, the short-term expedient is going to triumph over quality, profit is going to win out over ethics, and ambition is going to overrule teamwork.

When there are clearly identified values and attention paid to how these values are implemented, then values such as quality, ethics, and teamwork have room to grow and shine. As a supervisor, it is your job to hold the space and time for the values of the team. Talk about them. Ask your staff how they demonstrated a certain value over the last week. Remind your team how your organization's values improve the work of the team and the organization in the long run.

As a leader, remind your organization to take time for values. Show your staff what is of core importance by structuring in time for what you value. Make your work together intentional. It's about holding the space for values.

Coaching Corner

- What does your organization value? Are those values both clearly articulated and actually held up as worthy of time and attention?
- What value does supervision hold for you, for the people you supervise, and for your organization? Does the time you spend on supervision reflect that value?

- When you think of "holding the space for values," do you feel resistance? Does it sound "soft" to you? Explore any resistance you have and see what information it has for you.
- What needs attention in your work and/or life in order to ensure quality? When can you schedule time for this? What are you willing to give up to ensure that your work and life is one of quality and intention?

TAKE FIVE MINUTES TO PLAY TOGETHER

As a supervisor, one of your primary jobs is to develop and support your team, whether your team is one or one hundred. Essential factors in this endeavor include being clear on the team's mission; having clear goals, roles, and responsibilities; and helping people be connected so that they can work well together. Taking time to play as a group is one of the most effective ways I've found to implement this connection.

In third grade, I had an assignment to draw a picture of heaven. I drew a girl standing in front of a huge closet full of games. I described heaven as a place where there were games to play and always someone willing to play with you.

I have not outgrown my childhood vision of play as heavenly. In my work life, as well as my personal life, I have seen how games set a tone that relaxes people. Games make it safer for people to be themselves. Laughter erupts. People who might not have much to say to each other interact and connect. People who have divergent views on life, politics, and religion can still play together, and through playing together can gain practice in interacting on common ground or for common goals.

In my work as a Human Resources Director, I included games and/or playing in every training and meeting I facilitated. I started every group activity with a "question of the day." Over and over, I saw magic happen, and usually it was only through dedicating a few short minutes to this kind of exchange. A room that felt heavy because it was full of people who were stressed and overwhelmed became lighter. People talked to others whom they did not work with directly. People became human to one another. The boss was not just the boss; she became someone who used to play with fire-flies. Staff members popped balloons and laughed together.

There is a connection formed in playing that is unique and powerful and can last long after the fun and games are over. From a space of connection, people work together better, longer, and stronger. It feels safer to take risks. It feels possible to trust a teammate. The days don't seem as long and people don't feel as isolated. People share a common purpose and they share good times and fun together. People become more real to one another. Integrating fun into the workday doesn't need to detract from productivity or cost extra. In fact, if you want your employees to be innovative and pro-ductive and to think outside the box, then fun is essential.

I wrote my master's thesis on the topic of play at work. In my study, I found that work groups that took just a few minutes to play together in regular staff meetings experienced the following benefits:

- ✓ The participants got to know each other better.
- ✓ The participants built connections that nurtured their working relationships.
- ✓ The participants identified and accepted different styles and opinions of their coworkers.
- ✓ The play provided insights into others' behavior and provided some employees with an opportunity for self-reflection on their own behavior.

These results can have profound effects on the workplace over time. Self-revelation, connection, respect for differences, and insight into behaviors are all integral steps to the caring and flexibility that is required for work groups to become collaborative teams that respond fluidly to changes in their membership and the environment. Participants also simply had fun playing at work, and this impacted their general experience of work and the motivation they brought to their jobs. Play can make going to work each day more enjoyable.

As a supervisor, consider bringing a few minutes of play to your regular staff meetings. You and your team will get to know each other on a human level while also building connections that will boost their ability to work well together. Adding a few minutes of fun can make the work more enjoyable and more successful.

Coaching Corner

- Do you allow playfulness in your life? If you do, what do you gain from it? If you don't, why not?
- Do you have a belief that play and work don't mix? How did this idea develop for you? What if the opposite were really true?
- What could be gained by your team getting to know each other and playing together periodically?

Ten Game Ideas

Any play activity needs to happen within a supportive and safe environment. Make it clear people can pass or sit out if they need to but that you encourage participation and that this activity is simply about having fun together. Any competition is trivial and irrelevant; the point is simply to play together.

1. **Question of the Day.** Start each meeting with a get-to-know-you question. Ask each person to answer the question in a quick direct answer. Participants can simply say "pass" if they don't want to play. Whatever other questions you come up with, make sure they are not too personal.

> What was your first car?
> What did you love to play when you were a kid?
> What's your favorite part of your job?
> What's a good movie you would recommend?
> What kind of music do you love to listen to?
> What were you doing in 2002?

2. **Waves.** This is a quick activity to loosen people up and get them present for meetings. It's an adaptation of the "wave" done at sporting events. Arrange everyone in a circle of 8-15 people. Start with the traditional ballpark wave of raising your arms, one after another, so that the motion waves around the room. Let it go around the circle once or twice until people get the hang of it. Then when it comes back to the first person, they start another motion (e.g., lifting their right foot or moving their arm in a circle over their head). Then when the

continued ⇨

wave comes back to them again, the next person does another motion. Go around the circle until everyone has a chance to start a movement.

3. **Birthday Arrangement.** Do this activity as one group or as teams of ten to twenty. Ask everyone to arrange themselves in order of their birth dates (not years) from January through December, without talking. This one can be adapted by having people arrange themselves alphabetically by middle name, for example. Whatever the task is, the challenge is to arrange themselves in order without talking (gesturing is okay).

4. **Would You Rather?** Have people gather in an open space in front of you. You will pose a few "would you rather" questions. Explain to the group that to answer, they will move to stand on one side of the room or the other. As you ask the "would you rather" question, point out which side of the room is which answer. Here are a few I have used, or make up your own. Make sure there is nothing too personal or too divisive.

> Would you rather work on a spreadsheet or rewrite a letter?
> Would you rather eat ice cream or cookies?
> Would you rather swim or jog?
> Would you rather be confronted by an angry coworker or a hurt coworker?
> Would you rather be on stage as an actor or a part of the stage crew?
> Would you rather have more time off or more retirement money?
> Would you rather take four short breaks during the day or one long break?

Would you rather wake up early or sleep
   in late?
Would you rather go out dancing or go to
   a movie?
Would you rather receive public or private
   recognition? Or a little of both? (This last
   question adds an option for people to
   stand in the middle.)

5. **Scavenger Hunt.** Break into teams of two to eight. (You
    need at least two groups.) Remind people to be safe—
    no running. Each team picks a captain who comes up to
    the front and retrieves a paper lunch bag with a list in it.
    Everyone has five minutes to see which group can collect
    the most items on the list first. (Token prizes, such as a
    bag of chocolate kisses, to the winning team are optional
    and fun.) List ten to twelve items such as:

    a quarter
    a business card
    a #2 pencil
    something green
    a large paper clip
    directions to or for something
    a photo of an animal
    a non-yellow Post-it
    something that makes music
    a symbol of the work of your organization

6. **Proverbs.** Have the team come up with a list of old sayings
   or proverbs.* Then invite sub-teams to pick three or four
   from a hat and turn the proverbs on their heads. What if the
   proverb revealed some wisdom that was quite different

continued ⇨

from what the traditional proverb says, but still had some truth to it? What would that proverb be and what wisdom could it hold?

> For example:
> "Business before pleasure" might become:
>   "Enjoy your work and you'll have fun all
>   day long."
> "A stitch in time saves nine" might become:
>   "A stitch in time prevents you
>   from enjoying the sewing."
> Try it for yourself:
> "Every cloud has a silver lining," might become:

_____.

*It is important that each team choose their own proverbs so that the dominant culture does not overrule the diversity in the group. Don't assume that the proverbs you know are common to everyone.

7. **Baby Animals.** This is a fun group activity. The task is to match the name of an animal with its offspring (e.g., cow and calf). This game is different than others I've suggested so far because there is a definite "right" answer. However, as a supervisor, your job is to make sure this is a fun group activity, not a quiz.

Put up a flip chart with a list of eight to twelve adult animal words. Pass out a mixed-up list of matching baby animal words. Together the teams work to figure out which baby goes with which adult. (This might be done as one team or several, depending on the size of your group.) Make it lighthearted and fun; it's not about counting right and wrong answers. Don't put anyone on the spot. Start with some easy ones like dog and puppy, cat and kitten. Then move into harder ones, like fox and kit. People will know some and the others will be a process of elimination. Have people talk among themselves and call out their guesses. No counting; no prizes—just a fun group process to get people talking and connected. After five minutes are up, reveal the correct answers, and let the teams compare and react to what they came up with. As an alternative or another round, you can also use animals and their group names (e.g., wolf and pack).

Here are some combinations you can use:

ADULT ANIMAL	BABY ANIMAL
alligator	hatchling
ape	baby
bat	pup
bear	cub
deer	fawn
goose	gosling
frog	tadpole
goat	kid
grasshopper	nymph
horse	foal
jellyfish	ephyna
kangaroo	joey
llama	cria
owl	fledgling
oyster	spat
platypus	puggle
squirrel	kit
swan	cygnet
tiger	whelp
turkey	poult

continued ⇨

8. People Scavenger Hunt. This is fun for a larger group. Start by making a list of identifying characteristics. Then make a copy of this list for each participant. Instruct each person to get a signature from someone in the group who meets each category. Each person can only sign once on any given sheet of paper. Either the first person who gets all the lines filled in or whoever has the most lines filled in correctly after a pre-set period of time wins.

> Someone with a July birthday
> Employee here less than six months
> Employee here for more than twelve years
> Someone with a middle name that starts
>   with A, M, or P (and what is it)
> Someone who has more than one dog
> A native of your state or city
> Someone wearing blue
> Someone with three or more siblings
> Someone whose first car was a Honda
> Someone who has snacks at their desk

9. Stand Up If You . . . This is a quick, fun icebreaker. Create a list of questions or use the samples listed here. Invite people to stand up if they've done something or fit a category as you read it out loud. This is a great get-to-know-each-other activity and can lead to revelations and conversations. Start with an invitation to play that allows for opting out. "I invite you to play but of course if you want to pass you can at any time."

> Stand up if you:
> Ate ice cream last weekend
> Have ever lived in New York, Chicago, or

Los Angeles (pick large cities far away
    from your location)
Have ever skydived or parasailed
Have ever taken dance lessons
Collect anything
Have ever gone scuba diving
Have ever been to China
Have ever played in a band
Have ever had three or more pets at once
Have ever been to Yellowstone
Have two or more siblings
Have ever broken a bone
Like to read mysteries

10. **A fun reality check!** This takes a little preparation and sleuthing from you before game time. Walk around the office and note ten to fifteen items that are in plain sight. Then put together a quiz to wake people up to how much they walk right by every day.

Samples might be:

What brand of toilet paper do we use?
What poster is near the watercooler?
Who has a Scooby-Doo figure on his or
    her desk?

Have people fill out the quiz on their own. Then just read the questions out loud, ask for guesses, then share the right answer. Don't put anyone on the spot by asking them what they answered. As always, make it fun!

THOUGHTS ON LEARNING

I recently learned a new card game and was immediately aware of some anxiety coming up that I might forget the rules or do something stupid. And soon I did both. Once I made the mistake, and nothing bad happened, I was able to relax and remember that mistakes are usually part of learning a new skill. In fact, I realized that when I forgot a rule or made a mistake, it helped me learn the rules better for the next time I played the game.

Learning is a part of every job. It is important to remember that learning sometimes produces anxiety and that people learn best when it is safe to make mistakes. We are all learners when we start a new job and hopefully will continue learning for the duration of any job. We can learn about what's new in our field, as well as about what's working and not working in our current job, and how to get along together to be more effective in our work. None of this happens in a vacuum.

Learning styles vary from person to person. Some people learn by reading, others by listening, and still others by doing or teaching. Others learn by doing research or through good, old-fashioned trial and error. But this knowledge remains theoretical until we try it out. For instance, I can read about changing a tire or watch someone do it, but until I actually try it myself it is unproven knowledge.

Adult learning theory teaches us that adults learn best when the subject is related to the real world, not theoretical or abstract. We all want to know, "How does this apply to me?" And in a team setting, "How does this apply to us?" Adults also need to be engaged and active in their learning.

When the training involves the whole team it can also connect the team through a shared experience, build a common language around the topic, and help people learn to work more effectively together.

So when you are teaching new skills or procedures to your staff, remember these lessons about learning:

✓ Make it safe.
✓ Make it relevant.
✓ Make it interactive.
✓ Give the information in various ways to allow for different ways of learning.
✓ Make it a team-building opportunity.

Coaching Corner

- When have you had a good learning experience? What made it work for you?
- When you offer directions to the people you work with, how do you adjust your instructions to work for different learning styles?
- Is there anything you've learned on your own recently that would benefit from being shared? Is there a way you can build an opportunity for sharing learning at work?

ONLINE LEARNING IS NOT A PANACEA

In the spirit of complying with mandated trainings, there has been a trend to conduct trainings online. Often the content is fine, and I know you can't beat the convenience, but there are other factors that matter at least as much as convenience. I have had the opportunity to go through an online training, sitting in my office eating a sandwich while I clicked through lists and graphics, videos and quizzes. I then reflected on the differences between that experience and an in-person training I attended on the same topic which had large and small groups listening, talking, and laughing together.

When people in an organization are in a room working together to learn and improve the ways things work, there is a lot of energy. Human connection gets lost when people sit alone in front of their computers. Adults learn by doing—on their own and with other people. Trainings that are done in person can be fun and interactive. Taking an online quiz may be technically "interactive," but it is in a flat and one-dimensional manner that includes no one else. People can easily "phone it in," by going through the motions but they don't have to think about applying the knowledge to themselves or their work situations. This likely means any knowledge gained will not be retained beyond the short term. True interaction happens when people talk about real situations and their own thoughts and feelings, which makes it more likely that true learning will take place as well.

In addition, when a team does a training together, the participants build personal connections and team identity. "We did this training together." "Remember what we all learned in that training?" Depending on the topic, group training can build a common language and approach to a subject matter. When I do my supervision trainings, the whole group learns a common approach that can then be supported and reinforced by the team.

In a real-time training, there is an opportunity to make things relevant. There is time for questions and answers. People can ask questions that are specific to their organization or situation. When I do sexual harassment training and we talk about the need to protect employees from external dangers, we can speak about what those dangers might look like for the particular group in the room. I develop scenarios that are specific to their industry and organization. When you do trainings at your site, you can tie them into your actual policies and procedures. How does this work **here**? What does **your** policy say? What situations have **you** actually dealt with?

When organizations choose to do an online training, it is hard to "sell" the training. No one can see the enthusiasm of the other team members. No one can see that senior management actively supports the training. Whether it's true or not, the perception is "We **have** to do this." It becomes something employees just want to cross off their lists.

Training is an important and ongoing component of organizational life. It can either help the team be stronger and more effective, or it can be an external requirement imposed on unenthusiastic participants. You, as the supervisor and leader, have a say in how it is delivered. Your enthusiasm, attention, and own experience of the training will be one of the most relevant factors in whether the learning sticks or not. Whether you do the trainings yourself, hire someone else, or even decide to do them online, find a way to make them real. Find a way to talk about the training topic as a group. Make it actually interactive. Make it fun!

Coaching Corner

- Think of a time when you attended a training. What was the format and how was your learning impacted by the format? What was the overall takeaway when the training was completed (i.e., not just what you learned but how you felt and how your work was impacted)?
- Is there any area of work in which you have been "phoning it in"? Is this a behavior you are modeling to others? Are there areas of your work where you are modeling enthusiasm?
- Are you being an active participant in the learning that happens among your team?
- If there are topics that are taught online to your team, how could you design a follow-up activity or conversation to bring the values of in-person training to the online activity?

THE POWER OF ROUTINES

Someone once asked His Holiness the Dalai Lama, "If you only had one word to describe the secret of happiness, and of living a fulfilling and meaningful life, what would that word be?" Without hesitating the Dalai Lama replied, "Routines."
—from *Less: Accomplishing More by Doing Less*
by Marc Lesser

When I first read this anecdote, it made me think about what I do routinely and what I'd like to do routinely. A routine is something we do automatically and consistently, without thought or decision. We brush our teeth, we brake when the light is red, we eat at certain times of the day, we go to work. These are activities that we don't have to decide to do every day. We've already made the decision that we will do these things and we don't have to think about it. For example, the people who make exercise a routine are the most successful at it.

The Dalai Lama says that routines are not just the secret to success but the secret to happiness! When I thought about how this could be true, I realized that there is a difference between those routines that are chosen by me versus those thrust on me by someone else or society. The former really could be the secret to happiness, while the latter can be a recipe for resistance and failure. Make sure that there is an element of choice in the routines you build and help your staff buy into the routines you want them to build.

In recognition of the power and potential of routines, what follows are essential routines to put in place in order to be an effective supervisor. Consider these a menu of options to consider. Don't let me stir up your resistance by telling you what to do. If you'd like to find a clear routine that you can build to be a better supervisor, these are some ideas. If one sounds good, choose to work on it and make it an internally driven routine.

✓ **Build regularly scheduled, consistent, one-on-one meetings with each member of your staff.** Make these meetings a priority by establishing a set time for them, whether they're weekly, biweekly, or monthly. Get them on your calendar and don't miss a standing meeting unless it is truly a rare and urgent matter.

✓ **Look for successes and address them.** Build a practice of noticing what is working. Say thank you. Say, "I appreciate the way you . . ." Say, "I want to acknowledge how effectively you . . ." Notice and comment, out loud, on what is working, in a specific and clear manner. Make it happen on a routine basis. Positive motivation tends to be much more effective than negative motivation.

✓ **Make clear agreements.** Spell out who is going to do what when. This is especially important when there has been confusion or misunderstanding in the past. End every meeting with agreements. End your one-on-one meetings with agreements. Make them explicit. An agreement requires a two-way conversation that ends up with two people understanding (and agreeing on) the same next steps. This is different than simply telling someone what to do.

✓ **Set a specific time to reflect on how you're doing.** Use a self-assessment tool, like the one in the sidebar, or just make time to thoughtfully sit in silence to help you check in about how you're doing. Put this on your calendar. The last Friday of the month at 4:30, for instance. Take ten to twenty minutes to think and make plans about what you want to focus on for the period of time until your next self-assessment.

Choose the routines you will use to be an effective supervisor. Choose routines to be successful, happy, and fulfilled.

Coaching Corner

- Which routines are working for you and which are not helping you to be the person (or supervisor) you want to be?

- Select one of the routines listed above (or another that you think of) that you do not already practice, or that you do not yet practice with the regularity of a routine, and make a plan about how you could incorporate it into your work. Find a way to acknowledge yourself once you start building the practice. (For example, put a star on your wall calendar to show your progress.) If you forget, just start up again.

- How do you react when you don't do what you committed to doing? Do you beat yourself up or shame yourself? What do you need to do to transform this reaction routine into a learning opportunity instead of a punitive response?

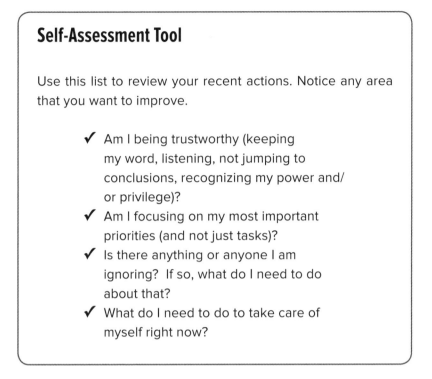

Self-Assessment Tool

Use this list to review your recent actions. Notice any area that you want to improve.

- ✓ Am I being trustworthy (keeping my word, listening, not jumping to conclusions, recognizing my power and/or privilege)?
- ✓ Am I focusing on my most important priorities (and not just tasks)?
- ✓ Is there anything or anyone I am ignoring? If so, what do I need to do about that?
- ✓ What do I need to do to take care of myself right now?

WHY DO I HAVE TO GO TO THIS MEETING?

Have you ever fallen asleep during a meeting? I've certainly been bored enough at times that I was on the verge of nodding off. Too many times meetings follow the same agenda every week with people only updating each other on things they already know. Or an item of discussion has already been beaten to death without any movement or conclusion, leaving people frustrated that no decisions have been made.

Welcome to the dysfunction of meetings in organizations! While it is important to have regular team meetings with your staff, it is equally important what happens in those meetings and how they are run. These factors make all the difference in terms of how effective they are and how people approach them.

Before you look at the meeting process, make sure you and your team can clearly identify who you are as a team and what you're about. What is the purpose of this group and how does this work support the mission of the organization? What are the essential outcomes that must be produced as a team? How will the team be successful? These questions might lead to a written team statement that can serve as both a guiding star and a touchstone for future decisions.

Consider the story of the team whose work was about finding jobs for hard-to-place clients (i.e., people with mental and physical disabilities). One year, the organization decided to reward this team with merit raises for those who found the most jobs for clients. Without a clear team statement to use as a touchstone for their work, the employees on this team inadvertently shifted the focus of the work to finding jobs for the most clients instead of focusing on those who found it most difficult to find jobs. If they had created a team statement and used it in regular meetings to guide their work, they could have recognized this shift earlier. As it was, at the end of the year their funding was in jeopardy because they had not met the specific goals they had committed to as an organization.

Once you have identified the purpose of your team, take time to identify the purpose of your meetings. Create space for your team to talk about what they find valuable in the meetings. Dedicate an entire meeting every year to this. When you give the team time to discuss what works and doesn't work about the current meeting structure, it creates ownership. Together you can forge a meeting plan that works for everyone, and everyone will be more motivated to attend and participate.

As the supervisor, you might lead the meetings and have a definitive voice about what any given meeting must include, but other staff should also be invited to voice what's important to them. Listen carefully to what they're telling you. Let them know ahead of time what kind of input you are asking for. Is this a vote about what future meetings will look like? Or are you asking your team for input that you'll consider when you decide what changes will be made, if any? To prevent confused expectations, be clear about the way this feedback about meetings will be used before the discussion happens. If, after listening and discussing, you decide you need to overrule the team majority, then be prepared to say why and how you've made that decision.

This annual meeting about the function and structure of your meetings can include discussion questions such as:

- ✔ Given the purpose of this team, what is the purpose of this meeting?
- ✔ What absolutely must happen in this meeting?
- ✔ What would be good to have happen in this meeting?
- ✔ Are relevant people in this meeting?
- ✔ How often do we need to meet?

The general answers to these questions should not change from meeting to meeting unless the team purpose changes. There may be shifts and different priorities from meeting to meeting but the overall purpose should remain firm. When the purpose and content of the meetings have been established, then you can move on to determining structure. Whatever structure you determine, the following roles within the meeting can help keep meetings timely and productive.

- ✔ Driver of Agenda
- ✔ Facilitator—one who will serve as the traffic cop for discussions and make sure everyone has a chance to participate
- ✔ Timer
- ✔ Note Taker/Agreement Catcher—one who will keep general minutes but also highlight agreements so there is a clear record of who committed to do what and when they committed to do it
- ✔ Game Warden—Someone who will bring a brief fun activity to start the meeting

Collaborating to examine your meeting process can help your team have much clearer, more effective, and more fun meetings that support their work together. And you, as the supervisor of that team, play the important dual role of being a leader and a participant at the same time. With the purpose and structure of the meeting established, they should be quicker and more engaging for everyone. And with the entire team involved in developing the meeting plan, people won't be wondering what they're doing there.

Coaching Corner

- When you think of boring meetings you've attended, what made them tedious? What was different about productive meetings you've attended? What made them work?
- As you've read this section, have you had any ideas about change you could make in your meetings?
- How open are you to hearing input about the meetings you run? What would you need to be able to sincerely welcome input while still holding the responsibility for any final decisions?

CHAPTER 11:

How You Think About You

AN ESSENTIAL SKILL: SELF-REFLECTION

Once I was asked what I considered to be the most important trait of a leader. My immediate answer was self-awareness. Without an awareness of how you act in the world, what your style is, and what pushes your buttons, you will be blindsided, ineffective, or incompetent. Or even worse, you will be manipulated by others who see your patterns while you don't.

How much time do you spend in personal reflection? Perhaps that sounds like a ridiculous question. Who has time to return their phone calls, never mind time to reflect on their actions? And yet, without some purposeful time to reflect and consider how you act in the world, you will not be a good leader.

Here's an example from my journey to leadership. When I was a new manager and a member of my organization's leadership team, I was hesitant. I didn't immediately share my ideas and there were times when I didn't trust myself. I was naïve in the ways of staff interactions and I was ripe for manipulation.

In one particular situation, I worked with someone who was friendly and extremely competent. After working with her for a few months, something shifted and I sensed that she was pushing me away and perhaps even lying to me. I asked her if everything was okay and she told me everything was fine. I believed her, even though my gut was telling me, "I don't think so." She was so good at her job that I wanted everything to be okay. As the tension mounted, I witnessed her making snide comments and not looking me in the eye. My intuition would read the signs and tell me to look at her actions. I continued to doubt my intuition to the point of being unwilling to examine the facts of the situation. Eventually this person left her job, but not before undermining my work and my reputation. After she was gone, I had a lot of damage to mend. Looking back a few months later, I could see my own part in the complicated relationship. I wanted to trust her and I wanted our working relationship to be a strong partnership. So I ignored the mixed messages and my own sense of unease, and by doing this I wasn't doing my job to its fullest. After this incident, I learned to trust my own awareness and to balance trust and optimism with a healthy dose of disaster preparation. I learned quickly that Human Resources is often about preparing for the worst that can happen while hoping and planning in order to bring about the best.

Here's another example where self-awareness was critical. I was coaching a supervisor who frequently had trouble with staff members who were people of color. Even though many of her employees had no previous problems in the workplace, this supervisor seemed to bring out the worst in them. One by one they would start to get warnings and poor evaluations. She saw problems where others had not. She was a kindhearted woman but she wanted things to be done her way. She wanted people to plan ahead the way she did, and for people to interact with others the way she did, specifically with a certain tone of voice and expression. When her staff did not mirror her style, she saw problems. The result of her supervision choices was that when she worked with people of color she was enacting a classic case of white privilege.

Her prejudices were not overt but they added up. I observed her in action and I noted her actions so I could point them out to her in a concrete manner. She used a directness of tone with people of color that she did not use with her white employees. I noticed intolerance for any deviation in style; she wanted things done her way, which was the mainstream, culturally dominant way, even if the alternative actions were effective and appropriate. And finally, when she met with these employees to explain the problems, she was often nervous, which manifested into an accusatory style that did not allow any dialogue.

Through coaching, this supervisor took time to reflect on my observations of her behavior. She practiced new ways of doing things and also learned a practice of self-observation that helped her be aware of her actions. Over time, she learned to make room for variations of style and to question herself about substance before she disciplined staff. She reflected on what led to her expectations and was able to change her approach and her actions.

These two examples were both difficult situations that took time to work through and required change. I had to learn to be more assertive and more aware, and the supervisor I was coaching had to learn to be more accepting of variations and look at her own internal assumptions. The level of self-awareness I am talking about is much more than knowing that you are an introvert or an extrovert, or whether you have a direct or accommodating style. That's a good start, but unless you learn and practice the fine art of deeper self-reflection, which will at times bring up painful truths, your habits and patterns of behavior will remain blind to you. Eventually, they will trip you up.

I know we are all staggeringly busy. The world is moving at a ridiculously fast pace. But without a few moments on a regular basis, you will not know yourself well enough to be an effective leader. Set up a regular, calendared "meeting" with yourself for five or ten minutes once a week to simply sit and ponder your actions during the preceding week. What worked? What didn't work? How could you have acted differently to be a more effective leader? Then take a few minutes in the midst of trouble to check in about your own actions. The self-awareness will make you a stronger and more effective leader.

Coaching Corner

- What assumptions do you make about people and situations without checking them out?
- Is there anything your intuition is telling you that you need to check against the facts?
- Were there emotionally charged points for you this week? What can these reactions tell you about yourself?
- How do you normally respond to conflict? Is this working for you? Is it working for the people with whom you have conflict?
- What is your part in a problem situation? When there is a problem or miscommunication, it is essential that a leader ask this question of themselves before they ask it of anyone else.

Reflection on Power and Privilege in the Workplace

Given that we all see the world through our own experience of the world, there are numerous opportunities at work to run into someone who sees things differently than you do. For those of us who are members of the dominant culture, we can simply look at that different perspective and choose to include it or not. People in the workplace who are not members of the dominant culture do not usually have the option to just ignore others' perspectives because the other perspective is often the default that makes the rules. Therefore when they bring a different point of view they are often seen as "making trouble" or "playing the race card" or "flaunting their sexuality."

This is not about politics or political correctness; it is about fairness in the workplace. When people make hiring or promotional decisions that are influenced by their membership in the dominant culture, whether consciously or not, they are perpetuating an unfair advantage that impacts every person in the work environment.

Consider:

- What parts of my experience place me in the dominant culture?
- What parts of my experience place me outside of the dominant culture?
- When I see people who are different than me acting in a way that challenges my perceptions, do I consider their views as viable or do I just dismiss them?
- What if their concerns were valid? What would that mean for our workplace and for my work as a supervisor?

continued ⇨

- When you hear someone say "That's just the way it is" (or hear yourself think it), ask yourself, "Why is it that way? How did this come to be? Who is being included or excluded by this practice?"

REFLECT AND CHOOSE

I stumbled onto a show on PBS one night called *Philosophy: A Guide to Happiness*. I was intrigued. I hated philosophy in college. If someone had told me philosophy actually held the secret to being happy, maybe I would have paid more attention! The thing that caught my attention was that both profiled philosophers (Socrates and Epicurus) said that a key ingredient to a happy life was reflection and choice. They both stated that an individual who takes time to reflect on life and lives in response to that reflection **will be happy**.

"That's what coaches help people to do," I thought. Perhaps that was why I love my work. I was happy to have made this connection! In supervision, as in life, it is imperative to reflect and make conscious choices. The most successful supervisors are the ones who take time to think about the work, the mission, and upcoming problems and potentials, and then they plan accordingly. The challenge in supervision, as in life, is to act on purpose, not accidentally or haphazardly.

Every supervisor I know has a full workload before they even begin supervising others. Organizations often reward good workers by promoting them to supervisory positions, expecting them not only to know how to supervise but also to fit the activities of supervision into their already overcrowded workday. It is often assumed that supervision, if done efficiently, does not take any significant time. I have often heard big bosses complain that supervisors are taking too much time supervising. Occasionally that can be the case. Some supervisors confuse "hanging out" with their staff with supervision. "Hanging out" with no focus, direction, or intention is not the same as building supervisory relationships that help people do their work more effectively. Most supervisors don't just sit around and waste time with their staff. There is a lot of pressure to manage people and to continue to be productive with the tasks you already have.

Good supervision takes time—time to know the people you supervise, time to meet with them, lead them, delegate, support them, and discipline as necessary. Time to listen to them and—perhaps most importantly—time to reflect and put all of the pieces together. What's working and what's not working? You must be clear about how your job and the jobs you supervise fit within the mission of the organization. You must ensure that your entire team understands this. You must think strategically. What is coming up and are you ready to deal with it? You must be able to find and work on any of your own biased or dualistic thinking about people or problems. You need time to recognize your own lens and how that is impacting your work. You also need time to look at your team: Are your people engaged? Are they sufficiently challenged? Who are you as a supervisor? How are you helping and how might you be hindering your team? And how do you choose to respond to all of these factors?

This seems like a lot to think about. For reflection to be helpful, however, it doesn't need to take hours every week. On a regular basis, with a team in place, you can mull over these questions for five to ten minutes a week. When you bring on a new team member, you might need to take a bit more time as you contemplate how to bring the new person into the team and how best to adjust the team. Two or three times a year, set aside a longer period of time to think about the big picture and do some long-term planning.

Having clarity about what you are doing and how you are doing it (the choosing part that comes after the reflective part) helps things move more smoothly. The ten minutes spent in reflection will be saved ten times over in efficiency and effectiveness if you reflect and choose. Otherwise you will just be letting things happen and then reacting to what comes up, including many problems that could have been prevented.

Invest time and attention in yourself. Invest in your team. Take time to think about what you believe and what you know, and then make conscious choices about how to proceed. Only then will you be sure that you are bringing your best to your work as a supervisor. Then you and your team can work productively, and maybe even be happy.

Coaching Corner

- How much time do you estimate you currently spend thinking about where your team is headed and how they are going to get there? Is it enough?
- Do you need to do anything to follow up or clarify anything from last week?
- What is coming up for you and your team—long-term and this coming week? Is everyone on the same page about what's ahead and their part in it?
- When can you set aside five minutes at the end of the week to reflect and prepare? (Put it on your calendar as an appointment.)

WHAT DO YOU NEED TO THROW AWAY?

Twice in the past week I found old keys. One of them was to my old office. I moved from that office nine months earlier. I had no idea what the other key was even for. The amazing thing was that I couldn't bring myself to throw either one of them away. It was quite silly. I knew where all the relevant keys in my life were located so there was no real concern that I might need either of the keys. It was simply that they used to be important for my daily routines so I was reluctant to let them go. I spent several minutes trying to convince myself to throw them away, but I couldn't, so I finally just threw them both in a drawer.

The keys made me think about ideas that we hold on to long after they're no longer of value to us. I thought about an old idea that I held for a long time: that if I disagree with someone, then that person won't like me. And that people must like me. This set of beliefs kept me restricted at various points in my life. It would get in the way and stop me from dealing with things I needed to deal with. Over time, I learned to deal with this belief. I realized that if I was going to be effective, I would inevitably do things, or say things, that people didn't like. And that it was impossible for every single person to like me. I learned to talk myself through it when those old ideas came up and to focus on dealing with the issue at hand. And I learned to tolerate my occasional discomfort of knowing people didn't like me or my ideas. Eventually, through reflective and persistent work, I had thrown this old belief and its limiting behaviors away.

What kinds of ideas are you holding on to that no longer serve you? Consider these beliefs that might get in the way of being an effective supervisor.

⊠ **Other things are much more important than supervision.** Deadlines. Production. Meetings. Paperwork. . . We all have so many priorities pressing on us that supervision becomes the passive part of our work. This leads to the critically flawed situation in which those you supervise say, "I only hear from my boss when there are problems." Your job as a leader is to lead—and that includes taking time for supervision and making it a top priority in your long list of priorities.

☒ **It will take too long to meet regularly with the people I supervise.** Almost everyone says they don't have time to hold regular meetings with their staff, until they start doing it. Then they tell me that the meetings have been extremely helpful and shifted the whole supervisory situation. It actually saves time in the long run, but it's hard to let go of the old belief that it takes too much time.

☒ **I'm afraid I'll do something wrong. The situation will just work itself out eventually.** When there is a problem, people often feel incapacitated by the idea that they might make it worse. Whether consciously or not, they hope that if they ignore the problem, it will go away. The problem won't go away! If you are polite, sincere, fair, and kind, you probably won't make the situation worse. Address the problem!

☒ **It won't make any difference what I do. People don't change.** People can often change if they are given adequate clarity about the need for change, the reason for change, and the understanding that they have a choice about what and how to do something. Some people **won't** change, but believing that people **can't** change is unfair to both of you.

☒ **My staff is fine. They don't want me to interfere with their work.** Meeting with people is not the same as interfering with their work. You can set up a clear agenda and make your meetings be a check-in. These meetings can be a time to touch base and make sure there are no problems coming up or changes that you have to consider. Trust me, your high-performing staff will appreciate the attention.

Any of these beliefs can get in your way and keep you from being an effective supervisor. Just because a belief might have been of value to you at some point doesn't mean you have to hold on to it. It's time to let them go. If you can't bear to throw them out, set them aside for now and just try on a new idea. Try a new way of doing things; it might just give you a new key to success.

Coaching Corner

- What do you prioritize over your tasks as a supervisor? What is the impact on your supervision of those priorities?
- Do you share any of the beliefs listed in this section? What are five beliefs that you hold about your role as a supervisor? How might these beliefs impact your staff?
- Some people do their best reflection at their desks. For others it's when they're running or in the shower or during meditation or during do-nothing time. What works best for you? If you don't know, experiment and find out.

BE WHO YOU ARE

My husband and I are probably one of the last couples in the country who sleep on a waterbed. The other night I was thinking about all the different kinds of beds people sleep in—futons, mattresses and box springs, sleeper sofas, air beds, etc.

It made me think about how we each have our own preferences and style. These styles show up in our choices, a few of which include our choices of bed, our food preferences, our partners, and our style of supervision.

There is room to be yourself while still being a good supervisor. You don't have to be just like the great supervisor who mentored you in your first job. Some supervisors are enthusiastic and charismatic. Others are warm and supportive, and others are a little detached and formal. Some are direct and rather strict, and others are disorganized and funny. Some are visionary and some focus on the project in front of them.

What's important is that you recognize and embrace the practices that support your individual style. How do you tend to accomplish things at work? How can your style be acknowledged and supported in a way that makes the whole team more effective?

An example of a style choice would be someone who knows they need time to themselves every day to be effective and builds a practice for that into their lives. Perhaps they have a "Do Not Disturb" sign on their door for an hour a day. Another example might be someone who loves the adrenalin rush of a deadline and therefore consistently asks for "all hands on deck" to meet the deadline. If your team understands these styles, then they can work with you. If you keep promising to plan ahead next time, then everyone will be disappointed, confused, and frustrated when the last minute rush happens again.

Recognize and build on your style preferences so that they'll help you be more effective. You also want to recognize and shift the unintentional habits that get in the way of being effective. You can be yourself and still recognize the need for improvement. If you've done a bit of self-examination, you may already know what your style preferences are; if not, you may need a little help getting your mind around this before you start to nurture the habits and styles that will support you and your team.

Here are a few reflection questions about personal style:

- ✓ Are you an introvert or an extrovert?
- ✓ Are you more comfortable being analytical or do you operate more intuitively? Or do you try to balance the two?

✔ Do you love processing information with a group or do you prefer to think things through on your own?

✔ Are you comfortable not knowing how things will turn out or do you like to get to resolutions **now**?

✔ How do you learn?

✔ How do you best deal with conflict?

✔ Do you like process or do you prefer product?

✔ What are the areas where you need to grow? Or to push yourself?

✔ Are you an optimist or a pessimist?

✔ What kinds of people or actions push your buttons?

✔ How are your people skills?

✔ How well do you know yourself?

✔ Are you comfortable with people questioning you?

Once you identify your style you can consider how you can work with your team using the strengths of your style. Start by asking yourself which styles support your work and which get in the way. And then consider how you might be able to communicate more clearly or tweak the "in-the-way" styles to make them more effective. For example, if you know that you learn best by reading, ask your staff to send you a written plan before you meet with them. Sometimes the most important step is to simply name your style so your staff knows. "I know it takes more time to prepare the plan before our meeting but it will help me be prepared and save us both time."

As long as you follow some basic steps and parameters of good supervision, you are free to be who you are and how you are. There are many styles of supervision and it doesn't work to try to be a style that doesn't fit you. Be yourself, while still being open to growth and change. Work with your strengths and you'll be much more effective.

Coaching Corner

- Identify a few examples of times when you had clear success in your job or supervision by really being yourself and using your own style.
- Is there a friend or colleague that you can trust to tell you when a habit is interfering with your effectiveness? If not, how can you develop and support this kind of feedback?
- Are there ways you need to communicate more clearly with your staff based on your actual style, to allow for processes to be more effective?

KNOW YOURSELF AND SHARE THAT KNOWLEDGE

When I took my last job as an HR director, I met with all the other directors one-on-one as soon as I started in the new job to talk to them about their needs and how I could support them. I also took time to give them an important heads-up about how I work. I let them know that I am a ponderer. I let them know that when they brought me a situation or a challenge, I would sometimes have an immediate answer for them, particularly if the question had to do with compliance or liability. But I wanted them to know that in many cases I would take time to consider the situation. I asked them to bring me developing problem areas as soon as they recognized them as such. If there was a complicated situation and nothing urgent was at stake, I forewarned them that I would likely take a day to think about it. I took time for two reasons: 1) I wanted to make sure I understood the situation clearly; and 2) I wanted to make sure that I had time to consider all repercussions of any action I would recommend or not recommend. I promised I would always follow up with them within twenty-four hours. And I did. With this, I set expectations, and made sure to follow through.

Setting my intention like this worked well for all of us. It gave me space to think, something I know I need. I don't like to be pressured into making hasty conclusions about complicated situations that can have huge impacts on the organization. I like time to let ideas meld, cook, form and re-form in order to make sure I didn't miss anything. Often my initial response to something does not change when I take a day to consider it, but sometimes I think of another wrinkle that I need to address, or another question I need to ask.

In giving my peers, and my staff, a heads-up about how I operated, we were all able to do our work better together. No one got worried when I said, "Okay, let me think about it." I had set a boundary, and with that came a certain sense of safety, in the promise that I would get back to them. No one wondered where I stood.

Think about how you operate. How do you make decisions? When and how do you do your best work? Under what conditions do you find yourself triggered or reacting? Under what conditions do you treat your team well, and when do you tend to treat them less well? How do you like to be approached with problems? When and how do you want to hear about mistakes? Is there a time of day when you're at your best, or worst? In what manner would you like your staff to let you know that they have a concern about something you're doing—or not doing?

One of the most important pieces of being a supervisor is that you understand yourself—that you understand your own reactions and practices and how you do your best work. You may realize that you need to change the way you do something. Maybe you need to set boundaries, invite questions, or communicate expectations in order for you to be able to do your best work while maintaining a sense of safety and trust with your team. It might be that explicitly sharing some more information about how you work could help your entire team be more effective.

Your staff may or may not be able to accommodate you, or they may wish you did things differently, but the act of revealing yourself and your preferred styles will help your team be stronger.

Think of this as giving operating instructions for working with you. Setting your intention is not the same as making a demand. It's simply sharing information about your own style and work process that will help your team work better together. Which is the point of it all, right?

Coaching Corner

- Think about how you operate. Review the list of questions in the fourth paragraph above and note the answers you know off the top of your head and note the ones you're not sure about.
- Consider how any of your answers to those questions affect your staff. Is there anything that you need to do differently? Do you have habits (like procrastinating until the last minute) that directly impact the workload or stress levels of your staff?
- What do you need to let your staff know about your operating instructions? When and how will you tell them?

SELF-AWARENESS IN THREE SCENES

A neighbor greets me on my walk.
A friend reaches up to push her hair behind her ear.
Playing charades—or any other guessing game.

These three vignettes offer a peek into the effect one person has on another and each is a reminder of how self-awareness is a critical skill of any leader.

Scene One

A neighbor down the street greets me whenever I pass him on my daily walk. I know he's trying to be friendly, but the impact of his approach makes me want to hide when I see him coming. The problem is that his greeting is always some kind of underhanded put-down.

"You've got a big coat on for such a mild day."

"Not exactly rushing yourself today, are you?"

"Haven't seen you out here for a while; you must be taking it easy."

I imagine he doesn't intend to insult me, but he's off-putting, and I've started avoiding him. This happens in the workplace too. Supervisors who don't listen to **how** they are framing feedback, or those who don't recognize other ways that they push people away can make it harder for their employees to hear and accept any appropriate feedback that they may have to give.

The self-awareness skill here is listening to how your words can be heard, not just what you are saying. This involves listening to yourself from another perspective as well as watching for people's reactions to what you are saying. Hearing yourself is just as important as listening to others to ensure healthy communication.

Scene Two

A friend recently rescued a dog from a shelter. Things were going well until she noticed that whenever she reached up to put her hair behind her ear, the dog would cower and shake. She realized that to this poor dog, the simple act of lifting her arm was interpreted as preparation to hit him. She adjusted her movements. With awareness, she started reaching up very slowly, and the dog was no longer reactive.

Her self-awareness in this scenario showcases the importance of observing your impact on others, even though this example is with a dog. We need to reflect on how our actions impact others. In this case, she wasn't doing anything wrong, but the dog clearly had a history of being hit and reacted to this simple movement. People are more complex, but they bring their wounds to their interactions just like animals. Of course that doesn't mean you're responsible for their reactions in these situations. But just doing the same thing over and over will not help you get your point across when there are patterns of negative reactions arising, nor will it help the team get the work done. Learn to pay attention to people's reactions and adjust if needed and appropriate.

Scene Three

I love to play games. I especially love guessing games—Charades, Pictionary, Password, Catch Phrase. Over the years of playing with family members and friends I've noticed that to be good at these kinds of games (and to have more fun with them), you have to be able to consider what the guesser is hearing and seeing, not just what you intend for them to see or hear.

If you draw a bird and they guess, "stove," it doesn't help to just draw the same thing again with more emphasis. You have to be able to look at the image through their eyes and adjust your actions accordingly. Maybe you're trying to get them to guess "fly" so you try to draw a bird and they don't get it. Then you draw a plane, and they still don't get it. Instead of assuming that the problem is that they're stupid, the challenge is to think, "What else can I do?" You may need to shift completely and draw a fly swatter and a little dot, and then they'll get it.

Playing these games can help you recognize other people's perspective and adjust your own perspective and actions to help them get where you want them to go.

You can't lead people if you aren't aware of your own impact on people. And you can't help others when they are having problems, if you can't see the world through their eyes to understand what the problem is. Their perspective matters, and if you can get that, then you can help them by adjusting your words or actions so they can hear you.

All of these stories are about practicing empathy—trying on another's perspective. Give it a try—through a game or simply by observing people's reactions. It will make you a better supervisor.

Coaching Corner

- Think of a time when someone didn't understand you. How did it feel? Getting in touch with that feeling can help you build empathy for when others don't understand you. Remember what it is like to feel confused and frustrated in that situation.
- Think of at least six ways you could get someone to verbally guess the word "plain." (See my ideas for this game on the next page.)
- How comfortable are you changing perspectives? When you think of trying to see something from another's perspective, what comes up for you? Do you think you are so clear that there should be no question about what you're asking? Does it just feel uncomfortable and irrelevant? Explore what comes up for you and see if you can gently remind yourself that there is no right or wrong here, it is simply a matter of trying something new to see how it works.

Six Ways to Get to Plain

1. It's another name for a prairie.

2. Iowa and Kansas have lots of them. It's a kind of flat land.

3. It flies in the sky and carries people to their destination. (In word games you can use homonyms!)

4. It's an adjective that means simple or even homely and often is paired with Jane.

5. It's the kind of yogurt that has no fruit in it.

6. It's the word used to describe leveling a piece of wood or surface.

CHAPTER 12:

How You Are Part of the Organization

SUSTAINABILITY BEYOND YOU AND ME

I once worked with a lovely woman named Janice. She was kind, funny, and friendly. She had worked with that organization for many years and was respected for the memories and history of the organization she knew and shared. Everyone in the organization loved Janice.

The only problem was that Janice was no longer effective in doing her work. The organization had grown and Janice's job was a substantially different job than when she first began. Janice was no longer supporting the work of the organization; in fact, the organization was now supporting Janice. Other people were not only working around Janice, they were sometimes doing her work.

Although we loved Janice and hated to cause her any personal trouble, there came a time when we had to let her go. We did it as kindly and as fairly as we could, but we had to remember that we were all there for the good of the organization and not vice versa. We gave Janice a goodbye package and a wonderful party but, of course, it was not easy.

All of us are ultimately replaceable. While we value and support our employees and hopefully mentor them to move on to bigger and better things when they are ready, the reality is that sometimes employees must go when they are not ready. If their work no longer benefits the organization, then it makes no sense to keep them just to be nice.

We get into trouble when we start thinking any of our employees, or ourselves, are irreplaceable. It can be an easy mentality to slip into. You have a great employee. Everything works so well with them on the job and you can't imagine running your organization without them. Or like the example of Janice, you really value the person and don't want to hurt them. They seem to be irreplaceable. But no one person should be irreplaceable. Any employee might choose to leave or you may need to let them go, and the organization should be able to go on without them.

If you, or anyone else in the organization, seem irreplaceable, then you are failing the organization. If you want your business to go on, it needs to be sustainable, and that means there needs to be a plan to replace people if/when necessary. Rarely should your organization rely completely on any one individual. It's got to be about the mission of your organization. People leave—they move, they accept new jobs, they want new challenges, they get sick. Every organization needs to be able to thrive despite the departure or even long absence of any individual.

When I was an HR director, my boss directed me to have a file in my desk that was called "the truck file." It was a rather gruesome file but once or twice a year I'd pull it out and update it. This file contained essential information from every employee about what to do if they got run over by a truck tomorrow and couldn't come to work for a while: What did we need to know? Where were their essential files? Who knew what they were working on? Who were their contacts? Who could take their place if they couldn't come to work for a while? Thank goodness I never had to use it!

That file was a morbid reminder of the fragility of life but having it and updating it was also a good business practice. If anything ever did happen, we would have a clue about where to start when we needed to. It was also a none-too-subtle reminder to every single one of us that none of us were irreplaceable.

While your day-to-day work needs to look at and support the individuals in front of you, including yourself, occasionally you need to look beyond the immediate future and think about the organization beyond the current workers. When you step back and look at the bigger picture, you can even ponder who might eventually take your place. It may not be tomorrow, or even in the near future, but having some sense of the organization beyond you as an individual helps you make sustainable decisions. Are you training your staff to back each other up? Are you building succession plans? Do you have so much institutional memory in your head that there would be no history left if you were gone? Get it out of your head! Write it down. Tell stories. Teach emerging leaders.

If you are relying too much on one person, start shifting that. Have them teach others some of what they do. Have them write a policy and procedure manual for their job. Have them show you their crucial files. Train them to think of the bigger picture as well as the work in front of them.

You don't have to tell them that they're replaceable—that is just mean and counterproductive. But you, as the leader, must act from that knowledge and prepare the organization for the potential loss of that particular individual. It doesn't have to be disaster-focused thinking; most employees don't stay at a job for their entire careers.

You may not need to actually develop a truck file but it is important to remember that none of us are irreplaceable.

Coaching Corner

- What concrete actions do you take to keep your staff grounded in the mission of the organization above their own individual needs?
- Do you feel irreplaceable? Does that make you feel important or trapped or something else?
- What is one step you can take in the next month to ensure that your organization could continue the work if you decided to leave the organization?
- Are you comfortable knowing that your staff members are simultaneously replaceable and valued individuals? Can you hold both seemingly contradictory truths at the same time?

REVEAL THE ELEPHANTS

There is a coffee shop in San Francisco that features a poster that states: "San Francisco has 15,000 homeless. Is that enough?"

I consider this a public disclosure of the elephant in the room. It speaks to an issue that most of us would be happy to not think about. When I saw the poster, it forced me to consider the issue of homelessness in a direct and surprising manner.

Every organization has elephants—those messy issues that we would just as soon ignore. Maybe we want to ignore the elephant because it makes us uncomfortable, or we don't know how to solve the issue, or we're tired of talking about it. Sometimes we ignore the elephant because we are just so used to working around it that we don't even see it anymore. Sort of like the invisibility of the homeless within our society.

Some organizations have huge elephants, like institutional racism. Other organizations have baby elephants, like unwieldy organizational structures that don't quite make sense anymore. The elephants can be ignored for a little while but if they are ignored indefinitely, they inevitably lead to trouble.

Whether the elephants are policies, practices, gaffes, people, incompetence, lack of fairness, or anything else, when an organization ignores an issue that is getting in the way of the work being done, they are tolerating, and in fact implicitly condoning, it. And when leaders tolerate anything getting in the way of the work being done, they have abdicated their leadership.

It is not easy to reveal the elephants. It can be scary to name the thing that everyone else is refusing to speak of. Or sometimes it feels like you are the only one who recognizes it, but that is rarely true. Some people are just so focused on what's in front of them that they don't notice the elephant. Other people get used to walking around it. Others feel it is not their job or within their power to point out the issue. However, when someone says, "Hey look, there's an elephant in the room," almost everyone breathes a sigh of relief.

Some people are better at naming the elephants than others. I have often been the person who did not see the elephant until a brave colleague pointed it out. Once it is pointed out, I can see it! I know that often those who are good at seeing the elephants get tired of being the ones to point it out, but they serve an invaluable service to our organizations. They are true leaders!

Sometimes the one who bravely names the elephant is promptly punished or silenced in response to their bravery. If you, the supervisor, or someone else with power in the organization immediately denies the elephant or does not follow up on the revelation, then you have surely taught every staff member an important lesson: Do not speak the truth in this organization. We do not tolerate anyone who is not going along with the status quo.

Some of the elephants you might see in organizations include an inconsistent application of rules, or job descriptions that make no sense, or an employee who is getting away with something. It's important to stop and look around periodically to make sure there are no elephants lurking. A good question to ask yourself or your team in the pursuit of revealing elephants is: What are we ignoring? This question opens the door for the elephant spotters to speak up.

Naming the elephant is often the most important step. As a supervisor, it is important to respond to this public baring of issues in a way that supports the rights of the one speaking up. Keeping your eye on the long-term consequences, you might want to acknowledge the bravery of speaking up. It may not be possible to address the problem immediately or to correct it to the satisfaction of everyone but you can be a supervisor who allows truth to be spoken to power.

Even if no solution is immediately apparent, just naming it helps people feel less crazy, and can start the process of looking for a solution. The problem can now be discussed openly and collaboratively. If nothing else, the team can identify what it is that they keep bumping into.

Coaching Corner

- Reflect on an elephant you have recognized. What was the impact of that elephant in the room? What shifted once the elephant was identified?
- Think of someone who seems to be an elephant spotter. Thank them for their service and ask them about their experience. What can you learn from them?
- How do you respond when elephants are revealed? Does your response depend on what your role is at the time (i.e., as a supervisor or in a group of peers in a management meeting)?
- What are you ignoring? What makes it difficult to address the issue or task? What is one step you can take to address the issue?

THE BLAME GAME

I read once that some languages have no concept of blame! The language will state, for example, that the lamp was broken but there are literally no words to say, "You broke the lamp!" This is an amazing, and foreign, concept for our society. If there is a problem, someone must be to blame for it. This shows up in our litigious habits, our politics, and in our workplaces.

Some workplace cultures are infused with blame. No matter what is going on in the organization, the focus seems to be on figuring out who did something wrong. Not to fix the problem, but simply to assign blame. This happens with major issues like how we got into this precarious financial situation, for instance, but also with seemingly minor issues, like whose turn it is to clean the kitchen. Major amounts of time and energy are spent by employees and managers, trying to figure out who is to blame. People talk about it—directly and indirectly. Interrogations happen. Evidence is gathered. And sometimes there is even proof about whose fault it is. Then everyone feels better, for the moment, but it still doesn't fix the problem nor prevent the next one from arising. Everyone feels better, that is, except the "guilty" one. Whether it was a simple mistake or downright incompetence, the one who caused the problem is made to feel wrong and bad.

The taxes were not filed in a timely manner. Everyone is talking about whose fault it is. It is clear that John was the one who was responsible for filing the taxes electronically and it was not done on time. John is assigned blame and everyone else goes back to work. Now, if John maliciously delayed filing the taxes for no good reason, there might be ample reason to hold John responsible and to expect him to accept the consequences. But if John could not file the taxes because he was missing important information from other people, then how does it help to blame him for the late returns?

Blame is a toxin in the workplace. It makes people afraid to act and it sets colleagues against each other. It causes employees and the entire culture to face backward, trying to figure out not just what happened, but who is to blame. Once someone is blamed then the organization often stops analyzing the cause and effect of the problem because they think that assigning blame is all that matters. There are times when people make mistakes or cause problems and removing them from the situation, the job, or the organization solves the problem. But more often than not, the problem is not simply the result of one person's actions. There are often contributing factors that make the solution more complicated than simply removing one person. In these situations, the same problem or a very similar one arises again within a few months. So the next time, it's not the taxes that are late but vendors who are complaining about not being paid. And then the blame game starts again!

Is the problem in this scenario John, who has the final step of filing the taxes and writing the checks, or is there something else that needs to be considered? Maybe there are structural delays in the steps leading up to the filing or check writing. Maybe the payments weren't authorized. Maybe there was missing data that John was waiting to collect from several different people. Maybe John's supervisor was not available to support John when he asked for help. Maybe there was not enough money in the account to pay the bills.

Blaming is very different than addressing what needs to happen in order to actually solve a problem. Problem-solving involves many kinds of actions: discussions, questions, and decisions. It's focused on figuring out solutions, not assigning blame. Problem-solving may investigate the past, but the purpose of this investigation is to fix the issue and prevent a repeat in the future. Whereas blame focuses all the attention and energy on the past, problem-solving keeps the team and the organization moving forward.

A problem-solving focus asks pointed questions: Why were these payments late? What was going on? Who else was involved in each step of the payment process? Does John have the authority to take other steps when obstacles get in the way? When we ask these kinds of questions, we might find out that there were five people involved in the process before John could actually pay the bills. Again, the goal of this conclusion is not to spread the blame, but to be able to brainstorm how to make the process simpler or more efficient from now on. We can recognize and address the entire system of bill paying to make it work more smoothly.

The ironic thing is that when there is a true search for a solution, it is much more likely that employees will actually accept responsibility for actions that happened. And from there, staff can work together to correct the problem.

Here are some forward-facing questions to ask to refocus yourself and your team on solutions anytime you notice a blame game is starting:

- ✓ What do we need to do so this won't happen again?
- ✓ How can we improve our work design?
- ✓ Is there anything in the system that contributed to this problem?
- ✓ Are there any lines of communication that need to be strengthened in order for this to work more smoothly?
- ✓ Does everyone understand now how to get support if this problem happens again?
- ✓ Have I been clear on my expectations about reporting concerns to me before they become large problems?

Part of this analysis and discussion may include looking back to gather information to solve the problem, not to shame and blame. Part of the solution may include individuals taking responsibility for mistakes, accepting consequences, or even corrective action, which may occasionally be discipline or even termination. But the point of this solution-oriented analysis is not to blame or punish someone, but to understand what happened, discover the various factors that were involved, and change whatever needs to be changed to prevent this from happening again.

There is a crucial distinction between blame and problem-solving that creates a vastly different workplace. In the blame-focused workplace all attention focuses on the past. People get stuck in the past and blame becomes part of the language. This gets in the way of individuals and the work moving forward, and it also discourages people from coming forward or accepting responsibility for mistakes they do make. In the problem-solving workplace, the focus is on the future. In the forward-facing organizations, it is much more possible for people to work together to build solutions, improve processes, and become more effective and efficient in the work. This creates a positive energy that infuses the work.

Pay attention to how you address issues. When there are mistakes or problems, you are better off cultivating a workplace that focuses on solving problems by facing the future.

Coaching Corner

- Which way are you facing when you deal with problems? How is this orientation working and how is it not working?
- Are you comfortable holding people accountable without blaming them? Is the distinction clear to you? What are the words you use when you slip into blaming mode and what can you change to remind yourself to translate blame into responsibility?
- Are you attentive when questions arise regarding ways your own actions may have contributed to problems? How can you manage any defensiveness that may come up so that you can address the problem?

THREE QUICK LESSONS ABOUT CULTURE AND CHANGE

Organizational culture is the phrase used to describe the unique combination of factors that make up the experience of working in a particular workplace. It includes the systems, symbols, practices, vision, values, level of formality, style of dress and language, and type of leadership that influences the day-to-day experience of working in a given place. In short, it is "the way things are done here." For example, a culture might be described as "mission focused and employee friendly" or it might be "authoritative and punitive." The culture might have been intentionally designed and built or it may have just evolved on its own. Culture happens whether there is attention to it or not.

There are nuances within workplace cultures, as well as layers of influence. Leaders and supervisors have a big influence on culture, but so do employees. No one owns the culture. As a supervisor, you will want to notice how the culture supports the work of the organization—or not!

Here are three lessons about culture that I learned from a recent trip to New Orleans:

Lesson One. The default culture spreads effortlessly.
Bourbon Street is the central street in the French Quarter of New Orleans. It's closed to traffic, the bars are open all hours of the day and night, various kinds of music issue from each establishment, drinks are creative and to-go, there are "adult" shows offered in all kinds of variations, and it's loud, crazy, and fun.

It was amazing to me when I went to visit that no one told anybody how to act on Bourbon Street. It has a very different culture than most American cities. But every day and every night visitors from all over the world arrive and within minutes they're joining in the fun. That's how dominant culture works! It just spreads. You watch, you notice, you hear things. You might learn something explicit, like "you can get your drinks to go here," but most of the culture is spread in much more informal ways.

The same is true of workplace culture. It is noticed and adopted very quickly when someone new joins an organization. Whether you talk about it or not, the organizational culture is present and spreading. If you, as a leader, want to have some impact on the culture, any changes need to be intentional, timely, explicit, and consistent or the default culture will continue to be dominant.

Lesson Two. Name the change.

Driving in California after returning home from New Orleans, I kept feeling like something had changed. Did our neighbors cut down a tree? Is that a new building? Did that store paint their exterior? I had only been gone a week, so I knew it was unlikely that there were many changes.

But I continued to have a vague feeling that things were different. After a time, it hit me. It was my own perspective that had changed. In New Orleans, I'd walked around the city a lot. I was surrounded by buildings, two- or three-storied buildings in the French Quarter and skyscrapers downtown.

Back in my little hometown, I saw trees and the sky and the horizon. Everything looked and felt different to me. Once I identified what was going on, I could enjoy the difference, but until I named it, I was experiencing a mild sense of unease that confused me.

Name the changes happening in your organization. Changes are noticed and experienced whether they are large or small. It is important to comment on changes and to give people a chance to respond to them. This is true whether you are changing forms or changing the culture. Identify the change and give people a chance to respond and adapt.

Lesson Three. New habits are easier to adopt when there is a path.

I wear a Fitbit that counts my daily steps. I thrive on games in general, and since Fitbit offers a gamelike structure, encouraging people to move more, it's great for me. On most normal days in California I walk between five thousand and eight thousand steps. I aim for ten thousand, but it is not yet my routine most days.

In New Orleans, I walked between fifteen thousand and nineteen thousand steps a day. It was not a conscious goal; it was simply that I had places to go and things to see! We didn't have a car and the area was walker friendly so I walked.

Chip Heath and Dan Heath wrote a book called *Switch: How to Change Things When Change Is Hard,* in which they talk about the three components of making a change. The last component they discuss is making a clear path. No matter how much I want to walk ten thousand steps in an average day at home, I usually fail. But when I had interest and time and a reason to walk, I did. This was a clear path. There were no obstacles between me and (over) reaching the goal.

Clear paths are essential for organizations that want to institute a change, like shifting the culture. Make a clear path and it becomes easier to accomplish. For example, you might decide you'd like to encourage more recycling in the office. So you put out more recycling cans. You make it easy to do what you want to see happen.

As a supervisor, you have an important role in the culture of the organization. Whether the current culture supports the work or impedes it, it is important for you to remember these three lessons: the default culture spreads effortlessly; name the change that is taking place; new habits are easier to adopt when there is a clear path.

Coaching Corner

- How would you describe the culture of your organization? Does the description you give match the experience of the staff? Is this culture intentional or unintentional? Is it supporting the work or impeding it?
- Have you ever experienced a disconcerting change that might have been easier had it been identified in a straightforward manner?

- Are there any changes that you need to name, for yourself or your staff?
- Have you ever experienced a clear path to change that worked? If so, what were the elements that made it successful? How can you keep that in mind for other endeavors?

DO NOT PASS GO

Those of you who have played the game Monopoly will recognize the title of this section. Monopoly is a board game that is set up as a real estate challenge in which a player buys properties with play money and then collects rent from other players who land on their property. Occasionally during the game, a player will draw a card that randomly sends them to a jail space on the board. That card reads: "GO TO JAIL: Go Directly to Jail. Do Not Pass Go. Do Not Collect $200."

When I was an HR director, I used the phrase "Do not pass go!" to remind the managers that there were some situations that were so serious they needed to come directly to HR for help. It was like a little mantra I had to remind them to come to me with their problems. "Go directly to HR," I would say. "Do not pass go! Do not collect $200." The reason for this caution stemmed from something an attorney once told me: "It isn't HR that is going to get an organization in trouble. HR knows the dangerous areas. It's your frontline supervisors who respond in the moment, or who don't respond at all, that can make or break an organization."

I wanted to make sure all the supervisors in the organization were alert to the primary danger areas they might confront in their work. I also wanted them to know they were not alone. So I taught them six critical areas to watch and listen for.

The six areas that often sneak up on an unprepared supervisor are:

☒ Discrimination
☒ Injury, illness, or a request for an accommodation
☒ Harassment
☒ Leaves of absence (LOA)
☒ Grievance
☒ Violence (or any threat of violence)

Let's see how you would respond if these scenarios showed up in your staff:

Discrimination

A staff member tells you, "I'm offended by what I've heard you say. In fact, I think you've discriminated against me."
Your response:

A. "Don't be ridiculous!"
B. "I'll have you know I am a member of the ACLU and have supported diversity for decades."
C. "Let me get you a grievance form."
D. "Really? Tell me what happened."

Injury, illness, or a request for an accommodation

A long-term staff member was diagnosed with arthritis last year. She could no longer reach up over her head to put things away so you had someone else do that task. Then she couldn't comfortably bend over to pick things up. You told the other staff that they needed to help her out. "After all, we're a team," you tell them. Now she has told you she needs some time off to deal with all her medical issues.
You tell her:

A. "Take all the time you need."
B. "No. I've adjusted the job as much as I can. If you can't do it with the help of the team, then this job isn't for you anymore."

C. "I'll talk to the staff and see if we can cover for you for a little while."

D. "Let's talk to HR and see what we can do."

Harassment

An employee who works with young people tells you she is feeling harassed by a client. You ask her what's happening and she tells you that one of the young clients she works with keeps asking her out. You tell her:

A. "You're the grown-up here. Tell him you're not interested but don't come on too strong—you don't want to drive business away."

B. "Okay, I'll tell him to back off."

C. "What do you want to do about it?"

D. "Let's talk to HR about this. We will work with them to investigate the situation and then we'll decide the next steps. In the meantime, I'll have your coworker work with that particular client until we figure this out."

Leaves of absence (LOA)

You have an employee who started working last January. She just found out her mother is ill. She asks you if she can take some time off to care for her. You say:

A. "Okay, as long as you don't use paid time."

B. "You can only use your Paid Leave Time, but when that's done you must be back here."

C. "Of course. We have an FMLA policy so I'm sure it will be fine. Go ahead and buy your ticket and I'll bring the paperwork to HR for you."

D. "I know leaves are complicated. Let me find out where we stand before you make any plans."

Grievance

An employee is unhappy with how overtime has been distributed. He tells you he knows his rights and wants to file an official grievance.
You say:

>   **A.** "No!!! Don't do that. I'll fix it."
>   **B.** "Go ahead—see if I care!"
>   **C.** "A grievance? Really? After all I've done for you? If that's what you want to do, you know where HR is but don't think I won't remember this."
>   **D.** "I really want to hear what your concerns are. Let's talk to HR and look up the grievance process in our handbook and see how we proceed from here."

Violence (or any threat of violence)

A person who was terminated has been posting mean things on her Facebook page about the organization and your boss. One day you notice that she has posted "I'm going to make them sorry that they ever messed with me!"
In response, you:

>   **A.** Click the like button.
>   **B.** Post a message on her wall saying, "You better stop posting these kinds of comments."
>   **C.** Ignore it.
>   **D.** Report it to HR, your boss and security.

In my fictional scenarios, the best initial response for each one, as you likely gathered, is D. Any other responses could open the door for liability on behalf of the organization, or you could be setting bad precedents on behalf of the organization. Even when you're being nice, it can still be a problem for the organization. Even if you know you've done nothing wrong, your response could be a problem. The bottom line action that you need to take after these situations is always the same: Do not pass go! Do not collect $200. Go straight to HR!

When any of these situations come up, you should see them as flags reminding you to respond carefully. Run the situation by HR, your boss, a consultant, an attorney, or someone who knows about the procedures and legal issues here. What you say and do in these situations matters. Do not respond automatically. Do not pass go! Get help.

Coaching Corner

- Would it be hard for you to tell a staff member to wait while you figure out how to proceed? Do you feel pressured to give an answer immediately? What does it mean to you if you have to defer to someone else?

- Do you know what your resources are if a situation like one of the presented scenarios came up? Who would you talk to? If your organization is small and has no HR department, think about how you could build a support team for times when tough calls must be made or research must be done.

- Do you believe that an organization should support an employee at any cost? Or that the employee should walk away if they cannot give 100 percent to the job 100 percent of the time? Or do you believe the response needs to be somewhere in between those two extremes?

Remember the Danger Words

Sometimes it is helpful to have a silly phrase in mind to help you remember key words. Here is one to help you remember the six danger areas that would send you directly to HR:

Did **I**saac **H**ave **A**ny **G**reen **V**egetables?

D—Discrimination
I—Injury, Illness, or Accommodation
H—Harassment
A—Absences (Leaves of Absence)
G—Grievance
V—Violence

CONSIDER THE SYSTEM

The death of Trayvon Martin in 2012 was just one of many racially charged killings in which an African American youth was shot and killed. In this case he was killed by a Latino man who was just another civilian who saw Martin walking down the street. There were conflicting stories about what happened. Many witnesses indicated that the victim was simply walking home from the store with Skittles and an ice tea. He was unarmed. The man who admitted to killing him had called the police because Martin looked suspicious and said that he acted in self-defense when he shot Martin. Conflicting stories.

Conflicting stories arise in workplace situations also. Two people have a confrontation and there are conflicting accounts of what happened. In both the world at large, and the workplace, it is important to step back and consider the system in which the incident happened. Then we can make a more informed judgment about what might have happened. In this case, there were two broader systems at play. One, the shooting happened in a state that has a "Stand Your Ground" law, which proclaims that in any situation in which self-defense is the justification, the benefit of the doubt will be given to the one who shoots. And two, our society as a whole has a deep history of racial injustice and white privilege, and continues to struggle with race relations. Within this system young black men like Trayvon Martin are inequitably targeted by the criminal justice system. They also experience poverty, violence, and housing and employment discrimination, and are subjected to a pervasive stereotype that they are dangerous.

When you overlay those two elements in this system, and look at the components of a story that are part of those systems, it is hard to dismiss the possibility that one citizen killed another (younger and unarmed) citizen because he was standing his ground against the "threat" that Martin was a young black man—and therefore didn't belong in that neighborhood and was presumed to be dangerous.

We live in a society infused with institutions and practices that impact different people in different and often unfair ways. We live in a society, and operate within workplaces, in which some people have privileges and others have hurdles, both of which are based on how they look or how they are perceived within the larger system, not on their individual performance.

People are sometimes treated unfairly within workplaces because others don't like the way they look or their mannerisms, not because of their performance. Women still make significantly less money than men. Black and Latino workers make less than white workers. The black unemployment rate is consistently twice as high as the white unemployment rate. People of color and women still disproportionately work in jobs with low pay. These kinds of discriminatory actions are problems with the system.

System problems can also show up when management treats people differently based on personal relationships or non-job-related characteristics. An example is when merit raises are given based on evaluations but everyone knows that one manager is an "easy grader" and his colleague is a "hard grader." When the rating system is flawed, so are the results. Another example is when there is no oversight to control or monitor individual hiring and salary decisions; a manager can simply hire her friends and pay them what she wants. And often, in workplace systems with arbitrary merit or hiring decisions, the results mirror the disproportionate pay and representation within the larger society. System problems go beyond individual actions and point to a lack of consistency and fairness. Such problems cannot be fixed only by addressing individual components of the system.

The courts have recognized the impact of systems on work actions. One of the ways that discrimination shows up in the workplace is in what's called "disparate impact." This means that while there may be no individual action or an organizational intention to discriminate, the entire system is impacted by discrimination. Historically, this has been documented in tests that on their surface look neutral, but in fact end up displacing a certain group of people in a higher percentage than would be expected. Think of the concept of the "good old boys' club" that relied on word-of-mouth hiring and therefore hired very few women or people of color.

The system is responsible for this. Yet, when we are part of a system, and especially when we are in a position of power, we share responsibility for addressing these issues. Even if societal injustice or workplace disparate impact is not created intentionally or by specific individuals, it can be changed by individuals and intentionality. Systems don't change themselves; they just keep rolling in their status quo, even if that status quo isn't fair.

Often, however, we don't immediately see the systemic issues. In fact, generally when we are part of privileged groups within the system, we have to learn—and work—to see the problems in systems. When we reap the benefits of unfairness, we can be blind to what's actually going on in the system, believing it to be neutral when it's not. Being part of the system requires us to look at it and at ourselves with a critical eye. Often we need someone outside the system or with another perspective of the system to help us see the problems. That can be a consultant who is not a part of your organization. Sometimes it can also be different voices within the organization, which clearly see the inequities because they are being treated differently and "somehow" are consistently ending up with the short end of the stick. Because the systems of the broader society will flow into workplace cultures and systems (unless the workplace has intentionally and regularly worked to build an alternate and more just workplace system), that means that within organizations white employees, employees of color, male workers, and female workers will often see different versions of how the system works.

Because systems historically (and still) benefit white and male voices as being the standard of the system, it's a good idea in your workplace to pay attention and listen carefully to complaints or perspectives from women and people of color—as well as other voices that are historically left out (LGBT voices, immigrants, disabled people, people from non-Christian backgrounds, etc.).

This doesn't mean that an employee is automatically right if they are, say, black or gay. It means it's a good time to make sure you are really listening, pausing, and self-reflecting. If you make a habit of listening it means you can hear if there might be any issues of actual or potential discrimination happening in the system (if so, discuss it right away with HR). But it's not just about catching overt discrimination. Listening is an important part of building trust, enhancing collaboration, and creating more safety in the workplace. It can be a way to begin to understand more about the whole picture that you might be limited from seeing based on your specific perspective. Listening and honestly sharing your own perspective on the organizational systems is a necessary first step to any change taking place.

The truth is that people can be good workers and still not succeed. Organizations can try to be fair and still not recognize the dangers of their systems. The system influences and impacts individual actions. And the consequences of those actions matter.

Look hard at the systems within which you work and live. See what works and what doesn't. Ask people who look (or speak or worship or act) differently than you how they see things. What workplace problems are caused or perpetuated by a biased system? Does racism infect your workplace organization in subtle or overt ways? How do you know? Are there changes that could be made to the system that could create a healthier and more effective workplace—for everyone? See the system and work to change what is not fair, and perhaps not even seen.

Coaching Corner

- Does the word "racism" make you uncomfortable? Think about what associations you have with that word and notice if you are resisting the word because it feels like a judgment. Does "systemic racism" have any different meaning to you? (Understand that I am describing the impact of unrecognized systems, not the actions of any one individual.)
- Can you think of a time when the system (in the workplace or in society at large) got in your way? A time when you tried to do the right thing as an individual but were thwarted by actions that you could not control? How did that make you feel? How did you react?
- Are there any reoccurring problems in your organization that might be bigger than the individuals involved in those problems? If so, how can you start the process of looking at the system? Do you need to bring in an outside perspective to support this process?
- As a supervisor, how can you ensure that all the voices on your team are being heard and that everyone has a safe space to address any real concerns they might have? Do people know they can talk to you or someone else about the organizational system? Does

your staff know they can bring up problems with you? Have you made it clear through your behavior and communication that you will listen if someone comes to you with a perspective different from yours?

KEEPING THE COCKPIT SAFE:
THE VALUE OF POLICIES AND PROCEDURES

Recently I was flying in a small plane when I noticed a flurry of activity at the front of the plane. Apparently the pilot had to go to the bathroom. Both flight attendants went to the front of the plane. One traded places with the pilot, entering the cockpit while the pilot exited and the copilot assumed control of the plane. They locked the cockpit door after they exchanged places. The other attendant stood at the front of the plane and kept all passengers from the area, turning away one person who unknowingly chose that moment to go to the bathroom.

When the pilot exited the tiny bathroom, the attendant used the phone to call into the cockpit. The flight attendant inside the cockpit looked through a small window to verify it was the right person before she opened the door and exchanged places with the pilot again. It was all done quietly, efficiently, and with no fanfare. I appreciated that there was a procedure to guard the cockpit. The woman in front of me exclaimed, "I feel so safe!" And I did too. The team took no chances and followed a clearly delineated procedure. They did their safety checks and followed safety procedures. It enhanced my trust in the system.

Policies and procedures are often denigrated as the unnecessary bureaucracy of any organization. Many people think procedures slow things down and make people jump through hoops just to make "others" happy, meaning the administration or a higher power in any given organization.

And yet, it is often those "others" who are responsible for thinking through the necessary steps to protect individuals and organizations from worst-case scenarios. As an HR director, I was often in a position to consider and write policies and to administer procedures. I would hold fire drills and check references. I would train staff on safety procedures and harassment. I would constantly be thinking about what could go wrong and how we could systematically prevent problems. I would work with affected staff to develop and disseminate a plan.

Policies and procedures are implemented to follow labor laws, prevent trouble, and ensure consistency and fairness. In the best of cases, staff can feel the results. When there are clear policies and procedures that are followed consistently, staff will trust their work environment more. Discrimination or harassment is much less likely to occur when there are established practices than when each manager does things the way she or he thinks best. Consistency enhances trust.

Of course, there are times when policies and procedures (and administrators) get too caught up in the rigidity of rules and forget the purpose of the practices. That's why the best organizations review and update their practices on a regular basis.

When they are written and practiced well, with intention and thoughtfulness, policies and procedures keep us all a little safer. And just as important, they build trust within the organization that no one is exempted from the rules, that people are treated the same, and that fairness is valued.

It was good to know that someone had thought through the process for a small airplane crew to safely transition through a simple operation. At no time was one person left alone in the cockpit and at no time was the cockpit left unlocked. We were safe and we felt it. Do your employees deserve any less?

Coaching Corner

- Are there policies and procedures that you skip because they are cumbersome or get in your way? Consider the impact of your actions on your staff and the organization. Are there steps you can take to update the procedure or change your actions?

- Is there anything in your sphere of influence that could benefit from a clearly formulated procedure? Who would you work with to develop the procedure? Who would potentially feel safer and more trusting if you made this happen?
- Think of the administrators in your organization. Take a moment to consider how they work behind the scenes to keep your organization safe. If you feel so inclined, find a way to thank someone.

LOOKING THE OTHER WAY

I don't know any organization that officially tolerates problem behaviors. But there are practices that inadvertently encourage staff to look the other way when there are problems. Ignoring problems may look innocuous, but over time it can poison a culture and lead good employees out the door. Here are three ways in which this plays out:

☒ **An overemphasis on being nice.** This is the organization that values "niceness" above all. They talk more often about "getting along" than about being effective. This is the organization where it looks like everyone is happy but it is an artificial harmony. Unspoken problems clog the work and lead employees to disengage, if not actively walk way.

When open disagreements are not permitted, or encouraged, in the workplace, it doesn't mean that conflict goes away. It simply goes underground. And then it's fairly common for passive-aggressive behaviors to develop.

Consider the following scenario:

Mary has a problem with Skylar but instead of addressing the disagreement/hurt/boundary/concern, she quietly bites her lip and goes about her business. The next time she sees Skylar, she may make a snide comment, murmur under her breath, or just ignore her. Maybe she'll tell her friends about her issue to make sure they see her side of things. Staff takes sides and alliances start to form around Mary and Skylar. Even staff who try to stay neutral get drawn into the underground conflict when they are around either Mary or Skylar. The initial disagreement didn't go away, it is just underground and eroding the trust and collaboration of the team.

☒ **Authoritative/bullying behavior.** Some people avoid problems by simply being so loud and aggressive that no one dares to disagree with them. Their aggressiveness might be verbally loud, or it may be "loud" in their tone of voice and behaviors, making it clear that anyone who disagrees with them is an idiot. When this happens, it shuts down problem-solving because disagreements don't even get voiced. Whether or not these bullying behaviors are directly coming from management, if they are tolerated then the message is that management agrees with this tone.

The organization may say that it values suggestions, feedback, and even complaints, but when someone actually brings one up, they are shut down so fast that it teaches them and everyone else not to go there—ever!

Look at this example:

In a staff meeting, Amy suggests how the organization might improve customer service. Before anyone else can say anything, Jake speaks up in a sarcastic voice, "Well, why don't we just offer them valet parking while we're at it! This is just such a stupid idea that I can't believe it made it on the agenda. Surely we're not seriously considering it."

It's bad enough that Jake has responded this way, but acceptance of the behavior is cemented when the leader of the meeting simply says, "Does anyone else have anything they want to say in response to the suggestion from Amy?"

If they did, they're certainly not going to now. And do you think Amy will **ever** make another suggestion, or that anyone else will bring up their thoughts on improving customer service?

☒ **Tolerating emotional blackmail.** Emotional blackmail happens when an employee is so volatile that it scares everyone else from confronting him or her. People are so uncomfortable with the possibility of what that person's emotional reaction might be that they avoid any interactions that might upset this person. Whereas the bullying behavior is aggressive, emotional blackmail may take the form of sadness, persistent moodiness, or volatility that affects the work of this employee and those around them. This is different than an authentic display of emotion that is appropriately expressed and then the person moves on. In that case it does not negatively affect their work or force others to deal with the emotions.

The emotional blackmailer impacts the work environment in manipulative ways. Sometimes even supervisors feel like it's not worth the consequences of crossing this employee. They will rationalize that the problems are minor, and while that might be true, with people who are allowed to emotionally black-mail others, their behaviors may escalate as they begin to push the boundaries.

Here's one way this might play out:

Shelly is a good worker but she is consistently late on Monday mornings. It's not a huge deal because she's good when she gets to work, but it does cause disruption because Monday morning is when the team has a staff meeting. When she is late, everyone ends up sitting around waiting for Shelly to show up to start the meeting.

When her supervisor brings it to her attention, Shelly gets quiet and then starts to cry softly. She agrees to do better. For the rest of the week she walks around with her head down and barely talks to any-one. Shelly is overly formal with the supervisor and does not talk to her unless she is asked a direct ques-tion. People can see she is sad and everyone is wor-ried about her. The supervisor decides that Shelly is too sensitive and does not want to deal with address-ing the next problem. So the next week when Shelly is once again late, nothing is said to avoid "hurting her feelings."

Within a few months, not only is Shelly late to the meetings, several other staff members also come in late on Mondays because they know the day will not begin on time. And now Shelly is also often tak-ing extra-long lunch breaks. When the supervisor made a comment about this, Shelly snapped that she was always being picked on by everyone and was being treated unfairly. The supervisor decided it was best not to rock the boat more, so again, the behavior didn't change.

The way to deal with any problem like the ones above is to address them. Tackle them head on. Not in an aggressive manner, but in an objective neutral tone that clearly states what the problem is, how it relates to the work and the mission, and what your expectation is going forward. This puts you, as a supervisor, clearly on the side of addressing the problem, not colluding with problem avoidance.

If you don't address these behaviors, you are tolerating them, which translates quickly to condoning them. And you are ceding power to the employee whose behavioral patterns are not supportive of organizational health.

Instead of avoiding the issue, tell staff how you expect them to deal with conflict and other problems. Show staff how to address disagreements directly. Hire someone to train them in conflict resolution. Talk clearly about your expectations in this area.

When there is conflict, whether direct or underground, one of the first questions to ask is: How does this action impact the work? If you can identify how something is impacting work, either directly or by impacting teamwork, then you need to address it. First get clear yourself about what the situation is, the impact, and the expected change, and then communicate it simply and clearly to staff (either to the individual displaying these behaviors or to the team if the entire team is participating in the problem behaviors):

1. Here's what I see happening.
2. This is how it is impacting the work.
3. Here's what I expect to see in the future.

If you can't identify how a situation impacts the work, then it might not be any of your business. (For instance, two employees who used to be friends are barely talking to each other now. But their work is not impacted and they are not pulling people into their fight. It doesn't involve you.)

When you are clear about your expectations and you address

the problem directly, you are acting as a good supervisor and a true leader. And you are also modeling how to address problems in a direct and respectful manner, in service to the mission.

Coaching Corner

- Is there anything about addressing problem behaviors head-on that is hard for you? In reading this section, were there any areas where you felt nervous or tense?
- Have you been tolerating any of these kinds of behaviors? What has stopped you from acting? What do you need to do to take action?
- Have you been clear with your team about how you expect them to handle conflict? Write out your expectations and make a plan to talk to your team about it.

PAYING ATTENTION

Recently my husband and I went outside at midnight to watch a meteor shower. It was a clear night and we reclined in our lawn chairs and saw a few shooting stars. We chatted in the dark as we kept our attention on the sky to watch for more. After about a half hour of watching, I looked away to watch a car drive by and when I looked back at the sky, I realized that we couldn't see any stars! Not one! During that half hour we'd been looking, the fog had rolled in, obliterating any view we had. But the amazing thing was that we hadn't noticed it. We had literally been staring at the sky the whole time and we didn't notice the stars disappearing.

The lesson here is that even when you are watching, you might not realize what is going on. In an organization, this can be a real problem. Here are just a few examples of how this might show up:

- ☒ Actions that start out as playful teasing can morph into harassment.
- ☒ Minor infractions can become major problems.
- ☒ Small performance issues can accumulate into deal-breaking performance issues.
- ☒ Seemingly minor comments can be lumped together throughout the organization and become a pattern of discrimination.
- ☒ Supervisors who are not very "user friendly" can ferment disgruntled employees.
- ☒ Inconsequential exceptions and adjustments can lead to some employees feeling unappreciated while others feel like they can get away with anything.

The list could go on and on. We must certainly pay attention and watch for major issues, but that in itself is not enough. We must also be proactive in addressing minor problems and preventing them. To be safe, and to prevent selective blindness, it is also a good idea to step back and look at things from a different perspective. In our backyard, looking away and then refocusing on the night sky helped me see things differently.

In an organization, there are all kinds of ways to step back and get a different perspective. You might develop an annual employee satisfaction survey that will tell you how people are feeling about their work. You could walk around and talk to people you don't usually talk to. Have a consultant or a colleague come in and conduct an employee assessment. Consider running a campaign to remind employees about policies and procedures for addressing problems to make sure they know that you really do want to hear about any problems that are impacting their work. Encourage the organization to keep training all supervisors and establish standards of supervision so this aspect of management is recognized and practiced.

Another thing to do is to take time every few months to get your team out of the office and look at things together—sideways. It doesn't have to be a daylong retreat (although it can be!); you can go out to breakfast and talk. You don't need to have a big structured agenda but can instead encourage people to talk about how things are going. What are people thinking? Do they have any concerns? What have you all been doing lately to catch problems and celebrate success?

Watching closely for shooting stars isn't enough. You have to occasionally shift your perspective so that you can notice the changes that happen over time.

Coaching Corner

- Have you ever experienced watching for something and then realizing that you missed it? What did it feel like? Looking back, what could you have done differently?
- How can you intentionally build a process to make sure you step back and look at things from a different perspective on a regular basis?
- Type "monkey business illusion" into your search engine and watch an amazing demonstration about the phenomenon of selective blindness. How does this apply to your work and/or life?

BULLIES IN THE WORKPLACE

We watched a beautiful bird with orange and brown coloring and a dappled belly in the apple tree outside our bedroom window. I noticed it was flying away and then coming back to the same spot in the tree. It was building a nest! When I looked more closely, I saw that there were now two varied thrushes working together to build a home. We watched as the birds flew back and forth a half a dozen times gathering twigs and moss and leaves to start the foundation for their nest. It was starting to take shape. I was imagining waking up and watching tiny newborn birds in a few months. Then, all of a sudden, a large blue jay flew into the tree, jumped over to the nest, and tore it apart! Piece by piece he ripped the nest apart and dropped it to the ground. One of the thrushes tried to fly at him once or twice, but the blue jay was twice as big and soon the smaller birds gave up and flew away. "Oh no," I thought. "Those birds will not be back. They've met a bully and this is no longer a safe place." And so it was. We never saw the thrushes again.

This is what bullies do. They drop in and wreak havoc and then go on their way, leaving hurt and damage behind them. According to The Workplace Bullying Institute, 35 percent of workers in the US have directly experienced bullying at work. That is 53.5 million people! One definition of bullying is "repeated unreasonable actions of individuals (or groups) directed toward an employee (or a group of employees) which are intended to intimidate, degrade, humiliate or undermine, or which create a risk to the health or safety of the employee(s)."

A few other interesting facts from The Workplace Bullying Institute include:

- 62 percent of bullies are men; 58 percent of their targets are women
- Women bullies target women in 80 percent of cases
- Bullying is four times more prevalent than illegal harassment*

The impact of an unrestrained bully, or a workplace culture that tolerates or even encourages bullying, is huge. Absenteeism, reduced productivity, individual health issues, low morale, stifled innovation, and high turnover are just a few of the consequences.

If you supervise a bully, it is essential to give clear expectations about how you expect people to treat each other and work together. This isn't about being nice; this is about how their actions affect the work and the environment. People cannot do their best work when they are constantly looking over their shoulder, or feeling that they're walking on eggshells, afraid that their actions might make them a target of the bully. Energy available for the work is diminished. There will not be trust or cooperation when staff members are intimidating or insulting others.

As a supervisor, you might address bullying by saying something like: "You don't have to like your coworkers, but you must be respectful and interact in a calm and professional manner to get the work done." There are a lot of words in that expectation that need clarification: respectful, calm, professional manner, even "get the work done." It is up to you to set the acceptable standards of behavior with your team. "I expect you to talk to each other about the work, and to address each other directly and calmly. There is to be no yelling or eye rolling. You must respond to e-mails from each other within twenty-four hours and you must share information that other people need to do their job. I am going to hold all of you accountable for these standards of behavior."

Just as important as setting expectations is giving clear feedback when people cross the line. This can be difficult for a supervisor to do because you could be the next target of the bullying behavior. But it's still imperative that you give clear behavioral feedback: "I saw you interrupt Jim five times in the staff meeting and in the lunchroom you cut right in front of him. That is unacceptable. I need you to listen to your coworkers without interrupting them and take your turn like everyone else. These actions are impeding the work of the team and will not be tolerated."

Be sure to tie both the expectations and the feedback to the impact that the actions have on the work. Even if the bully turns his venom on you, you must hold him accountable for the expectations you have specified. If the actions continue, you might have to write him (or her) up and move into disciplinary actions. Get help from HR to address the problem with the individual employee and throughout the organization if it is a widespread problem.

Addressing the actions of a bully in the workplace can have far-reaching positive effects. Staff will see that you have their backs. They will see you are taking actions in a fair and direct way. They will see that you are committed to the work and to maintaining a safe space for that work to happen. This will build trust and loyalty from staff, perhaps even from the bully. And if the bully can't, or won't, change, then you have laid the groundwork for discipline and termination if it comes to that. (Remember to document your conversations so if it does reach the point of discipline you are prepared.)

I couldn't do anything for the neighborhood birds, but we can uphold standards in our work environment and make it safe for everyone to do their best work.

*Many people confuse bullying with harassment. Harassment is a legal term that refers to behaviors that are unwelcome and uncomfortable, impede the work, AND are targeted toward a member of a protected group. If the actions are directed toward an individual simply because the bully doesn't like them, that is not harassment. It is bullying and it is not okay!

Coaching Corner

- Have you ever been bullied or harassed? Remember, or imagine, how it felt to be targeted and unfairly picked on. Getting in touch with the pain of bullying can help you strengthen your resolve to address it.
- Is there anything you're doing that could be seen as bullying? How do you treat people you don't like, or those who are not living up to your expectations or trust? What can you do to remain respectful in the face of your own difficult feelings?
- Are there disrespectful actions that you have ignored? Has anyone complained to you about a coworker's actions and the impact of those actions on their work? If something is impacting the work, then it must be

addressed. How can you prepare for any difficult conversation you must have with a potential bully?

CREATING A BULLY-FREE WORKPLACE

Jeremy is a top performer. He does his work well and is a well-known member of the community. He is widely recognized as the public face of the organization. The only problem is that internally Jeremy is a bully. He orders people around in a brusque, demeaning manner. He dominates staff meetings. He doesn't show up on time for appointments or meetings. At least three staff members have resigned with the explicit disclosure that Jeremy made their work lives a living hell for them by singling them out for teasing and put-downs.

The organization that Jeremy works for has appropriate policies in place to discourage the kind of actions that Jeremy takes. His supervisor has counseled him, sent him to trainings, and even written him up for his actions. But when it came time to take the next step and actually terminate Jeremy, senior management balked. It would impact the work too much. It would cause a ripple of bad feelings in the community. He was too valuable to lose.

So Jeremy, and everyone else in the organization, is clear about the **real** values of the organization. They may say, on paper, that they value teamwork and cooperation and conflict resolution, but clearly they value Jeremy more. So Jeremy has a pass to keep behaving badly. Everyone understands that it does no good to complain about Jeremy's actions. And Jeremy's supervisor is now looking for another job because he too understands that he is only Jeremy's supervisor on paper, and that Jeremy is in fact one of the most powerful people in the organization.

A supervisor cannot always handle bullying behavior on their own. It takes the entire organization to build a bully-free culture. Too often there is subtle, or direct, reinforcement of the bully's behavior, especially if the bully is a superstar in terms of other performance indicators.

No organization officially endorses bullying, but too often an organization will publicly prohibit certain behaviors and then unofficially reward them. This creates a toxic culture because employees quickly recognize which behaviors are truly valued and they also recognize that the organization is duplicitous and therefore cannot be trusted.

Who is the human face of the "organization"? It's you, the supervisor. As a person with implied authority (whether you actually have authority or not is another question), you are seen as part of the problem. Even if staff know you are trying to do things differently in your department, they will soon conclude that you are powerless to change things when the culture continues to reward bullies.

Rewarding bullies can be literal: they get bonuses, promotions, and perks. Or it can be subtle: the behavior is overlooked, and the bullies are not held accountable to the written standards. Staff sees that certain people can get away with behaviors that other people can't. Some people can yell at others and nothing happens (or they are quietly told "you shouldn't do that" but there are no real consequences). Those people who get away with bad behavior might be top performers or they may be part of a privileged group: personal friends of the top managers, white people, men, or even long-term employees who know their jobs are safe.

Individual supervisors must hold their staff accountable to performance standards, which include behavioral standards. But furthermore, there needs to be unified, authentic action from the organization to create a bully-free environment. Leadership must identify how they expect people to treat each other. What are the standards of our interactions here? What is our code of conduct and how do we hold ourselves to it?

I read about one organization that instituted a 10/5 rule. When you came within 10 feet of a coworker you were expected to make eye contact, and when you were within 5 feet, you were to verbally greet the other person. The Veterans Administration launched a program called CREW (Civility, Respect, and Engagement in the Workplace). Their analysis of the program results showed reduced turnover, higher morale, less sick leave, fewer discrimination complaints, and higher patient satisfaction.

Here are a few steps an organization can take to keep the culture safe for everyone:

- ✓ Create a zero tolerance bullying policy. This policy should be part of a commitment to a safe and healthy workplace and must have the full support of leadership.

- ✓ When witnessed, bullying behavior should be addressed immediately—and publicly. This doesn't mean shaming the bully, but it does mean addressing the actions in a clear and direct manner: "That's not how we talk to our coworkers here."

- ✓ Train supervisors and managers in how to have difficult conversations and give hard feedback in a clear and respectful manner.

- ✓ Build a culture of respect. Train all employees how to communicate effectively and how to resolve conflicts, including how to get help when necessary.

- ✓ Establish an independent contact for employees (e.g., HR) so that everyone has a neutral and safe person to report problems to. Make sure HR understands the importance of neutrality and confidentiality.

- ✓ Create a Code of Conduct that defines professional behaviors and unacceptable behaviors. Have every employee sign a commitment to follow the Code of Conduct and make it part of the evaluation process.

When these steps are taken, the expectation is clear that bullies are not welcome in the organization and that bullying will not be tolerated. It supports you in your work with your staff. It makes the organization safer for everyone. And most of all, more time and attention can be directed to the actual work that needs to be done.

Coaching Corner

- No organization intentionally sets out to encourage bullying, but many inadvertently do. How does your organization as a whole respond to inappropriate actions? What behaviors are actually valued and rewarded?
- Are there other areas where your organization might have a written policy that is not truly reflected in the day-to-day culture?
- How can you initiate an organization-wide conversation about effectively supporting your employees to be safe, happy, and productive in their work?

HOW DID 100 PERCENT BECOME TOO LITTLE?

Michael wanted to inspire his staff. "I expect 110 percent from each and every one of you every day," he said passionately. "And I will be right there beside you giving 120 percent."

It is not possible to give more than 100 percent! One hundred percent is absolute—it is all. Supervisors who say, "I expect my staff to give 110 percent," think they are setting a high bar, but in fact they're setting an impossible bar. If we are expected to give 110 percent, we can never meet the goal.

How did 100 percent become too little? And what does it mean that it has? I think it means that people are stressed! It means that workers are expected to give and give and give. It means that good enough is never an option. It means that 24/7 is an accepted expectation of many workplaces, which again sets up an impossibility. And yet, we hear it so often that we buy into the normalcy of it. We think it is perfectly normal to check our work e-mail at midnight and again at 6:00 A.M.

At the same time "work-life balance" is the go-to perk of the best places to work. Many organizations are trying to implement a culture that encourages a work-life balance by focusing on work-at-home policies and flexible schedules. Rarely do they address the problem head-on and say, "We can't do the amount of work we are trying to do."

In this world of impossible standards, there is never enough of us to go around. People are stressed at work and at home and feel like they can never catch up in either venue.

According to Sara Robinson in her Alternet article "Why We Have to Go Back to a 40-Hour Work Week to Keep Our Sanity": "More than a hundred years of research shows that every hour you work over 40 hours/week is making you less effective and productive over both the short and the long haul."

Robinson writes about how Henry Ford figured out a long time ago that workers were more productive if they worked only forty hours a week. New studies confirm that this is still true, even though the work, and certainly the time pressures, have changed. This holds true for "knowledge" workers as well as manual laborers.

We need to be mindful of this truth, and of our unending desire to strive for more, better, perfect. This pressure for more-than-perfect often leads to our detriment. In baseball, .350 is considered a great batting average. That means that a player gets a hit 3.5 out of ten times at bat. That means that 6.5 times up at bat, they get out. Even the best players "fail" almost 70 percent of the time! While this is not a number that translates directly to other kinds of work very easily, the concept does. If you don't allow room for mistakes, misses, and learning, the work suffers. You cannot bat 1.10! You can aim for "good enough" or "my best" sometimes.

We may not be able to scale back the work of our organizations, (although if you're in a leadership position, don't write that off too easily), but we can begin to adjust and word our expectations in a way that set up our employees to achieve rather than fail.

To start, don't ever ask your staff to give you "110 percent" effort! Instead, let them know that you expect them to do good work and then go home and spend time with their families or time doing what they love to do. In the long term, everyone will most likely be both more productive and happier.

Coaching Corner

- When do you exaggerate or use superlatives to describe the work of your team? Think about the possible impact of what you're saying. How could you convey your meaning without the excesses?

- Where in your work is perfection required? What does "good enough" look like as a positive quality?

- How early/late do you check your e-mail? That is often an indicator of the degree of overwork we have. Do you expect your staff to answer e-mails after hours? If not, have you told them so? How can you be clear and realistic about work-life balance with your staff to help nudge things in a more sustainable direction?

Afterword

THANK YOU.

I often remind supervisors to appreciate their staff. So it's the end of this book, and I want to appreciate YOU. So much of the work you do is behind the scenes, unknown, unacknowledged, and unappreciated. So cheers to you—the unheralded supervisor—for the vital role you play in your organization.

Thank you for all the times you've oriented a new employee. For taking them around and introducing them to everyone else. Thank you for patiently explaining a concept to your staff, over and over again when necessary. The concept might be your vision for the department, the mission of the organization, or how to process a client through your system. Whatever it is, thank you for your patience.

Thank you for keeping the big picture in mind. Often people get so focused on the task in front of them that they lose sight of why they are doing the tasks they're doing or where the path is leading them. As a supervisor, you keep the big picture in mind, knowing where the team is headed and how you want them to get there.

Thank you for listening. As a supervisor, you listen to problems, explanations, concerns, chatter, and questions. You listen to the words, the tone, and the understory. You hear between the lines and ask the questions that need to be asked. In this listening, you are often the connection that keeps information moving, both up and down the organization.

Thanks for making decisions. With thoughtful reflection, you do your best to weigh out the possible scenarios of any given situation or problem and determine the best path to follow. You can't always know how it will turn out, but you use your best judgment and make a decision.

Thank you for accepting responsibility. As a leader—of the team or of the whole organization—you know that everyone has their piece of the puzzle, but that you, as a leader, hold a bigger share of responsibility. I commend you for apologizing when you make a mistake, acknowledging when things work and when they don't, and holding responsibility for the outcomes. Thank you for recognizing your power and holding it thoughtfully and responsibly.

I acknowledge you for having the hard conversations and, when necessary, disciplining and terminating employees while maintaining respect for the individual.

And you do all this with very few acknowledgements of your own skills and accomplishments. Take a moment to celebrate yourself! Even if you don't always do all of this, you can appreciate your successes while you commit to improvement. Your intentions, your focus, your commitment to being a good supervisor are to be commended. You make it all work. You hold it all together. Thank YOU for the work you do every day to make your team and your organization succeed!

APPENDIX:

How Big a Bite Do You Have Time For?

1 minute (300 words or less)

SIDEBAR: Remember the Danger Words
SIDEBAR: What Is a "Fair Period of Time"?
What Do You Believe?

2 minutes (301–504 words)

Relationships in Minutes
SIDEBAR: Reflection on Power and Privilege in the Workplace
SIDEBAR: Sample Questions for Intentional Conversations
SIDEBAR: Self-Assessment Tool
The Space Between
Thank YOU
Things I Know and Forget
Thoughts on Learning
Working and Playing for the Team

3 minutes (505–754 words)

Are You a Family or a Team?

Be Who You Are

Build a Vision for Your Team

Compared to Perfect

Curiosity: Wake It Up to Slow Down

Dangerous Dozen and Diligent Dozen

Do I Hear You Now?

Don't Just Complain About Your Staff

Don't Just Do Something, Stand There

Dualism Gets in the Way

A Formula for Giving Feedback

Getting Feedback

Give Them a Map

Goldilocks and the Three Supervisors

Good Morning

GPS and Mentoring

Hiking Together

How Did 100 Percent Become Too Little?

The Importance of Seeing

Intentional Conversations

It's About You

It's Simply Information

Keeping the Cockpit Safe: The Value of Policies and Procedures

Know Yourself and Share That Knowledge

Laugh a Lot

Making Room for Introverts

Moments of Wonder

My Way or the Highway

Online Learning Is Not a Panacea

Paying Attention

The Power of Routines

Praise and Thank-Yous

The Problem with Common Sense

Raucous Geese
Reflect and Choose
Reveal the Elephants
Rita's Rules of Engagement
Self-Awareness in Three Scenes
Show Up and Tell the Truth
SIDEBAR: Approaching Conflict: Ten Steps
SIDEBAR: Lessons from Baseball
SIDEBAR: A Sample Coaching Conversation
State of the Team
Take Five Minutes to Play Together
Tough Times Call for Tough Truths
The Transparent Supervisor
Triple Vision Required
Undervalued Team Members: Introverts at Work
What Are You Practicing?
What's in Your Pocket?
Who Does What?
The Words You Use
Working Together
"You've Got a Bad Attitude"

4 minutes (755–1,004 words)

Accidents Happen
Are You Playing the Same Game?
Avoid the Judges' Table
Avoid These Communication Traps
Beware of Shortcuts
Bullies in the Workplace
A Coaching Style of Supervision: Working Together for
   a Common Goal
Contain the Complaining
Creating a Bully-Free Workplace
Delegation Made Simple

5 minutes (1,005–1,250 words)

6 minutes (1,251–1,553)

Consider the System
Introduction: Supervision Matters
Looking the Other Way
SIDEBAR: Ten Game Ideas

Acknowledgments

I want to thank Mark, first of all, for all his support throughout the years. We always believed the point of our marriage was to help us each become more ourselves and in your love, I have done that. This book is one manifestation of that growth.

I appreciate all my clients who shared successes, joys, challenges and frustrations with me over the years as they worked tirelessly to make the world a better place. I am honored to have taught you and learned from you. In particular, thanks are due to San Francisco Neighborhood Centers Together (SFNCT) who hired me as their HR Circuit Rider when I was a baby consultant.

And even more specifically, thanks are due to my LEAP group (Leaders Emerging and Pioneering), who asked me questions and suggested topics that helped me know what I know. You are all in my heart and in my gratitude.

To my fellow consultants, I am grateful for the support and sharing and friendship that make this work less lonely and more fruitful. In particular, Margi and Emily who took me under their wings and applauded my flight. And to the PC Group who shares the road with me in our service to nonprofits. My office mates have added joy and comradery to my work and my life. Casi called me a mentor and we went on to built an intergenerational partnership. We are all committed to our work to make a better world and each of you lives it in your life and in your work. I appreciate every one of you.

Thank you to Susan Cain who helped me think about introverts at work through her breakthrough book, *Quiet: The Power of Introverts in a World that Won't Stop Talking.* Thanks also to Chip Heath and Dan Heath who wrote *Switch: How to Change When Change Is Hard* and Robert Maurer, who wrote *One Small Step Can Change Your Life—The Kaizen Way.* These books helped me change myself while thinking about change in organizations. Thank you also to my graduate school professors who have become colleagues and supported me long after school. And a special thanks to my first coach, Lisa, who reminded me to be curious and gave me a key to coaching and to life.

I am grateful to my former coworkers who trusted me with their problems and their paychecks. I learned what I was doing in order to support you in your work. A special thanks to my former bosses, Andrea and Helga, who trusted me to keep the organizations safe and helped me grow in my career and who both modeled strong female leadership. I would not be the person I am, at work or in my life, without the gift of Roberta and Barbara in my life. You opened my eyes to privilege and oppression and once my eyes were opened things never looked the same. Thank you.

I am extremely grateful to my children and grandchildren, who are the icing on the cake and the point of it all. I also learned so much about leadership and supervision through parenting.

Special thanks to Rachel and Masha for your excellent editing support. You made this book stronger and more relevant. Thanks also to Brooke for helping me turn my newsletters into a book and all the She Writes Press team for guiding me through the publishing maze. Thanks to my publicist who taught me how to show up in the world with a book in my hand.

I want to recognize my virtual focus group and thank you for your insights and opinions. Love and appreciation to my family and friends who I always know are in my corner. You know who you are and how much I love you. To Katie, who helped me take up space in the world.

And finally, thank you to my newsletter readers over so many years—those of you who are supervisors and those who are not. You encouraged me to think and write and share. You assured me that my work, and my words, matter.

Author Biography

Rita Sever has brought a unified approach to human resources and organizational development to nonprofit and business organizations for over twenty-five years. She has an MA in Organizational Psychology and is a certified professional coach.

Rita's business, Supervision Matters, focuses on the critical role of supervision in organizations. Through all her work, Rita sees the tremendous impact of supervision—both positive and negative. Too often, supervision is an auxiliary function added onto an already full job, but it is never an auxiliary function to those being supervised. Every action that a supervisor takes, or doesn't take, impacts the organization. Rita works with individuals, teams, leaders, and the entire organization to improve the culture and practice of supervision, thereby helping the organization to achieve its mission.

Rita is proud to work as an affiliate consultant with RoadMap Consulting, a national group of consultants committed to strengthening organizations and advancing social justice.

Rita worked at nonprofits for over twenty years, including nine years at an AIDS organization and another nine years at a community action agency. Rita has taught part time at University of San Francisco and Sonoma State University in California.

Rita lives with her husband in Sonoma County, California, and they spend significant time in Portland, Oregon, where their son, daughter-in-law, and grandchildren live. A daughter and her partner live in Germany and Rita and her husband appreciate the magic of computer visits with them.

Rita loves to read, play games, spend time with friends, and travel in her free time, preferably all at the same time.

Author photo by Katharine Kimball Photography

Selected Titles from She Writes Press

She Writes Press is an independent publishing company founded to serve women writers everywhere. Visit us at www.shewritespress.com.

People Leadership: 30 Proven Strategies to Ensure Your Team's Success by Gina Folk. $24.95, 978-1-63152-915-3. Longtime manager Gina Folk provides thirty effective ways for any individual managing or supervising others to reignite their team and become a successful—and beloved—people leader.

The Clarity Effect: How Being More Present Can Transform Your Work and Life by Sarah Harvey Yao. $16.95, 978-1-63152-958-0. A practical, strategy-filled guide for stressed professionals looking for clarity, strength, and joy in their work and home lives.

The Thriver's Edge: Seven Keys to Transform the Way You Live, Love, and Lead by Donna Stoneham. $16.95, 978-1-63152-980-1. A "coach in a book" from master executive coach and leadership expert Dr. Donna Stoneham, The Thriver's Edge outlines a practical road map to breaking free of the barriers keeping you from being everything you're capable of being.

Think Better. Live Better. 5 Steps to Create the Life You Deserve by Francine Huss. $16.95, 978-1-938314-66-7. With the help of this guide, readers will learn to cultivate more creative thoughts, realign their mindset, and gain a new perspective on life.

Stop Giving it Away: How to Stop Self-Sacrificing and Start Claiming Your Space, Power, and Happiness by Cherilynn Veland. $16.95, 978-1-63152-958-0. An empowering guide designed to help women break free from the trappings of the needs, wants, and whims of other people—and the self-imposed limitations that are keeping them from happiness.

The Complete Enneagram: 27 Paths to Greater Self-Knowledge by Beatrice Chestnut, PhD. $24.95, 978-1-938314-54-4. A comprehensive handbook on using the Enneagram to do the self-work required to reach a higher stage of personal development.